The Order
of the
British Empire

Queen Elizabeth II, wearing the Sovereign's mantle, leaving St Paul's Cathedral
after the 1988 Service of the Order

The Order
of the
British Empire

Peter Galloway

Printed for the Order of the British Empire
1996

ISBN 0 907605 65 6
Central Chancery of the Orders of Knighthood

Distributed by Spink & Son Ltd, 5–7 King Street, St James's, London SW1Y 6QS

Printed in Great Britain by Stephen Austin and Sons Ltd
Printers at Hertford since 1768

CONTENTS

FOREWORD

His Royal Highness The Prince Philip, Duke of Edinburgh, KG, KT, OM, GBE, AC, QSO, Grand Master of the Most Excellent Order of the British Empire

It may seem a bit early to write a history of the Order considering that it has only been in existence for almost eighty years, but the early years of any institution are usually the most interesting and certainly the most formative. This is definitely the case with the Order of the British Empire. The concept was simple enough, but bringing it to fruition and then to completion proved to be immensely complicated. It taxed the minds of many senior and experienced administrators, politicians, churchmen, architects, designers and both King George V and Queen Mary. Later both King Edward VIII and King George VI were deeply involved. The originators were also seriously handicapped by the fact that, in 1916 and 1917, the Prime Minister and his Cabinet were pre-occupied by the need to prosecute the war against Germany.

It is not that there was any significant opposition to the concept, the problems stemmed from the very strong emotions that the idea generated, particularly on such delicate issues as political expediency, the relationship of the proposed classes of the Order to social classes and the need to define various levels of merit and courage. All this on top of a radical departure from traditional perceptions of the much older Orders of Chivalry. It would include women and previously unimagined numbers of 'ordinary' people. It is interesting to see that the idea of popular nominations, introduced in 1993, was already envisaged in the very early days.

It was difficult enough to arrive at an agreed name and structure, but it proved to be just as difficult to settle all the ancillary problems of insignia, robes, banners, ritual and the choice of a Chapel.

Weaknesses and anomalies were bound to arise in the early years, but I believe that the originators would have been well pleased with the undoubted success of their brain-child. The Order has made it possible to recognise contributions to the public good by people from all walks of life. It has given many thousands of people immense personal satisfaction and a comforting sense of belonging to a company or fellowship of good citizenship.

The Revd Dr Peter Galloway has obviously done a great deal of meticulous research, and produced a record that will be interesting for contemporary readers and a vital source material for future historians.

LIST OF ILLUSTRATIONS

Frontispiece Queen Elizabeth II, wearing the Sovereign's mantle
Between pages 84 and 85

The highest reward for a person's toil is not what they get for it,
but what they become by it.

John Ruskin

ACKNOWLEDGEMENTS

I acknowledge the gracious permission of Her Majesty The Queen for the republication of material which is subject to copyright, from the Royal Archives.

I am grateful to His Royal Highness The Prince Philip, Duke of Edinburgh, Grand Master of the Order of the British Empire who, despite a busy schedule, kindly agreed to read the text, and to write the Foreword.

Admiral Sir Anthony Morton, GBE, King of Arms of the Order, and Commander Sir Robin Gillett, GBE, Gentleman Usher of the Purple Rod of the Order, both read through the text and offered useful suggestions for improvement.

John Morton of the National Art Library supplied information about the professional career of Miss Elinor Hallé, CBE, designer of the old pattern insignia of the Order. Stephen Connelly of Spink & Son, and David Thomas of Garrard & Co. provided information about the insignia of the Officials of the Order. G. P. Dyer, Librarian and Curator of the Royal Mint, supplied information relating to the work of Colonel Sir Robert Johnson, KCVO, KBE, Deputy Master of the Mint in the 1920s, George Kruger-Gray, CBE, designer of the Collar of the Order, and Langford Jones, designer of the re-formed Medals of the Order in 1922. Brian Toye, of Toye, Kenning and Spencer, supplied information relating to the manufacture of the Mantles of the Knights and Dames Grand Cross in 1959–60.

Alan Tabor of Spink & Son painstakingly photographed the insignia of the Order over several sessions. Philip Way, Photographer to the Dean and Chapter of St Paul's Cathedral, supplied the illustrations of the Chapel of the Order and the Altar Plate. Charles Green photographed the Grand Master and Officials of the Order. Terry Fincher of Photographers International, supplied the illustration of Queen Elizabeth II leaving St Paul's Cathedral after the 1988 Service. The Public Information Department of HQ London District supplied the illustrations of Dame Mary Donaldson, GBE and Sir Alexander Graham, GBE. The illustrations of the old pattern diamond insignia appear by courtesy of Christie's, London.

The following individuals helped with information about the Australian Associations: Brigadier Charles Flint OBE, of the Australian Capital Territory Association; Mrs Patricia Bridges OBE, President of the New South Wales Association; Dr Sam Mellick CBE, of the Queensland Association; D. H. M. Roeger MBE, Honorary Secretary of the South Australian Association; Mrs Barbara Sattler, Honorary Secretary of the Tasmanian Association; David Mandie OBE, President of the Victorian Association; and Commodore R. H. Percy CBE, President of the Western Australia Association.

Nicholas Davidson, Lecturer in History at the University of Leicester, enlightened me on the use of the word 'Empire' in the Europe of 1534. Michael Hyde shared his memories of the life and work of his grandfather Sir Robert Hyde, KBE, founder of the Industrial Society. Bill Macall, formerly General Secretary of the Institute of Professional Civil Servants, kindly agreed to discuss his personal criticisms of the distribution of honours. A number of the 'records' established by members of the Order, and included in Chapter Six, were originally unearthed by Russell Malloch and used in an article in the *Journal* of the Orders and Medals Research Society.

Raymond Foster, Brian Johnston, William Stewart, John Tamplin, TD, and Lieutenant Colonel Robin Charley helped in the task of tracing the years of birth and death of the Knights and Dames Grand Cross of the Order.

The design of the book is due to the expertise of Tony Kitzinger. Richard Russell of Stephen Austin & Sons, gave much wise guidance to an author inexperienced with the technicalities of the printing world. David Lee provided the index.

Lieutenant Colonel Anthony Mather, OBE, Secretary of the Central Chancery of the Orders of Knighthood and Registrar of the Order of the British Empire, and the staff of the Chancery, were unfailingly prompt, patient and courteous in answering my frequent requests for sometimes obscure information.

Mrs Ruth Gardner, LVO, OBE, formerly Assistant to the Ceremonial Officer in the Cabinet Office, spent many hours sharing her invaluable experience of the Order, accumulated over a period of many years. She learned well and wisely from her mentor, Sir Robert Knox, KCB, KCVO, the first Ceremonial Officer 1936–65. Knox had been Private Secretary to Sir Warren Fisher, GCB, GCVO, Head of the Home Civil Service 1919–39 and Secretary of the Order 1922–39; and Fisher had known and often corresponded with Sir Frederick Ponsonby, GCB, GCVO, who played a prominent role in the creation of the Order in 1916–17.

Although he died in 1935, Ponsonby helped to form much of the content of this book. His many surviving letters, preserved in the Central Chancery of the Orders of Knighthood, and the Ceremonial Branch of the Cabinet Office, proved to be an invaluable chronicle of the early history of the Order. Often exasperated by those who could not, or would not, accept his point of view, he had an impressive knowledge of the subject of honours, and many of the problems that beset the Order in its earliest years might have been avoided if his advice had been more readily heeded. As I read his letters, his words to Sir Douglas Dawson remained a constant encouragement. 'I am . . . anxious that everything should be done according to the book as all this may one day be interesting historically.'[1] He was quite right.

In 1967, on the fiftieth anniversary of the foundation of the Order, the Reverend Canon Frederic Hood, CBE, a Canon Residentiary of St Paul's Cathedral and Sub-Dean of the Order, wrote a short guide to the history of the Order, its insignia and the Chapel, copies of which have been available to members of the Order ever since. As the Order has now passed its seventy-fifth anniversary, it seemed appropriate to look again at its history, its insignia and its chapel and, by producing a thorough and more detailed study, to correct misconceptions, to enlighten enquiring minds, and to stimulate interest in this, our national Order.

Peter Galloway

ONE

Conflict and Reward

THE FOUNDATION OF THE ORDER

Of course any idea of medals or rewards is ridiculous at the present moment, but all sorts of crude schemes for new Decorations are being quietly discussed and I feel that unless we have some sort of idea of what we are going to do, we shall, when the end of the war is in sight, be swept off our legs by a rush for Decorations in all quarters.

Sir Frederick Ponsonby to Sir Douglas Dawson, 6 December 1915

The origin of the Order of the British Empire can be traced directly to that European maelstrom known as the First World War.

The war began after the assassination of the Archduke Franz Ferdinand of Austria, and his wife Sophie, Duchess of Hohenberg, in Sarajevo on 28 June 1914. The archduke, and the Austro-Hungarian Empire over which his family ruled, are now distant memories, but the year of his death has come to be seen as an historic milestone in European history. The assassinations in Sarajevo provided the cause for the launch of a cataclysmic war, after which Europe was never to be the same again.

The war was the first for a century to be fought on a European scale, and because of the development of increasingly sophisticated weaponry, the loss of human life was on a scale never before seen. Every section of society in the United Kingdom played a role during the four long years of war. The entire nation took part in the 'war effort', and it soon became apparent that some way of rewarding the nation would need to be devised, because the United Kingdom honours system in 1914 was both rarified and restricted. Certainly by December 1915 the need for a new honour was the subject of informal discussion.

A number of people feature in the story of the foundation of the Order of the British Empire, the most prominent being Sir Frederick Ponsonby (1867–1935). Fritz Ponsonby was the son of Sir Henry Ponsonby, long-serving Private Secretary to Queen Victoria, and he first joined the Royal Household as an Assistant Private Secretary to the Queen in 1895 after his father's death. He was appointed Keeper of the Privy Purse in 1914, and remained in office until his death in June 1935. Ponsonby was independent in thought and speech, often stubborn in determination and purpose, and sometimes self-opinionated; but he was usually right. His memoirs, *Recollections of Three Reigns*, remain a refreshingly candid source of information about his forty years of service in the Royal Household.

Sir Frederick Ponsonby

Ponsonby's knowledge of Orders and Decorations was prodigious. He had played a leading role in the creation of the Royal Victorian Order in 1896, and in the institution of its Collar and Mantle in 1911. On his own evidence, there was much informal discussion about the creation of a new honour in 1915, but it is he who can take credit for leading and structuring that debate into the foundation of the Order of the British Empire on 4 June 1917. The task was not easy and, beginning it with the enthusiasm of a committed volunteer, he eventually shed it with relief as a wearisome burden.

On 6 December 1915, Ponsonby wrote to Sir Douglas Dawson, Secretary of the Central Chancery of the Orders of Knighthood:

All sorts of crude schemes for new Decorations are being quietly discussed and I feel that unless we have some sort of idea of what we are going to do, we shall, when the end of the war is in sight, be swept off our legs by a rush for Decorations in all quarters.[1]

He enclosed a memorandum, dated November 1915, in which he outlined his personal proposals for what was to become the United Kingdom's most well-known national Order. Although debate was still informal and embryonic, Ponsonby recognised that the length and severity of the war would require a new and widely available honour. 'Some form of recognition must be devised for all classes and indeed for a considerable proportion of the population.'[2]

The need for a new Order

Ponsonby's memorandum outlined the various options under discussion at the time, and was effectively a foundation paper for the many months of discussion that lay ahead. At the root of his argument for the creation of a new honour lay a critique of the existing honours system.

He rightly argued that because honours were restricted to a small minority, a decoration was not within the reasonable expectation of ninety-nine per cent of the population, 'and moreover Decorations are given to men at a time of life when such things are ceasing to attract'. Turning to European comparisons, he pointed out that the United Kingdom was the only country in Europe which had no general Decoration specifically for services to literature, science and art; and people unconnected with public services to the State had little or no chance of being honoured. There was no decoration 'definitely associated with philanthropic and charitable work'. There was no decoration for foreigners, 'and it is thought that the practice of other countries especially at International Exhibitions, is a severe handicap to our success'. So narrowly defined were the criteria for award that, for example, the merchant navy was not even eligible for naval decorations. The Order of the Star of India and the Order of the Indian Empire were mainly confined to ruling princes and Anglo-Indian officials, 'and the host of small native officials are not considered'. There was no method of honouring low ranking members of the diplomatic service. There was no decoration for junior consuls and vice-consuls, 'and in cases where foreigners are appointed, this omission prevents us from obtaining the best men, who naturally serve other European countries by preference, in order to receive decorations'. With the exception of the Order of the Crown of India, the Order of Merit, the Imperial Service Order, the Royal Red Cross and the Order of St John, and despite examples of eminently distinguished service, women were not eligible for any Decoration.

These are some of the considerations which have created a demand for a new Decoration. The present time seems opportune for establishing a new Order, which might in its initial stages be connected solely with the War and later be developed to suit the conditions of Peace.[3]

Ponsonby's initial proposal

Ponsonby's personal proposal was fine in principle but short on detail, and it bore no resemblance to the Order of the British Empire that appeared twenty months later, but it was the starting point for debate. He envisaged an award of three grades. The first grade would be an 'International War Medal' with a design and ribbon approved by all the Allies. 'This . . . would only be given to those who had actually taken part in the fighting and would therefore constitute the most valued medal of those generally distributed.' Although the Crimean (1854–6) and Egyptian Wars had set the precedent for British soldiers being allowed to accept foreign medals:

the conditions are now different; our men could not be allowed to wear the medals of five or six different nations, and if we were offered a certain number of medals by our Allies there might be invidious comparisons . . . the Montenegrin Medal, for instance, would hardly rank with the French or Russian.

The second grade would be a 'distinctly British medal' for those who had offered to risk their lives but had not actually been under fire. Ponsonby envisaged that these recipients would have enlisted for general service, but had not been employed abroad. The third grade, 'the most difficult to define' could be called the 'War Star', and would be for those who had performed services indispensable to the war, including those in the Territorial Army, munitions workers, 'and other civilians whose good work it was considered desirable to recognize'.[4]

Another, unidentifiable, source, apparently not Ponsonby, had suggested the creation of a new order, to be called the Order of the British Empire, to be given for 'voluntary services of a national or Imperial character', and Ponsonby agreed.

An Order of the British Empire

It is thought that a new Order with some such title would go far to solve the difficulty of rewarding those who had performed special services in the war and for whom the War Star alone would be inadequate.[5]

The Order should be open to women, and that on reaching the higher grades, they should be allowed to assume the title of 'Dame'.

But opinion is divided as to whether women would prefer a separate Decoration of their own. In recent years the Suffragette movement has rendered it difficult to create such an Order, or even discuss its creation in a calm atmosphere, but now the difficulty does not arise.[6]

The title 'Order of St Margaret' had been suggested, and Ponsonby endorsed this: 'St Margaret is the only British female Saint, and she was a member of the Royal Families of England and Scotland'.

The British Red Cross Society was anxious to have a Decoration of its own.

There is at present the Royal Red Cross for Nurses, but no Decoration for men; and it is thought that the services of Doctors and Surgeons, who in most cases are unpaid, the Orderlies, Stretcher Bearers, Volunteer Drivers of Ambulances, Workers in Stores and Ambulances, Organisers of Supply Parties and searchers after the missing and dead should be suitably rewarded.[7]

Dawson's reply was encouraging, and endorsed most of Ponsonby's points.

I like your idea of the three classes, the trouble will be in the accurate and equitable definition of each class. . . You rightly say we have no decoration for foreigners. But who has? and if they had would it be valued? Is it not the fact that the foreigner gets what we wear that enhances its value in his sight. Would we not treat with even greater indifference than we do now a foreign Order if we knew it was not worn by the denizens of the Power conferring it on us. . . For women we have nothing, except for wives of Viceroys in India. . . We withhold till too late the junior classes of our Orders, the result being that while our Minister at Brussels or even Tehran has a simple Civil CB on his breast, his Russian or German equivalent is covered with Stars and sometimes even sashes.[8]

Ponsonby's memorandum and Dawson's reply are the first known steps in the lengthy process leading to the creation of the Order of the British Empire. Much ground was to be covered throughout 1916 and the first half of 1917, before the Order became the recognisable entity that it is today. Although it is certain that the debate continued throughout the early months of 1916, little paperwork has survived to provide an accurate chronicle of developments at this point.

Early in 1916 a small committee was appointed to make preliminary recommendations to the Cabinet. The three members were Ponsonby, Sir Edward Troup, Permanent Under-Secretary of State at the Home Office, and Maurice Bonham Carter, Private Secretary to the Prime Minister, Herbert Asquith. By May 1916, the three men had decided that the new decoration should be styled an 'Order', and that it should be given only for the duration of the war, and not permanently added to the existing Orders of Chivalry. Troup saw no need for it to be anything more than a one-class Order; but Ponsonby was firm in his view that it should consist of several classes.

One of the principle (*sic*) reasons for its institution was that it might be given to foreigners. We have at present nothing to give to the multitude of small officials who have been of service to us in France and the Mediterranean. Now anyone acquainted with this type of Foreign official will know that a one-class Decoration would never please them. If we gave the General commanding the Garrison at some port the same Decoration as the head of a boot factory, or the Locomotive Superintendent at the Railway Station, the former would hardly be likely to appreciate the honour. . . At home it is really the type of man for whom the 4th or 5th classes of the Victorian Order are suitable that we have no Decorations for. The CB (Companion of the Order of the Bath) and CMG (Companion of the Order of St Michael and St George) are too exalted and the ISO (Companion of the Imperial Service Order), is restricted to members of the Civil Service.[9]

Ponsonby was aware of contemporary suggestions, no doubt based on convenience, that the addition of an extra class and a medal to the Order of the Bath and to the Order of St Michael and St George, might go some way towards satisfying the need, but he was adamant that such a move would have a cheapening effect on those Orders in particular, and on the United Kingdom honours system in general.

If the prostitution of those Orders is to be avoided, a new Decoration must be started and given only for the war. That is the only solution that will save our Decorations from sinking to the level of Foreign ones. In this way as this generation dies out, there will be every chance of British Orders resuming their normal proportions.[10]

This was not to be his last word on the subject. By the following year he was convinced that both Orders should be transformed into five-class Orders to match the new 'democratic' Order of the British Empire.[11]

Having abandoned his first thought of three types of medal, Ponsonby proposed a new four-class Order to be called 'The Order of the Empire'. The number of appointments would be unlimited, and both women and foreign nationals would be eligible for admission. The four classes would be designated as follows:

GCE	Grand Cross	CE	Commander
KCE	Knight Commander	ME	Member

There should, additionally be an associated medal, to be styled, 'The Medal of the Order of the Empire'.[12]

Sir Edward Troup issued his own proposals, in which he still clung to his belief that a one-class order was quite adequate.

In this way we should avoid the very great difficulty of assigning the recipients of the Order to the several classes. This difficulty is a great one, even in the case of existing Orders, when guidance is given by the official position of the recipients and when a person placed in a lower class can always look forward to promotion to a higher. It would be almost insuperable, in the case of a new Order, to be given to some thousands of persons for the several classes.[13]

Ponsonby was quick to spot the fallacy of this argument. In the socially stratified age of 1916, he saw no difficulty at all in assigning people to particular classes of an Order: 'If an Admiral of the Fleet jumps overboard and saves the King's life, he gets the Grand Cross; if a Midshipman rescues the Monarch from the deep, he receives the lowest class'.[14]

Ponsonby, Troup and Bonham Carter met in May 1916 to finalise their recommendations to the Cabinet, and in a spirit of compromise, agreed on a three-class Order. Within a few days Ponsonby had revised his thoughts again, and proposed a five-class Order to Troup and Bonham Carter.

One of the crying needs we unearthed during our enquiries was the want of Decorations for the class of man who receives MVO 4th and MVO 5th, yet here we are proposing an Order on the same lines as the Bath and the St Michael and St George, both of which do not go low enough. The danger of having only 3 classes is that the 3rd class will become like the CB, and be reserved for men of a superior class, in which case the 4th class man will again be squeezed out. With foreigners I have no hesitation in saying that 5 classes are best. All Foreign Decorations are divided into 5 classes and in giving the new Decoration to foreigners you only have to ascertain what class he has of the Decoration of his own country and you give him the equivalent of the new Decoration. If he is dissatisfied, you tell him the rule and he can only grumble against his own Government for not having recognised his claims to a higher grade. . . Here at home the delicate distinctions between the five classes may present some difficulties, but it is not impossible to draw up some fixed rules. . . If we have 5 classes . . . we might work on the principle of the Legion of Honour (the national honour of France), which is really the mother of all foreign Orders:

Grand Cross	Officier
Grand Officier	Chevalier
Commandeur	

The difficulty will be in providing an equivalent to the 2nd class. The letter 'G' being associated with Grand Crosses should not, if possible, be used with a 2nd class. We might then have:

Grand Commander	Officer
Distinguished Officer	Associate
Commander	

One point worth consideration is that the name 'Order of the Empire' when translated into a foreign language, does not say what Empire. The British Empire would therefore be preferable. We should then have:

GCBE	OBE
DOBE	ABE
CBE	

DOBE and OBE are preferable to DOOE and OOE.[15]

Troup agreed with Ponsonby's subsequent thought that even this was too complicated, and that perhaps the simplest arrangement would be for the letters OBE to designate and to be used by all classes. Although eventually abandoned, his view has survived in the sense that the letters 'OBE' still stand, in popular belief, for 'Order of the British Empire'.

Ponsonby believed that the Order would have to be located within the Table of Precedence.

It is the custom in most of the Colonies to work out precedence with meticulous precision and if the new Order is not mentioned in the lists of precedence, Colonial Officials will think very little of it . . . if we do not give precedence now, we shall be forced to do so later.[16]

Troup was opposed: 'I am against giving precedence unless it is forced upon us. The CB and still more the Colonial CMG will not like having innumerable OBE's thrust in over his head.'[17]

On 10 June, Ponsonby had produced a rough draft of the proposed report to the Prime Minister and sent copies to Troup and Bonham Carter, with an accompanying note urging swift action.

They are screaming for decorations in France and so the matter presses. As it is it will take nearly 6 months to produce the Order in any large quantities. . . I have tried to bring out all the various points without being too verbose, but of course a great deal might be written. It is however a tedious subject and people with brains are bored stiff with it.[18]

To the King By 16 June 1916 Ponsonby had discussed the new Order with King George V, who asked that a copy of the report to the Prime Minister be sent to him as well. The King was insistent on one point, namely that the Order be a permanent addition to the honours system, and not simply given for the duration of the war. Ponsonby duly relayed the King's view to Bonham Carter on 21 June.

The King said that once an Order like this was started, it would be practically impossible to stop it and that we had much better make one mouthful of it. Public opinion would force us to make it permanent eventually and we had therefore much better do it at once. . . His Majesty very much doubted whether a Decoration which was not a permanent one, would be acceptable to foreigners. . . This rather changes the whole question, but I see no great difficulty in altering the report accordingly.[19]

King George V took his role as the 'fount of honour' very seriously. He was keenly interested in the new Order, and his advice that it be established permanently was the first of many sensible suggestions that he brought to the debate during the succeeding twelve months.

To the Cabinet The Committee sent its final report to the Cabinet on 8 July 1916, emphasising the distinctive purposes of the new Order. Firstly, it would be available for foreign nationals. Secondly, it would recognise the work by women. Thirdly, it would be given to minor officials outside the civil service. The report specifically discounted any enlargement of the Orders of the Bath or of St Michael and St George, citing the belief that to do so might be to depreciate the value of those Orders. And so came the firm and final recommendation of a five-class order, to be called 'The Order of the British Empire', 'this title having been selected because in addition to its general suitability, the use of the letters OBE would avoid confusion with any existing Order'.[20] In an appendix, the authors recommended that future consideration might be given to absorbing the Imperial Service Order within the Order of the British Empire. This was included as the result of a conversation between the King and Ponsonby, the latter suggesting the expansion of the Imperial Service Order instead of creating the Order of the British Empire. The King thought that this proposal would cause too much confusion, if the ISO were still to be given for twenty-five years in the civil service and additionally for distinguished service in the war. The King proposed that the members of the civil service should be eligible for the Order of the British Empire, and that the ISO be allowed gradually to pass into desuetude.[21] The proposal anticipated a decision made in 1993 to cease recommendations for the ISO.

Among the recommendations of the report was one that became something of a tiresome red herring and wasted a substantial amount of time throughout the second half of 1916 and the early months of 1917. The committee recommended that none of the classes of the new Order should carry the honour of knighthood, which would therefore make the Order 'acceptable to many to whom this title is not an object of ambition'.[22]

The question of knighthood

Ponsonby admitted that this was something of an innovation:

but the general feeling seems to be that it is a distinctly good idea. There are a large number of people who dislike knighthoods, not only the Labour members, but such men as Arthur Balfour (First Lord of the Admiralty and a former Prime Minister), Walter Long (President of the Local Government Board), etc., and while they would like to have some Order, it would hardly do to relegate them to the lower classes.[23]

Ponsonby sounded a little less than entirely convinced, and it is possible that any concerns he voiced were over-ruled by Troup and Bonham Carter.

The obvious response to this proposal was made in a hand-written note on a copy of the report which, though unsigned, bears the style of Ponsonby.

By this procedure all persons appointed to the first Class, and who would still remain 'Mr Smith & Mr Jones' would be given precedence over all KCBs and KCMGs . . . , KCVOs, etc. etc. who are dubbed 'Sir' and, what is worse 'Mrs Smith' would have precedence over 'Lady Brown'. . . What is the fundamental objection? If the Order is to rank in its proper place with Orders and not be considered an inferior affair, the first and second classes would confer the honour of knighthood. . . Surely the dignity of the Order about to be created by the King should be considered and not the ambitions of the recipients.[24]

The thought of designating all five classes with same letters 'OBE' had been dropped by August 1916. The King, who had never liked the idea, believed that different classes should be indicated by different postnominal letters, as with all other Orders, and the Cabinet had agreed. Ponsonby told Dawson that the original proposal was 'insisted on' by Troup and Bonham Carter 'as being pleasing to the democratic world'.[25] Bonham Carter then suggested the following:

GCBE	Grand Cross	MBE	Member
SBE	Star	ABE	Associate
CBE	Commander		

There were to be many more changes before the question was settled.

After the committee had reported to the Cabinet in July 1916, it divided in two. Ponsonby and Dawson formed what was to become known as the Statute Committee, and were joined by the King's cousin, Prince Louis of Battenberg and Henry Farnham Burke, Norroy King of Arms. Sir Edward Troup was joined

The division of work

by Sir Thomas Heath, Permanent Secretary of the Treasury and Head of the
Civil Service, and representatives of the principal government departments, to
form the Departmental Committee. Broadly speaking, the Statute Committee
considered mostly ceremonial questions such as drafting the statutes and the
design and manufacture of insignia, while the Departmental Committee looked
at the wider issues of allocation and distribution. It was not an altogether happy
division of responsibility. Friction was almost inevitable, and the furtherance of
good relations between the two committees was not helped by Ponsonby's somewhat impatient attitude towards the civil servants.

From no knight-
hood to optional
knighthood

Debate on the issue of no knighthood resumed in the autumn of 1916 when
Farnham Burke raised objections to the idea. Working with an heraldic eye to the
minutiae of such matters, Burke thought that the creation of an Order without a
category of knight would create formidable difficulties, as Ponsonby reported to
Troup on 13 October.

Hideous problems of precedence which seemed to me quite inane were brought forward.
I quite realised, however, that although the points seemed to me ridiculous they might
possibly assume gigantic proportions in a small town. I therefore asked him to communicate his objections to our scheme to the Central Chancery . . . so that they might be
properly considered by people competent to express an opinion on such matters. Personally I was quite incompetent to venture even to consider such conundrums.[26]

Dawson illustrated Burke's objections in a memorandum dated 12 October 1916.
Essentially, they revolved around the practical difficulties of according precedence to a male unknighted member of the first class, and to his wife. The untitled wife of a member of the First Class of the Order of the British Empire would
have to be given precedence above the titled wife of a member of the second class
of the Order of the Bath 'or else she would, as the wife of Mr Jones, GCBE, have
no precedence at all . . . the same remarks apply to Mr Jones, GCBE, and Sir
John Jones, KCB.'[27]

Burke's opinion was subsequently conveyed to the King, who had always
thought that the question would have to be reconsidered. The King discussed the
problem with his new Prime Minister, David Lloyd George, on 3 October 1916,
and the two men agreed on a curious compromise, which only caused further
debate and delay. They decided that the first and second classes should, in common with the other Orders, carry the honour of Knighthood – for those who
wanted it. For those who did not, on ideological or other grounds, the option to
accept the Class but decline the knighthood was to be available. Although the
decision seems curious, and further debate brought the realisation that it was
unworkable, it was neither a foolish nor a frivolous proposal. The King and the
Prime Minister both wanted the new Order to begin its working life with the
widest possible spectrum of support.

Sir Edward Troup thought that the idea was radical but excellent, and told
Ponsonby so.

Why should the King . . . be rigidly bound by the Custom of the existing Orders? As for
the titles 'Sir' and 'Lady', there are two things that might depreciate their value – increasing their numbers unnecessarily – and forcing Knighthood on persons who . . . do not
desire the title . . . Members of the First and Second Classes of the new Order may be
offered and may if they desire accept the honour of Knighthood – but I think it should be

made quite clear that they will not thereby have any precedence over other members of the same Class . . . In short, the Knighthood would be independent of the Order, and merely conferred at the same time.[28]

It soon became apparent that the problems of relative precedence were not so easily solved.

The only way of designating unknighted members of the first and second classes was to call them just that – 'Members of the first class' and 'Members of the second class', and by 23 November, the designation of recipients of the fourth class as 'Members' (MBE), had been dropped in favour of 'Officers' (OBE). It was also felt that style of 'Member' (MBE) for the fourth class would imply that the recipients of the fifth class, 'Associates' (ABE), were not members of the Order. A further proposal was made to style the fourth class 'Companions' (CBE), the Commanders of the third class using the letters 'CrBE'.

On 5 December 1916, Prince Louis, Ponsonby, Dawson and Farnham Burke met to discuss the question of optional knighthood, and were unanimous in their decision that it was unworkable. At a meeting at Buckingham Palace the following day, the Statute Committee met in joint session with Sir Edward Troup and Sir Thomas Heath from the Departmental Committee to discuss three possible schemes:

Firstly, the Order should be instituted on exactly the same lines as the other British Orders, membership of the first two classes conferring knighthood. The group accepted that this would mean the creation of anything from 450 to 600 Knights, 'thereby depreciating the value of the honour of Knighthood.' Secondly, the Order should carry neither knighthood nor precedence. This would dispose of the question of the relative precedence of the CBE and the CB; it would prevent knighthood from becoming 'too common'; and it would dispose of the question of how to entitle ladies admitted to the first two classes.

The disadvantages of this scheme would be that it is doubtful whether an Order carrying no Knighthood and no precedence would ever be appreciated by the public. Women, who for the first time are being admitted to participate with men in a British Decoration, might resent this.[29]

Thirdly, that knighthood for the first two classes should be optional. This would have the advantage of satisfying those 'to whom the honour of knighthood was distasteful.'[30] But this option would only lead to more difficulties on the question of precedence. If men, admitted to the first and second classes, refused knighthood and had no precedence, they would rank after members of the fifth class of their own Order. If they were given precedence, members of the second class would rank before Knights Bachelor. 'This would be most unpopular, as the Knights Bachelor of this country were a most influential body and would inevitably resent such an innovation.'[31]

The joint committee was divided on which scheme to recommend. Prince Louis, Dawson, Ponsonby, and Farnham Burke held to their view of the previous day, that the idea of optional knighthood, although attractive in theory, would be impossible in practice. Prince Louis, Dawson and Burke favoured the first scheme, but were prepared to accept the second if the creation of so many knights was considered inadvisable. Ponsonby favoured the second scheme. Heath and Troup favoured the third scheme, but were prepared to adopt the second scheme if optional knighthood proved inadvisable. Although Bonham Carter was not present, Troup reported that his conversations with Bonham Carter indicated that the latter supported the third scheme.

These were the earliest signs of friction between the two committees. Dawson took the view that he, Ponsonby, Burke and Prince Louis, having been appointed by the King to draft the Statutes, were the 'expert' committee, and whatever views were held by the Departmental Committee should be formulated and laid before the experts. Heath and Troup had other ideas and, according to Ponsonby, seemed to think that the proposals of the Statute Committee should be submitted to them, and that the Statutes should in fact conform to whatever resolutions they had agreed. Ponsonby was in despair.

I had hoped to keep the two Committees quite distinct. . . I am afraid that a meeting of the two Committees would only end in chaos. There are already ten members of the other Committee and four of the Statute Committee. I will endeavour to try to get some solution of this difficulty settled out of court.[32]

The situation cannot have been helped by the inter-personal friction that existed, according to Ponsonby, within the Departmental Committee.

It is necessary to be careful not to call the Departmental Committee Mr Bonham Carter's Committee, as Sir Thomas Heath would strongly object to serving on a Committee under Mr Bonham Carter. He even objected to serving on the Committee unless he was in the Chair, and it was only when we agreed that there should be no Chairman that he consented to attend.[33]

Ponsonby was by this time becoming weary of the new Order, and had described himself on 28 November 1916 as 'the unfortunate individual who has to do with the Order of the British Empire'.[34] He went to the King and reported all that had occurred at the joint meeting of the Committees.

His Majesty said that he was not at all wedded to the idea of a Knighthood being included in the new Order. He thought that there were already too many Knights and that it would be a mistake to add to their number. It would only cheapen the honour of Knighthood and depreciate the value of the KCB.[35]

The King then decided that the new Order should not confer knighthood in any class, but that it should have precedence. The pitfalls of such an arrangement were there for anyone to see and, although with hindsight, we may wonder that so much time should have been spent on such a detail, questions of precedence mattered in 1916, more so than perhaps they did in subsequent generations.

Dawson warned that the whole thing was unworkable and advised an 'all or nothing' approach; either the Order should have knighthood and precedence, or it should have neither.

Any attempt to place Members of the Order of the British Empire, without Knighthood, in the same precedence as that accorded to those of other Orders would cause an outcry, not only from Knights Commanders of other Orders, but from the whole community of Knights Bachelors. Further it would cause endless confusion in assigning precedence at Functions, and give rise to bickering and annoyance. . . I believe that an Order of Chivalry without Knighthood, yet conferring precedence, would be proved, before the new Order was a week in existence, to be unworkable and unpopular, while it would become the object of derisive criticism.[36]

Were his advice to be ignored, the only way to avoid controversy was to place the whole Order below Knights Bachelor as follows:

GCBE should rank immediately after Knights Bachelor;

GOBE should rank immediately after GCBE and immediately before CVO;

> CBE should rank immediately after CVO and before County Court Judges;
>
> OBE should rank immediately after MVO (4th class);
>
> ABE should rank immediately after MVO (5th class) and before Baronets' younger sons.

Dawson had done the best he could in placing the Order within the national Table of Precedence, but the very low status now accorded to a brand new Order was not lost on one diplomat at the British Embassy in Petrograd.

> We are instructed to send in a list of officials we recommend for it. This is impossible unless we have some idea to what class of official each class is to be bestowed. As the first class of the Order is below Knight Bachelor, I suppose the 5th is for the Chancery dachshund?[37]

The matter was referred back to the King who agreed that Dawson's proposed precedence was the only practicable solution. But Ponsonby would have kept the King informed of the sharply differing opinions on the questions of knighthood and, although he had decided against knighthood but in favour of precedence, the King took the wise constitutional decision to refer the matter back to the War Cabinet.

Back to the Cabinet

In December 1916, Ponsonby prepared a full and careful account of the various steps that had been taken to institute the Order. 'I am afraid that if we omit any of these reports, the Prime Minister will be tempted to upset some of the decisions arrived at. After all, he can read as little or as much of it as he likes.'[38]

At this stage, there was still a clear intention that the institution of the Order should be announced in the New Year Honours List 1917, and Ponsonby sent his memorandum to Downing Street in good time for the Prime Minister to make an announcement. It was to no avail. The Prime Minister was occupied with other more pressing affairs, and by the middle of January, his private secretary reported that 'Mr Lloyd George has not had a moment of time in which to consider the New Order',[39] but hoped to be able to do so when the first lists of members were published on 25 January. In the light of the King's decision to refer the question of knighthood to the War Cabinet, the intention to announce the first appointments on 25 January was subsequently abandoned.

On 9 February 1917 Ponsonby was summoned to Downing Street to attend a meeting of members of the Cabinet to rehearse the issues yet again, and it was not a pleasant experience. He found himself confronted by David Lloyd George, the Prime Minister; Arthur Henderson, the Paymaster-General and Labour Adviser to the Government; and the formidable figure of Earl Curzon of Kedleston, former Viceroy of India, and now Lord President of the Council.

> It would be quite impossible to find in this country three men more incapable of expressing an opinion on the subject of Decorations. In the first place, the Prime Minister kept on alluding to a rosette in the buttonhole, which he seemed to think was the only thing that mattered. There was Mr Henderson, who had not the foggiest idea of what we were talking about the whole time, as Orders and Decorations had never come his way. Lord Curzon had some idea of Decorations from India, but as he explained, he had only been referred to in cases of Grand Crosses, and knew very little about the lower classes. The Prime Minister explained that he had had no time to read any papers on the subject, although copies of the proceedings of the various Committees had been sent to him. I am

told that he never reads anything, and therefore that it was not likely that he would read through a large mass of papers of this description. I felt like a man being court-martialled as I came into the room, and was told to take a seat at the far end of the table. There were a host of Secretaries and shorthand-writers, and Curzon sat on one side of the table, with the Prime Minister and Henderson on the other. . . From the questions that were being asked I could see that, with the exception of Curzon, I was not being understood at all.[40]

Ponsonby's analysis proved correct. To his dismay, the three men decided that knighthood should be optional for the first two classes of the Order, and that unknighted members of those classes should enjoy the same precedence as knighted members. Ponsonby's comment to C. A. Harris on 16 February summed up the situation.

The whole question of the institution of the Order of the British Empire under present conditions is bristling with difficulties, and the decision which the War Cabinet arrived at . . . makes it even more difficult.[41]

Dawson and Prince Louis helpfully produced yet another set of postnominal letters. Clearly unknighted members of the first two classes could not use letters traditionally indicating knighthood, and some distinction would need to be made between the two sections.

	Knighted	*Unknighted*
1st class	GCBE	GMBE
2nd class	KCBE	SCBE
3rd class	CBE	CBE
4th class	OBE	OBE
5th class	ABE	ABE

The knighted members were brought into line with existing Orders by the use of the letters 'GC' and 'KC', while the unknighted members were to be known as 'Grand Members' and 'Star Commanders'. Ponsonby was not in agreement with the choice of GCBE and KCBE. He feared a confusion with the Order of the Bath (GCB and KCB), 'and when you have to write to Sir John Jones, KCB, KCBE. it may sound ridiculous.'[42]

Ponsonby believed that the War Cabinet's decision to choose optional knighthood was hasty and taken without serious consideration of all the ramifications. His 'court-martial' experience diminished his confidence in the ability of politicians to understand the delicate matters of honour and precedence, in which he was an undoubted expert. But their 'hasty' decision, and comparatively superficial interest in the new Order needs to be set within context. A few days before Ponsonby's meeting with Lloyd George, Henderson and Curzon, Germany had declared unrestricted U-Boat warfare, the United States had broken off diplomatic relations with Germany, and the Prime Minister and his Cabinet could not reasonably have been expected to accord a high priority to reading papers about the institution of the new honour.

Ponsonby was certain that it was quite impossible for unknighted members of the first two classes to be given the same precedence as knighted members and, at a subsequent meeting, he tried to impress on Curzon the impossible situations that would arise. Unfortunately for Ponsonby, someone had told Curzon that there was a precedent for 'unknighted knights'. Clergy admitted to the first two classes of the Royal Victorian Order never received the accolade, and did not use the title of 'Sir'.

He kept on quoting the case of the clergy who had been given the KCVO, and was so much pleased at his cleverness in thinking of this that he was convinced he had satisfactorily disposed of all the difficulties.[43]

The case of unknighted clergy knights was in fact a socially awkward and unresolved issue. Should Mrs Dalton, the wife of Canon Dalton, KCVO take precedence over Lady Parratt, wife of Sir Walter Parratt, Knight Bachelor? 'It was a question which had shaken Windsor to its foundations, and, as nothing was laid down on the subject, these two ladies were quite unable to meet at dinner.'[44] Managing only a ten-minute meeting with Ponsonby, Curzon promised that he would think further about the problem.

Curzon duly thought about it, and Ponsonby was summoned to another meeting on 5 March.

I found that the Prime Minister was away, and Bonar Law took his place. In addition to Curzon and Henderson there was Milner (Minister without Portfolio and a member of the War Cabinet), who is just back from Petrograd. Curzon, who appears to have been the only member of the War Cabinet who had taken the trouble to master the contents of our recommendations, spoke at some length in the subject, and was followed by Milner. . . Henderson then applied for a one-class decoration, and I had to explain all over again why this was impossible. Bonar Law then cross-questioned me on several points, and having a virgin mind on the subject, appeared to think that a decoration with no Knighthood, was the best solution. After some further discussion, in which all the members of the War Cabinet joined, Bonar Law began to announce that he had decided in favour of Knighthood but Curzon forcibly pointed out to him that, if every time the War Cabinet met they came to a different conclusion, there would be no finality in any of their decisions.[45]

The Cabinet concluded that one of its members should meet with members of the Statute and Departmental Committees, and try to come to a final decision. After Henderson had 'flatly refused', the choice fell upon Curzon, and Ponsonby rather wearily prepared himself 'to go all over the ground again.'[46]

Curzon appears to have given so little time to devote to the issue, that Ponsonby was forced to write to him on 21 March.

Lord Curzon's report

Is there any prospect of your being less busy? Will there be any lull in the war of politics which will give you sufficient desire to decide this tiresome question of knighthood. . . All the Government departments are getting impatient, and want to know when the new Order, which was promised at the beginning of the year, will be available. . . Until a certain number of people in this country have received the Order, it is impossible to give it to foreigners.[47]

The two men met on Monday 26 March in the Privy Council Office. Curzon, accompanied by Sir George Cave, the Home Secretary, represented the Cabinet. Prince Louis, Ponsonby, Dawson and Burke, represented the Statute Committee. Sir George Fiddes of the Colonial Office, Sir Thomas Heath and Sir Edward Troup, represented the Departmental Committee. The meeting decided to abandon all idea of optional knighthood. The Order of the British Empire should be a five-class Order, either with or without knights. If it was to have knights, then another one-class decoration, to be called the War Service Order or the National Service Order, should be created.

Curzon duly submitted the recommendations in the form of a memorandum, dated 1 April 1917, to a meeting of the War Cabinet. His memorandum is a frank exposition of the diverse problems. The Cabinet, he said, was faced with the task of establishing an honour which would be suitable for presentation to a number of entirely different classes, and would satisfy those classes. Quite apart from foreigners, there would be persons 'who attach a good deal of importance to social precedence and to titular prefixes to their names'. There would also be persons of distinction 'to whom it would be absurd to offer the style and title of Knight'; and there would be those 'who would not refuse a decoration but would, for reasons entirely honourable to themselves, abjure a title'. Curzon advised that to satisfy the claims of all these conflicting parties was an almost impossible task.

We decided to submit two alternative schemes to the War Cabinet, for both of which there is something to be said, but neither of which is free from objection. Objections, indeed, are inseparable from any solution that can be proposed.[48]

There were only two clear options. Either there should be a five-class Order of the British Empire, without knights and with precedence that recognised that fact; or there should be a five-class Order of the British Empire with knights and a one-class War Service Order (or National Service Order if continued in peacetime) that bestowed neither title nor precedence. 'The two schemes are submitted with no sort of exhilaration. . . Were it not for the insatiable appetite of the British-speaking community all the world over for titles and precedence, the first would be unhesitatingly recommended.'[49] Ponsonby reported to Dawson that the King was 'much amused' by this final comment by Curzon.[50]

The War Cabinet met on 6 April 1917 and decided in favour of the second scheme. The Order of the British Empire should be a five-class order, with knighthood for the first two classes, and for those who did not wish to be knights, there would be a one-class National Service Order.

No more need be said about this National Service Order. From this point onwards it acquired a history of its own, culminating in the establishment of the Order of the Companions of Honour on the same day as the Order of the British Empire. Its function was simply to provide a decoration equivalent in rank to the first two classes of the Order of the British Empire, for those who did not wish to have a knighthood.

More letters   The postnominal letters were settled by the War Cabinet in accordance with Curzon's recommendation:

GCBE	Grand Cross	OBE	Officer
KCBE	Knight Commander	ABE	Associate
CBE	Commander		

The letters were to be the same for women members, with the exception of the second class, where the appropriate letters would be DCBE. By 23 April 1917, the King had requested that the designation of the fifth class be changed from 'Associate' to 'Member', leading to the familiar 'MBE' of today.[51]

The letters 'GCBE' and 'KCBE' lingered in use for a few weeks longer until Ponsonby issued a circular letter, reporting a general feeling that the selection of letters so closely resembling those of the Order of the Bath was open to criticism. His respondents were in agreement with his suggestion that the letters 'GBE' and 'KBE' should be used instead. A number of them pointed to the remaining possibility of confusion between the CB and the CBE but, as the India Office remarked, 'that can't be helped as "BE" would mean nothing'.[52]

No matter how well formulated the plans for the establishment of postnominal letters, they were not speedily implemented. In the summer of 1918, Ponsonby noticed that Sir Arthur Pearson, President of the National Institute for the Blind, and one of the first Knights Grand Cross of the Order, was using the letters GCBE after his name. He wrote to Pearson pointing out the error, and received the reply: 'the reason why I put the letters GCBE after my name is because these are the letters embossed on the cover of the case given me by the King and containing the Decoration'.[53]

The problem of precedence was not confined to the issue of unknighted members of the first and second classes. The relative precedence of the new CBE caused expressions of disquiet in certain quarters. With the title and precedence of 'Commander', the third class of the new Order would rank after the third class of the Victorian Order (CVO) but before the third class of all the older Orders (CB, CSI, CMG, CIE). The issue was raised by Sir Thomas Heath in November 1916. He warned that the existence of the CVO:

The precedence of Commanders

is a great anomaly, and has caused much feeling among the Companions of the older Orders, particularly among the CBs. . . I hope it is not too late to see that the 'Cs' are Companions and below the CB, etc.[54]

Ponsonby acknowledged that the precedence of the CVO before the CB was a valid question. It had been discussed in former years, and suggestions made that the CB should be worn from the neck and converted into a Commandership. 'Foreigners were quite unable to understand why we attached so much value to a CB, which was worn in a place usually associated with the smaller classes of their own Decorations' (as a medal on the chest). 'The King, however, was reluctant to change in any way one of most ancient Orders, and said that if foreigners did not like it, they should not be given it.'[55] The only solution was to raise the status of the CB from 'Companion' to 'Commander' and add another class below, but then the same procedure would have to be followed with the CMG. Heath, realising that he had moved into deep waters, was satisfied.

It would be a great pity to alter the number of classes of these older Orders in any way. It is . . . a much lesser evil . . . that the CBs, CMGs etc., should suffer the slight disadvantage of having a few more Commanders ranking above them.[56]

Ponsonby proposed the obvious course of converting the CB, CSI, CMG and CIE into neck decorations. There would be no need to make them into Commanders, and the old word 'Companion' could be retained, with perhaps one or two lower classes being created. His proposal was discussed and accepted at a meeting chaired by Viscount Sandhurst, the Lord Chamberlain, on 18 May 1917.

The admission of women to the new Order provoked an unprecedented area of debate. Queen Victoria had vehemently opposed admitting women to the new Royal Victorian Order in 1896, and women were eligible for admission to only a few Orders created specifically for that purpose and none of them carried a distinctive title. Should admission to the first and second classes of the new British Empire Order carry the right to use any title equivalent to 'Sir', or should these lady members be left untitled?

The titles and precedence of ladies

The issue was batted back and forth for almost as long as the debate on knighthood. Ponsonby had proposed the title of 'Dame' in November 1915. The issue was raised again in October 1916 when the title 'Lady' was proposed. By December 1916 Prince Louis was pressing for 'Dame'.

Want of precedence may be put forward as an objection, but it only means establishing another class in existing female hierarchy. A number of Peeresses in their own right have always existed... If a woman can be called 'Countess of Cromarty' or 'Baroness Beaconsfield', why not 'Dame Johnston?' – while her husband remains a commoner.[57]

Sir George Fiddes, Permanent Under Secretary of State at the Colonial Office, was against the idea.

Is it really intended that women should be knighted and be socially known as 'Dame Anne' etc.? I must be pardoned for suggesting the possibility that public ridicule may kill this part of the scheme.[58]

The title of 'Dame' was not in fact an innovation of 1917 but, arguably, a revival of medieval practice. Although the wife of a knight has been styled 'Lady Smith' since the 17th century, the alternative style of 'Dame Anne Smith' survived well into the 16th century.

Sir Edward Troup consulted three ladies prominent in the war effort, though he did not divulge their names. The first was happy with the right to wear insignia, but had 'the gravest doubts' about the use of the title 'Dame'. The second was against a title of any description: ' "Mr Jones and Dame Jones" would not only complicate our visiting cards but embitter countless homes.' The third said that she personally was against the title of Dame but thought it would be quite popular among a considerable number of women. 'The people who would press their claims to it most strongly will be the ladies who have managed the worst canteens.' Troup also consulted the Home Secretary, who was 'very decidedly against the proposed title'.[59]

In his report to the War Cabinet, Curzon, who disliked 'Dame', recommended that it should be allowed, but should be optional. The title of 'Lady', he thought, might become 'a fruitful source of domestic perturbation'.[60] The Cabinet decided that, although women should be eligible for admission to the first two classes of the Order, and be listed as Dames Grand Cross and Dames Commanders, and be allowed to use appropriate postnominal letters, they should not assume any title. As Dawson remarked to Ponsonby on 2 May, 'We shall have the fat in the fire. Precedence to mere men & not to females. But if the excellent idea of "Dame" is blackballed there is no alternative.'[61]

Dawson's point was well made. The conferring of a title on a gentleman GBE and the withholding of a title from a lady GBE would have caused resentment among women when set against the background of the suffragette movement with its demand for the right of women to vote. To admit women to all classes of the nation's first national Order, but simultaneously to refuse to accord them titles similar to those borne by men in the same grade, would at the least have been inauspicious, and at worst would have probably caused an uproar. For the first time large numbers of women were to be honoured for their achievements, and to style a woman recipient of the first class, 'Mrs Jones, GBE' would transform her into a second class member in a painfully obvious way. But what should she be called? The style of 'Lady' had been proposed at an earlier date and it was pressed again in May 1917 by the Lord Chamberlain's Office and the College of

Arms. Both felt that ladies should receive some form of title, but both disliked the innovative title of 'Dame'. Ponsonby, who was by now very familiar with every view of every aspect of the Order, regarded it as 'an exceptionally tiresome question'.[62]

The King was sensitive to possible criticism in the press, and asked for the matter to be reconsidered. Ponsonby, Prince Louis, Dawson and Burke met on 15 May and recommended that the title of 'Dame' should be restored.

As the inclusion of ladies in the Order is a feature to which it is desired to give prominence, it is thought that it would not be moving in the right direction were ladies, who for the first time are included in an Order which gives precedence to its members, not accorded similar precedence as the male members of the Order. It is therefore suggested that the decision to suppress the title 'Dame' . . . might be carefully reconsidered.[63]

It would also mark the fact that the ladies would be given a distinctive title recognising that they had been honoured for their own service. The King himself had never much cared for the title of 'Dame' which he thought 'smacked too much of the Primrose League',[64] but he realised that there was no satisfactory alternative, and he had 'reluctantly' accepted the title of 'Dame' by 24 May.[65] On 31 August 1917 Norroy King of Arms issued his opinion that Dames Grand Cross and Dames Commanders should be verbally addressed as 'Dame' followed by the Christian name, and this was approved by the King early in September. 'Dame Elizabeth Jones is preferable to Dame Jones and it is the equivalent to Sir John Jones who is not Sir Jones.'[66] The practice has continued to the present day.

It is often assumed that the title of 'Dame' indicates a female knighthood, but this is not the case. There is no provision for a woman to be made a knight of the realm by receiving the accolade. The title of 'Dame', introduced with the Order of the British Empire in 1917, and since extended to other Orders, is simply a way of entitling a woman when admitted to the class of an Order which will confer a knighthood and the title of 'Sir' on a man.

The final title

In common with many of its fellow Orders, the title of the Order of the British Empire was prefixed by a superlative. 'Most Glorious' had been suggested, but whether the allusion was thought to be too warlike or too heavenly, it was dropped and, by Letters Patent dated 4 June 1917 and gazetted on 24 August, 'The Most Excellent Order of the British Empire' was finally, formally and publicly brought into being.

The eighteen months of prolonged debate about such technicalities as the styles of 'unknighted knights' and lady 'knights', had been wearisome enough for all concerned, but still greater problems lay ahead. It was one thing to create a new Order, but quite another to decide who should have it and, more importantly, how many should have it. In one sense, the problems were just beginning.

TWO

Allocation and Management

THE SIZE AND ORGANIZATION OF THE ORDER

We do not propose to limit it very much, but we ought to have an idea of how far we are going, or otherwise we may suddenly find that the number is so great that the Order will be considered of no value at all, and nobody will take it. I have been trying to think that out, and the difficulty I have found is that there is no standard to go upon at all.

Sir Frederick Ponsonby, 1 May 1917

On 26 January 1917, Ponsonby sent a circular letter to the departmental permanent secretaries asking them to give some thought to their rights of nomination for membership of the new Order.

The Departmental Committee on Decorations is considering the scope of the Order and endeavouring to frame the principles on which it may be granted. It would be of considerable assistance . . . if you could roughly indicate the nature and the extent of the claims which your Department is likely to put forward. It is not asked that individuals should be named.[1]

Having already alerted government departments as early as September 1916 to the fact that a new honour was about to be instituted, Ponsonby now found himself in the unenviable position of having to field repeated requests for further information, and the non-appearance of the Order in January 1917 caused the first hiccup, as Ponsonby reported to Curzon.

Several government departments omitted from the New Year's Honours all persons whose services could be rewarded with the OBE . . . under the impression that a Gazette for this Order was shortly coming out. It has, therefore, made their awards at present, uneven and illogical.[2]

The lack of any sense of urgency on the part of the Cabinet, together with the protracted and tiresome debate about optional knighthood, caused Ponsonby to issue a cry for help to Curzon on 30 March: 'The War Office and Admiralty are screaming for decorations for Foreign Officials who have helped us'.[3]

On 26 April 1917 he circulated another memorandum, outlining the criteria for awards.

The Order is to be given in the first place for non-combatant services in connection with the War, and will be open to foreigners. After the War it is proposed that it should be utilised to reward services to the State, construed in a wider sense than is possible in the case of the Orders of the Bath and of St Michael and St George. It will include distinction in the Arts, Literature and Science, as well as public service rendered by persons outside the ranks of the civil service, who are at present ineligible for the CB or CMG. . . The Order will, for the present, be given solely for services in connection with the War. Only persons should be recommended whose service under ordinary circumstances would be worthy of some recognition, and the First Gazette will be framed with a view to including as many distinguished names as possible.[4]

A further memorandum, dated 27 April, added that the Order 'should not be given to those who already have other British Decorations, or, even to those who have reasonable expectations of receiving the Bath, or St Michael and St George.'[5]

The next stage, fraught with difficulty, was the convening of a meeting of heads of departments to take the discussion a stage further. Ponsonby decided to seek the King's approval to hold the meeting at Buckingham Palace. 'Owing to the jealousy of Government Offices I find it quite impossible to hold the meeting at any particular Government Office.'[6] The King approved the request, and the Master of the Household offered the Household Dining Room, adding, 'I have also warned the Senior Gentleman Porter that the Grand Entrance will be required'.[7]

The meeting was held on 1 May 1917, and the verbatim report runs to twenty-eight pages of typescript. The first part of the debate centred on the relative status of the National Service Order and the Order of the British Empire. It was agreed by all present that it should be equal in rank to the first two classes of the British Empire and used 'to meet the cases of conscientious objectors to knighthood'. Then Ponsonby raised the perplexing question of the size of the membership of the Order.

We do not propose to limit it very much, but we ought to have an idea of how far we are going, or otherwise we may suddenly find that the number is so great that the Order will be considered of no value at all, and nobody will take it. I have been trying to think that out, and the difficulty I have found is that there is no standard to go upon at all.[8]

A new departure

The Order of the British Empire was a bold development in the United Kingdom honours system, and it attracted criticism from those who failed to appreciate the principles on which it was founded. In the years after 1917, the distribution of the Order reached a level that was unprecedented within the United Kingdom, and by February 1921 membership stood at the figure of 25,419. Such a rapid increase in size brought forth allegations of unnecessary profligacy, and later even corruption, and the Order suffered a certain amount of scorn and ridicule throughout the 1920s. But the burgeoning of the Order can only be understood when set within the context of the unique circumstances of the First World War, and the reaction to that burgeoning when comparing the distribution of United Kingdom honours with European honours.

In 1921 the publishers of *Burke's Peerage* produced *Burke's Handbook to the Order of the British Empire*, a massive biographical directory of the living members of the Order at February 1921. The book was an attempt, in the words of the editor, 'to extend and give permanency to the scattered records of those who have been admitted to the Order in recognition of important services to the Empire in the hour of its greatest need'. He praised the Order as 'the British Democracy's own Order of Chivalry', and produced a true, if somewhat emotional, comment on its origins.

The entire British nation . . . was fully mobilised for war . . . all were harnessed to its remorseless wheels. The war had become an intimate part of everyone's life. Its demands were inexorable and insatiable. . . All the energies of the State, all the energies of industry, all the energies of individuals were directed towards the carrying on of a devouring and devastating struggle. . . The womanhood of the country was marshalled and mobilised as never before. . . Such were the conditions to meet which the new Order was instituted, for in a nation thus mobilised for war service how else could just recognition be made of those who were rendering signal service to their country?[9]

There is no doubt that the event of the First World War made the creation of the Order an absolute necessity.

The United Kingdom and Europe

Criticisms of the widespread distribution of the Order need to be set against the very un-European restrictive scope and distribution of United Kingdom honours before 1917. The one-class Orders of the Garter, the Thistle and St Patrick, with twenty-five, sixteen and twenty-two members respectively, were the national Orders of England, Scotland and Ireland. The twenty-four strong Order of Merit recognised artistic, scientific and military merit of the highest eminence. The small three-class Order of the Bath (c.2,300 members), was principally the preserve of the armed forces and the civil service. The Order of St Michael and St George, also a small three-class Order (c.2,200 members), recognised overseas service. The Orders of the Star of India, the Indian Empire and the Crown of India had an obvious geographical limitation, and the Royal Victorian Order was for the Sovereign's personal use. All these Orders were created to satisfy perceived, but quite specific, areas of need. There was no 'national' Order to recognise 'national' service.

As well as a restriction of scope, there was also a restriction on numbers that was without parallel elsewhere in Europe. The following table shows the relative distribution of Orders by the major European powers on the eve of the First World War.

Country	Orders awarded annually
Germany	29,000
France	22,000
Russia	16,000
Austria-Hungary	970
United Kingdom	320

The table shows the gulf between the practice of the United Kingdom and, with the possible exception of the Austro-Hungarian Empire, the other European powers in the award of Orders. As Ponsonby remarked to his fellow delegates, 'It becomes a question of whether we are right or the Germans are right'.[10] The scarcity of United Kingdom Orders was well known in Europe, and Sir Frederick Ponsonby, who accompanied Queen Victoria during her visits to the south of France in the 1890s, remembered the behaviour that surrounded the Queen's departure. 'There was always much ado about Orders and presents when the Queen left, as nearly everyone wanted an English Order, which was like a rare stamp or an unknown egg to collectors.'[11]

First proposals on numbers

Ponsonby initially suggested that the size of membership of the new Order might be as follows:

Grade	Numbers
GBE	100
KBE/DBE	300
CBE	600
OBE	1,000
MBE	1,500
Total	3,500

With foresight, a number of the other delegates thought that the numbers assigned to the fourth and fifth classes were too small. The Order was designed to cope with the emergency of the war, and to reward citizens, not only of the United Kingdom, but also of the Dominions and of India, and of the allied powers. Ponsonby then suggested doubling the numbers of both classes, the OBE to 2,000, and the MBE to 2,500 or 3,000. The figures of 2,000 OBEs and 3,000 MBEs were agreed, bringing the total membership of the Order to 6,000.

The remainder of the meeting was spent on the allocations to the government departments and to India and the Dominions. Sir Thomas Heath of the Treasury suggested that each government department should estimate the numbers that it would put forward for admission to the new Order. Ponsonby interposed to say that he had sent a circular to the departments earlier in the year asking them to do just that, 'and they failed absolutely. The Munitions Department told us they had 600,000 workers, and the Red Cross said they had 120,000; and everybody said, "We do not know who we should pick out".'[12]

Allocations of quotas

Allocation to the Dominions was a problem at the opposite extreme. Sir George Fiddes of the Colonial Office reported that mostly unhelpful replies had been received from the Governors-General.

Australia said she could not do it for the first Gazette, but would do it as soon as possible. That only means the Governor-General, because the political conscience of the present Commonwealth Ministry does not allow them to make any recommendations for honours at all. Then South Africa is in a difficult position owing to the English and Dutch there, and so on . . . Mr Massey, of New Zealand, whom I consulted, did not want to put forward any names at all. He is not a conscientious objector, but he realises that his party would not like it if he took the decoration. He was willing to put forward a few ladies – one was Lady Liverpool, because Lord Liverpool would not recommend his own wife, and Mr Massey said she had done a lot of work out there, and he would like to put her name forward. In the case of Newfoundland, I had a discussion with Sir Edward Morris [Premier of Newfoundland]; he said he did not wish to have any reward for war work. . . I went to Sir Robert Borden [Prime Minister of Canada], and the upshot of a long discussion with him was that whereas the Duke of Devonshire put forward a list, he had thrown in eight names with no discrimination of Classes, and as far as I can interpret his telegram they were all to be G.'s. . . Moreover, Sir Robert Borden said he was not quite satisfied with the Duke's list, because he noticed there were no French names in it, and he thought it wanted looking at.[13]

This debate took place less than five weeks before the institution of the Order and the announcement of the first appointments, and it was clearly going to be impossible to include any names from the Dominions. The meeting took Fiddes' view that the first list of appointments should be accompanied by a statement to the effect that the Dominion and Colonial List would be published later.

If you do not do that, people here and elsewhere will say, 'You have not properly recognised the Dominions or properly balanced the claims of one against another,'. . . It would look as if we sitting here had once more outraged the Dominions.[14]

Window-dressing The meeting concluded that the first gazette should be very small; all members of the civil service, and permanent officials should be excluded, although they could be considered for future gazettes; a sub-committee under the chairmanship of Sir Thomas Heath should determine the allocation of numbers of each class to government departments; the first gazette should be produced on no particular principle, but with the view of associating the Order with eminent persons; in all subsequent gazettes, each government department would be given the exact numbers of each class allotted to them, and would be asked to submit recommendations accordingly.

Throughout the discussion, Ponsonby referred to the first gazette of appointments as the 'window-dressing gazette'. He rightly predicted that the choice of the first names would be crucial, as the public would estimate the worth of the Order on the evidence of the names of those who had been selected. 'We propose to go in entirely for "window dressing", in order to make the new Decoration attractive. Later on we shall extend it in various directions, but of course the great point with an Order is to produce heartburnings; there is no greater happiness in this world than for a man or a woman to be anxiously expecting a Decoration for two or three months, and then, finally getting it.'[15]

I want to deal with this window-dressing gazette before we go to the other propositions, because it is so urgently required abroad. They keep on asking me for it . . . they want it all over the place, and we have nothing at present to give them. That is why I want to get this window-dressing gazette out as soon as possible, right or wrong . . . the names should be jumbled up together – I mean they should not be gazetted under 'Admiralty,' 'Board of Agriculture' and 'Colonial Office'; but the names should be put down as 'Jones,' 'Smith,' and that sort of thing, one after the other, with a description of what he was doing, otherwise you would get the British public making calculations.[16]

As Prince Louis of Battenberg remarked to Ponsonby on reading the report of the meeting, 'We always felt that the practical application of this new Order bristles with difficulties and I wish the Home Secretary joy'.[17]

The fourth day of June 1917 had been settled on as the date to announce the creation of the Order, but by 30 May the names of the first appointments had still not been settled, chiefly due to a delay imposed by the Prime Minister. When he saw the list of proposed appointments, Lloyd George decreed that it was not democratic enough, and Ponsonby complained to Dawson on 31 May that the Order 'has been hung up by the Prime Minister'.[18] He had written firmly to Lloyd George on 30 May urging that the list should appear on 4 June.

It is essential that the OBE should appear with the other lists on Monday; otherwise people will imagine it is not a *bona fide* Decoration. The First Gazette is merely a 'window-dressing' list, but if you could take out names which you think might give a wrong impression, and add others which would be more suitable, I could still manage to get it into the Gazette. The first list must contain names the public knows, and as this is the first time women are included, the names should meet with the general approval of the majority of women in the country.[19]

Lloyd George was not to be moved. Despite Ponsonby's urging, the Prime Minister refused to authorise a list for publication on 4 June and referred the issue to a meeting held on 7 June in the Privy Council Office. Those present were Lord Curzon, Christopher Addison (Liberal MP for Hoxton and junior minister at the Ministry of Munitions), George Barnes (Labour MP for Glasgow Blackfriars and junior minister at the Ministry of Pensions), Sir Edward Troup, Edmund Phipps (Secretary to the Ministry of Munitions), J. T. Davies (Private Secretary to the Prime Minister) and Ponsonby.

Our instructions were to reconsider the lists of recommendations, and to see whether we could not give it a more democratic aspect. I insisted that if the OBE was to be a success it would be necessary to include in the first list, names of well-known public people . . . but if the Committee insisted on having Mrs Jones and Mrs Smith in the First Gazette, it might kill the Order, stone dead. . . I had some difficulty in keeping these eminent men from doing something foolish, as they had not the foggiest ideas of the difficulties relating to Decorations. I am glad to say that I was able to keep in all the big names I wanted.[20]

The committee also agreed that responsibility for submitting names for the Order should be handed over to the Home Office.

Ponsonby's patience with the Prime Minister's insistence on a 'democratic' list of names was wearing thin, as he intimated to Charles Harris at the War Office on 25 June.

I have been trying to instil into the Prime Minister the right way of democratising an Order; this is not done by giving a chimney sweep a Grand Cross, but by ensuring that every man in the community should be eligible for some Class of the Order.[21]

Although the Letters Patent creating the Order were passed on 4 June 1917, and the date is recorded as the foundation day of the Order, a delay of eleven weeks occurred before the public was aware that there was a new Order. The Statutes, together with the first appointments, did not appear in the *London Gazette* until 24 August 1917. The long delay was partly due to the re-consideration of the first list of appointments, and partly due to a desire to wait until Parliament had adjourned for the summer recess, thereby ensuring 'more room in the press'.[22] On publication day, it was announced that the appointments should date from 4 June to link the new Order, retrospectively, with the Birthday Honours List. The first appointments included 13 Knights Grand Cross, 6 Dames Grand Cross, 43 Knights Commanders, 5 Dames Commanders, 79 Commanders, 70 Officers, 53 Members and 52 awards of the British Empire Medal.

The first appointments

There is little to be gained by a detailed analysis of this 'window-dressing' list. The names are now largely forgotten and their war efforts are history. The list of Knights Grand Cross was headed by the King's sole surviving uncle, the Duke of Connaught. Among the Knights Grand Cross were Viscount Gladstone, Chairman of the War Refugees Committee; Lord Emmott, Director of the War Trade Department; Lord Moulton, Director-General of Explosive Supplies, Ministry of Munitions; The Honourable Arthur Stanley, Chairman of the Joint Committee of the British Red Cross and the Order of St John; Sir Eric Geddes, First Lord of the Admiralty; Sir Arthur Pearson, Chairman of the Blinded Soldiers and Sailors Care Committee; Mr Justice Sankey and Mr Justice Younger, Joint Chairmen of the Advisory Committee as to Internment and Repatriation; and Alexander McDowell, Joint Director for Ireland, Ministry of Munitions.

Among the Dames Grand Cross were Lady Lawley of Queen Mary's Needlework Guild; Lady Paget of the Serbian Relief Fund; Lady Reid, for special services in connection with the Australian forces; and Mrs Katherine Furse, Commandant in Chief, Women's Voluntary Aid Detachment.

Ponsonby had had enough experience of the Prime Minister's office to be clear on one matter. The Order of the British Empire had to be removed from what he called 'the chaotic establishment at 10 Downing Street'.[23] Although the committee chaired by Lord Curzon on 7 June, had accepted Ponsonby's proposal that the Home Office should be the department responsible for the collection and submission of names, the decision was subsequently overturned by Lloyd George.

I thought that a decision arrived at by a Committee composed of three Cabinet Ministers was sufficient authority to work upon. Apparently however the Prime Minister on the advice of his Private Secretaries annulled this decision, and determined to take over the management of the Order at 10 Downing Street.[24]

The first Officials   Ponsonby's strong feelings on this subject influenced the arrangement and appointments of the ceremonial officials of the Order. Although all other United Kingdom Orders of Knighthood are attended by one or more 'officers', whose duties are mostly ceremonial, the use of the title 'officer' for members of the fourth class of the Order of the British Empire, required a different designation. Consequently, the 'officers' of this Order have always been styled 'officials'. A preliminary paper, dated November 1916, envisaged three officials: a King of Arms, a Registrar and Secretary, and a Gentleman Usher of the Purple Rod.

Dawson thought that the Order, 'shorn of so much that would popularise it',[25] would benefit from the appointment of a Grand Master, and that the office should be held by the Prince of Wales. Prince Louis agreed that this was a good way 'to raise the dignity of the Order as much as possible'.[26] The King consulted his uncle the Duke of Connaught, himself Great Master of the Order of the Bath, who agreed to the proposal.

The Statutes of 4 June 1917 established the three offices of King of Arms, Registrar and Secretary, and Gentleman Usher of the Purple Rod. By Statute 26, the King of Arms was required to do no more than 'sedulously attend the Service of the Order'. By Statute 27, the conjoint Registrar and Secretary was to:

record all proceedings connected with this Most Excellent Order in a register to be appropriated for that purpose and shall, under the directions of the Grand Master, prepare all Warrants and other instruments to be passed under the Seal of the Order and engross the same, [and to] summon the Knights Grand Cross to attend the Sovereign at all investitures of this Order. . .

Statute 28 described the insignia of the Gentleman Usher of the Purple Rod, but assigned him no duties. By Statute 29, all the officials were commanded to 'execute diligently whatever the Sovereign or Grand Master may be pleased to command touching the interests of the said Order', and all three offices were to be held 'during good behaviour'.

Dawson proposed to Ponsonby that Lord Lurgan, the former State Steward at Dublin Castle, who had offered his services, should be the King of Arms; the office of Registrar and Secretary should be held ex officio by himself; and the office of Usher should be held by an official at the Home Office. Ponsonby concurred in the suggestion of Lurgan, but he could see the flaws in Dawson's proposal to assign anything other than a minor and nominal official to the Home Office. Dawson was essentially unwilling to agree that real responsibility for the organisation of the Order should lie anywhere other than at the Central

Chancery. Ponsonby suggested the division of the conjoint office of Registrar and Secretary, and patiently explained to Dawson the logic of his proposal. There were two separate functions connected with organising the Order. Firstly, an official who collected recommendations, prepared lists of appointments for submission to the King, and who generally supervised the machinery set up to decide who should be given the Order. Secondly, an official who supervised the manufacture of insignia, ensured that a sufficient supply was kept in stock, attended investitures, and was generally responsible for the actual bestowal of insignia. The first official would be on the staff of the Home Office, and the second official would be on the staff of the Central Chancery.

The Secretary of both Indian Orders is at the India Office and I am sure that if the Home Office runs this Order they will name the Secretary. . . As we are starting a thoroughly up to date Order it would be perhaps best to place the Officers of the Order on a thoroughly logical footing. . . I hope . . . that you will hang up this question until the Home Office has definitely taken over the Order. There are two difficulties yet to be overcome. One is that the Private Secretaries at 10 Downing Street are anxious to keep the Order in their own hands and appear to be very reluctant to hand it over to the Home Office; the second is that the other Government Departments may resent being placed under the Home Office for the purposes of this Order. Until all this has been definitely settled, it would perhaps be unwise to appoint the Officers.[27]

It was not until 15 November 1917 that Ponsonby gave the matter further thought. He reiterated his belief that the offices of Registrar and Secretary should be separated and that, additionally, the Order should have a Prelate, and offered the following provisional list of appointments.

Grand Master:	The Prince of Wales
Prelate:	The Bishop of London
King of Arms:	Lord Lurgan
Registrar:	The Secretary of the Central Chancery
Secretary:	The Home Office official in charge of the Order
Gentleman Usher:	Sir Frederic Kenyon, Director of the British Museum
	or
	Sir Cecil Smith, Director of the Victoria and Albert Museum

By February 1918 it had been agreed that the Secretary should be the Permanent Under Secretary of State at the Home Office, and the provisional list was forwarded to the King for his approval. The King selected Sir Frederic Kenyon in preference to Sir Cecil Smith, but decided against Lord Lurgan, and favoured General Sir Arthur Paget instead. Formal letters of appointment went out on 7 March, and the appointments were announced on 9 April 1918. The revised statutes were gazetted on 12 April 1918. Apart from the changes to the ceremonial officials, the Viceroy of India and the Governors-General of Canada, Australia, New Zealand and South Africa, were empowered to conduct investitures on behalf of the King, and certain heraldic privileges were extended to members of the Order. No duties were assigned to the Prelate. The Registrar was charged to:

record all proceedings connected with this Most Excellent Order in a register to be appropriated for that purpose and shall, under the directions of the Grand Master, prepare all Warrants and other Instruments under the Seal of the Order and engross the same, that he shall summon the Knights Grand Cross to attend the Sovereign at all investitures of this Order.

The Secretary was required to 'collect and tabulate the names of those persons who are to be submitted . . . for admission to this Order or to be awarded the Medal'.

To Downing Street again

Moving the Order away from the control of the Prime Minister's office was not as easy a task as Ponsonby had hoped. He informed the King of his plans, and the King suggested that Ponsonby himself should run the Order with the assistance of the inter-departmental committee.

> I have put this proposal forward to the Prime Minister, but as it is unlikely that I shall receive any reply I propose going to 10 Downing Street myself, and fixing up the whole question if possible, with him, if not with one of his secretaries.[28]

Ponsonby had been to No. 10 by 20 September, but with little success. Lloyd George being away, he had an exasperating and unsatisfactory meeting with William Sutherland, MP for Argyllshire and the Prime Minister's Parliamentary Secretary. Sutherland had acquired a dubious reputation of hawking baronetcies around the clubs of London, and was probably only one of a number of individuals who brought the honours system into disrepute during the premiership of Lloyd George. Whether or not Ponsonby was aware of that, his encounter with Sutherland was less than successful.

> He certainly did not impress me as being a man of any capacity, and his ignorance on all questions relating to Decorations was pathetic. He suggested that he and I should run the Order, and that there was no necessity to consult anyone else. He said he was very much opposed to Committees, and thought it far simpler for the Prime Minister and the King to keep it entirely in their own hands. I refused even to consider this proposal, and said that the King would run it with the Committee composed of representatives of the principal Government Departments: after some discussion he more or less agreed to this, but said he must first consult the Prime Minister. . . He had absolutely no idea of the difficulties of distributing these decorations evenly, and having been two years ago associated with the Ministry of Munitions, he appeared to think that that was the only Department that required decorating. . . I am sure that if the Prime Minister will agree to my running the Order with the Committee, and doing everything according to the book, we shall get to work and produce another list, but if it is left in the hands of this secretary, we shall get nothing done at all.[29]

Ponsonby was not alone in his feeling that nothing was being done. Lloyd George's decision to retain the Order at Downing Street was not helped by the fact that his private secretaries omitted to tell the committee, or indeed anyone else. Lord Derby, Secretary of State for War and Vice-President of the Army Council, wrote to the Prime Minister, asking when the Order was to be transferred to the Home Office, and received no reply. Arthur Balfour, First Lord of the Admiralty, wrote pointing out the unsatisfactory nature of the existing arrangement. Walter Long, Secretary of State for the Colonies also voiced his unease. The absence of any list of appointments from the Dominions was beginning to cause criticism and Long felt that urgent and decisive action was needed to place the organisation of the Order on a clear and firm footing.

> I cannot usefully ask the Governors-General to submit lists until I am in a position to tell them how many honours in the several Classes will be available for each of them; and this again cannot be determined until some scale of proportion has been established as between this country on the one hand and the Dominions and Colonies on the other. I have consulted my colleagues of the Home Office, Foreign Office and War Office and I

find that they are experiencing similar inconvenience... We consider that the Home Office is the natural and best office for the purpose. In the absence of such an arrangement things seem to have come to a deadlock, and we urge on the War Cabinet the importance of taking the course suggested without further delay. Until this is done, I see no prospect of getting the matter out of its present chaotic condition, and I fear that grave scandal may ensue.[30]

The issue was discussed by the War Cabinet, but Lloyd George refused to give way, arguing that the other government departments could not be controlled by the Home Office; only the office of the Prime Minister could do this. He then adjourned the discussion saying that he would consult the three living former prime ministers, Arthur Balfour, Herbert Asquith and Lord Rosebery.

Back to numbers and allocation

On 28 September, two days after Long's memorandum, and the day following the first investiture of the Order, the departmental committee was convened at 10 Downing Street to bring some degree of order out of the prevailing chaos regarding allocation and numbers. The results were communicated to William Sutherland in a memorandum dated the same day. Since the Order of the British Empire was intended primarily for civilians contributing to the war effort, the committee began by estimating the percentage of decorations and medals to men in the field at 2½ per cent. Applying this formula (twenty-five per thousand) to the home services, it became clear that the numbers of the Order of the British Empire would need to be radically increased. It was claimed, for example, that the Ministry of Munitions now employed 750,000 people (an increase of 150,000 on the figure quoted on 1 May!) which would make their allocation 18,750. Even allowing for the fact that three-quarters of these would be medals, there would still be 4,000 admissions to the Order from that one department. The committee concluded that the size of the membership originally envisaged would be totally inadequate, and recommended that the numbers of the CBE, OBE and MBE classes should be doubled in size to 1,200, 4,000 and 6,000 respectively. They agreed that the numbers of the GBE, KBE and DBE grades should not be increased, because of the possibility of depreciating the value of a knighthood.

A complicated mathematical formula divided the numbers between the various departments and between the United Kingdom and the Dominions and India. The numbers would be divided between three gazettes, and 70 per cent of each gazette would go to the War Office, the Admiralty, Munitions, Shipping and Air Board, and the remaining 30 per cent would be distributed among the other departments. The population of the Dominions being approximately one-quarter of that of the United Kingdom, the committee recommended that one-quarter of the numbers of the United Kingdom should be allocated to the Dominions, the Colonial Office subdividing this allocation on the basis of the population of each Dominion. Although India had several well-established orders and medals, it would have been open to misinterpretation to exclude her, and it was agreed that the numbers available to India should equal those of Canada, the largest of the Dominions. One-twelfth of the total numbers calculated for the United Kingdom would be allotted to the Crown Colonies.

The Order would be available to civil servants, but only for work directly connected with the war. 'It is particularly important that women in the Civil Service who have rendered services in connection with the war, should not be excluded.'[31]

Awards to the Allied powers should be made on the basis of half the numbers available to the United Kingdom. 'It is important that the high standard of British Decorations in Europe should be maintained, and therefore the numbers should be limited.'[32] The task of dividing the numbers among the various allied countries was devolved to the Foreign Office.

A certain number of members of the Diplomatic Service had been included in the first gazette 'with a view to give the Order its proper status in the eyes of foreigners on whom it might be conferred'.[33] This had apparently been resented by some of the recipients in the belief that it would render them ineligible for the Order of the Bath. It was therefore agreed that while both the Diplomatic Service and the Consular Service should still be eligible, the practice of awarding the Order to the Diplomatic Service should gradually be discontinued. 'The Consular Service is however on an entirely different footing from the Diplomatic Service, as they rarely rise to sufficient eminence to be considered for the Order of the Bath.'[34]

The committee discussed the possible award of the Order to officers of the armed forces, but decided to make no recommendation for the time being. The Army Council would need to decide whether to differentiate between officers serving in the theatre of war, and those serving in the United Kingdom, and if there was to be a distinction, then the Order might be an appropriate award for the latter. For much the same reason, the Order should not yet be given to foreign serving officers in the allied armies. To avoid the danger of compromising their neutrality, the apportion of decorations to neutral countries was deferred until the end of the war.

The committee found it impossible to draw up any regulations governing the distribution of the Medal of the Order, because the conditions of service varied so much in government departments, and a sub-committee was appointed to consider proposals relating to the Medal. On the subject of the Medal, Ponsonby believed that with a five-class Order of 11,600 members in the United Kingdom alone, it would be too much for the King personally to present the Medal.

Already His Majesty has as much as he can do to keep pace with the Military Decorations. I would suggest that the Lord Lieutenant of the County, or the Mayor of the town should be given authority to present the Medal in a suitable manner.[35]

Ponsonby's concern for the King's ability to cope with the presentation of a vastly increased quantity of honours was borne out by a letter from Colonel Clive Wigram, the King's Assistant Private Secretary, to the Central Chancery in February 1923.

When sending warrants of appointment to the various Orders, please do not send the King more than fifty at a time. An enormous batch of Warrants for appointment to the Order of the British Empire arrived this evening, and there were too many for His Majesty to tackle at one sitting.[36]

The size of the membership of the Order of the British Empire was unprecedented in the United Kingdom, and the 'window-dressing' list of 24 August 1917 gave no true indication of the lavish scale of appointments that was to follow. Whether they were generous or whether they were irresponsible depended on the extremes of opinion, but one thing was certain, neither the King nor the country were prepared for what they were about to receive, and well before the publication of the second list in January 1918, expressions of unease were beginning to be heard.

THREE

Anxiety and Concern

THE PROBLEMS BEGIN TO SURFACE

A new decoration is a delicate thing, and unless it is launched under favourable circumstances it may be looked upon with suspicion, and even ridicule.
Sir Frederick Ponsonby to David Lloyd George, 30 May 1917

On 10 October 1917, Sir Douglas Dawson wrote to Ponsonby with a worrying account of a meeting he had had with Lieutenant General Sir John Cowans, Quartermaster General to the Forces and Sir John Stevens, a retired judge.

They are loud in their denunciation of the Prime Minister keeping the British Empire in his hands solely. They say all letters awarding the honour are *signed by Lloyd George*. They say it is absolutely essential that this Order be released from its *political* tie. . . Now it is absolutely essential to drag this away from L.G. Surely the King, as sovereign of all the Orders, can insist on this. Cowans tells me Derby says he is powerless, but he promised to speak again to Derby, and if necessary try & see the King himself. He says immense harm has been done already by the political tendency given in selection. . . Can you do something to help this, it is time a strong hand was put down in the matter. The King will probably hear shortly from Derby, at least if Cowans does what he said he would. When we meet I can speak more plainly than in a letter.[1]

Although forceful and forthright, Ponsonby was a well-trained courtier with a very sensitive early warning system. The slightest intimation of a potential conflict between the King and the Prime Minister, provoked by a third party, was enough to start the alarm bells ringing. He was in no doubt that control of the Order should be removed from the office of the Prime Minister. On more than one occasion he referred to the 'chaotic establishment' at 10 Downing Street as ample justification for moving the Order to the Home Office. But whatever the rights or wrongs of the behaviour of the Prime Minister and his staff, the King must not be drawn into a political dispute. His reply to Dawson was sent by return of post.

I am most anxious that the King should not at present be mixed up with the question of who should have the OBE. It is a matter on which the P.M. apparently feels very strongly and I should be sorry if he and the King came to loggerheads over such a trivial matter. . . It is very difficult for me to move unless I know that the War Cabinet approves of my dealing with the matter.[2]

It is well known that King George V was alarmed at the distribution of honours by his maverick Prime Minister, yet he was conscious of his circumscribed role as a constitutional monarch and anxious to avoid a clash with the head of a demo-cratically elected government. Although he had no liking for his Prime Minister, King George V behaved with impeccable constitutional propriety throughout, and treated Lloyd George with unfailing courtesy. Sadly, the reverse was not true and Lloyd George's attitude to the King was cursory and increasingly neglectful, at least of the royal prerogative to be consulted, and he discharged his duties to the King only when it suited him. In April 1917 Lord Stamfordham complained that 'His Majesty is pained at what he regards as not only a want of respect, but as ignoring his very existence'.[3]

Ponsonby was concerned to keep the King well clear of any political dispute, but he was a loyal courtier and had no intention of allowing the King's prerogatives to be eroded, and he enlisted the aid of the Earl of Crawford and Balcarres, Lord Privy Seal.

In the first instance the present Prime Minister was induced to make a formal submission to His Majesty, and the creation of the Order . . . was officially sanctioned. I am constantly asked whether the proposals put forward by the Committee have received the Royal Approval, and I have had to reply that, so far as I know, they have never yet reached the King. Would it be possible for you, as the Minister of Cabinet Rank, responsible for the Order, to make a formal submission to His Majesty on the subject.[4]

Lloyd George and the Order

The Order of the British Empire was unfortunate in being created during the time of David Lloyd George as Prime Minister, and he remained Prime Minister for the first five years of the Order's existence, until ousted by a backbench coup in 1922. Lloyd George was a man of undoubted ability and powerful oratory, but his tenure of 10 Downing Street was clouded by his reputation for countenancing a practice known as the sale of honours. This highly disreputable practice is well known and well chronicled, and led directly to the Honours (Prevention of Abuses) Act 1925. There was almost an air of comedy about the way in which honours were sold for contributions to party funds, which made the Prime Minister seem not unlike W. S. Gilbert's impecunious Duke of Plaza Toro, who raised funds to support himself by the unscrupulous use of his position.

> Small titles and orders
> For Mayors and Recorders
> I get – and they're highly delighted –
>   They're highly delighted!
>
> M.P.s baronetted,
> Sham Colonels gazetted,
> And second-rate Aldermen knighted –
>   Yes, Aldermen knighted.

Was the Order of the British Empire tainted by the scandal of the sale of honours? The question is impossible to answer without undertaking the massive task of a detailed enquiry into each of the 25,000 appointments to the Order in the years that Lloyd George was Prime Minister. There were probably some 'political' appointments to the Order in the years 1917–22 as there have been ever since, but whereas the post-1922 appointments for political service have been subjected to rigorous scrutiny by the Political Honours Scrutiny Committee, the pre-1922 appointments were subject to no scrutiny whatever. There is an account of one recipient who, at his investiture, was asked by the King why he had been appointed to the Order, and he replied that he did not know. Ponsonby conducted an investigation on behalf of the King, and it transpired that the recipient's name had been added to the list at the last moment by William Sutherland, one of the Prime Minister's parliamentary secretaries.[5]

It is difficult to state categorically that the Order was not part of that abuse of honours, but it can be asserted that it is unlikely to have been so. The sale of honours involved substantial sums of money, and substantial sums were only to be gained by the offer of substantial titles. In fact there had to be a title involved – a peerage, a baronetcy or a knighthood – for money to exchange hands, and the most desirable honours were those of an hereditary nature, i.e. peerages and baronetcies. Knighthoods, being non-hereditary, came some way down the list of coveted honours, and knighthoods in the grade of Knight Bachelor, or even in the Order of the Bath or the Order of St Michael and St George, were much more desirable than the new and very humble Order of the British Empire. In 1922 during a debate on honours in the House of Lords, the Duke of Devonshire read out a letter from a tout who had a knighthood for sale – 'not of the British Empire, no nonsense of that kind, but the real thing'.

Nevertheless, the large number of awards of the Order were set against this scenery of a cavalier attitude towards the bestowal of honours, and the Order inevitably suffered by association. If peerages were for sale, then everything was for sale, and with such vast numbers of OBEs and MBEs being given out each year, there crystallised a suspicion that all was not above board with the Order of the British Empire. There were those who suspected that the Order, like so many honours during Lloyd George's premiership (1916–22), was given in return for political services, whether financial or of another kind, and had nothing to do with war service. This latter suspicion possibly lay behind a curious and circuitous question in the House of Commons on 3 July 1918. Lieutenant Colonel Henry Croft, Member of Parliament for Christchurch, rose to ask the Prime Minister:

how many male recipients of the Order were under military age; and whether he will give an undertaking that in future this Order is not extended to those who are unwilling or unable to serve their country in the field.[6]

The reply, given by the Home Secretary on behalf of the Prime Minister, was categorical and unequivocal: 'There is . . . no foundation for the suggestion that the honour has been conferred on any person unwilling to serve his country in the field.' Remove the Order of the British Empire from the equation, and Croft's question, conceivably, might be taken to refer to conscientious objectors. But the overt complaint that this Order in particular was being used to reward such people, indicates the low level of esteem in which it was held, and it was to be many years before the Order was able to escape from this dark cloud of disdain which hung over it like a curse.

It should be stated, in fairness to Lloyd George, that he was head of a government that was in the throes of the worst war in European history, and the Order of the British Empire, as with so many other things, was a means to an end. He was consumed with the task of winning the war, a task he was not prepared to leave to professional soldiers, and he had neither the time nor the interest to concern himself with the intricacies or principles of a new honour. He was not a Ponsonby or a Dawson, with the time and the interest to fuss over the details of the appearance of the insignia or the allocation of numbers. He was concerned above all else with winning a war, and victory was by no means certain throughout 1917 and the early months of 1918. The Order was one of many tools that he used to increase morale to win the war, and use it he did.

The War Cabinet met on 17 October and accepted the departmental committee's report of the 28 September, but with three exceptions. Firstly, the Secretaries of State for India and the Colonies would vet the recommendations from their *Lord Crawford's report* departments and then send them through the Prime Minister's office to the King. Secondly, Ponsonby's belief that the control of the Order should rest with the Home Office was firmly rejected. It was thought desirable that the other government departments should send their recommendations to the Prime Minister 'for his scrutiny, and amendment if necessary'.[7] Although it was pointed out that this would entail an enormous amount of labour for the Prime Minister and his staff, the reply was that the burden would substantially decrease after the war when it became simply a matter of filling the vacancies.

The Prime Minister urged the importance of vesting in the hands of the Prime Minister the final decision in regard to the recommendations for such Honours, as it would be impracticable to detail the Head of one Government Department to adjudicate on the claims put forward by the other Departments, and that a Prime Minister was independent in such matters.[8]

Thirdly, the committee's revised and increased limitation on numbers was not accepted, on the ground that it was impossible, even approximately, to assess the number of people eligible, since it could be said that the whole nation was eligible.

On this last point, the Cabinet charged Lord Crawford with producing new recommendations. Crawford was not overjoyed at the task of sorting out the new Order as he confided to Ponsonby on 23 October 1917. 'The more I contemplate this infernal problem the bigger does its stature grow.'[9] He submitted a provisional report to the War Cabinet on 25 October urging a control on numbers of appointments, and an efficient co-ordination of recommendations.

Many complex and delicate problems arise on which I shall send a subsequent report, but I desire to invite an early decision on one or two matters of urgency. In order to have names ready for the coming New Year's Honours List, it is necessary to establish in a general manner the total number of decorations to be conferred, the percentage to be allotted to various services, and the number of gazettes into which this total is to be divided. . . It is specially important for the Foreign Office, India Office, War Office and Colonial Office to receive their instructions forthwith.[10]

Crawford recognised that Ponsonby was an expert in such matters and carefully consulted him before submitting his final report. On the question of numbers Crawford agreed with Ponsonby's recommendations of 28 September, but added the numbers of appointments that would be allocated pro rata to the Dominions, India, the Colonies and the Allied Powers.

Grade	Ponsonby's recommendation to the meeting of 1 May 1917	Decision of the meeting of 1 May 1917	Decision of the meeting of 28 September 1917	Lord Crawford's calculation of 25 October 1917 (including Dominions)
GBE	100	100	100	195
KBE/DBE	300	300	300	585
CBE	600	600	1,200	2,350
OBE	1,000	2,000	4,000	7,830
MBE	1,500	3,000	6,000	11,250
Total	3,500	6,000	11,600	22,210

The allotment of numbers to the various government departments also occupied Crawford's mind, but it was an impossible subject to resolve to everyone's satisfaction, and poor Crawford found himself tackling the problem alone, though with advice from the ever-helpful Ponsonby. The Admiralty was allotted 25 per cent of the appointments, which Crawford thought 'excessive', and he wanted it made clear that the percentage would be subject to review. On 27 October he went to see John Davies, the Prime Minister's Private Secretary, to seek his aid in dealing with the problem, but found it a waste of time. 'I went to see him yesterday & found him quite as bewildered as I am myself.'[11] Crawford was certain that mutual jealousy among government departments was a sufficient reason for them not to be told each other's share or quota, but, as he told Ponsonby on 7 November, the Prime Minister had to lay down the rules as quickly as possible.

But when will he be able to attend to it? He won't be back for several days, & on his return will be immensely pressed on very urgent things. I asked Curzon if the Cabinet could act to give me authority to go ahead – Curzon doesn't think so & in any case is in bed. He referred me to Bonar Law, who hasn't answered. I am really afraid of some scandal which may be caused by the names being rushed at the last moment.[12]

Crawford's final report to the War Cabinet, dated 11 November 1917, was a model of its kind and indicates that he had listened carefully to Ponsonby's points.

I remind the Cabinet that when complete the Order of the British Empire will have a roll of 22,000 Members. The risks involved are as obvious as the scale of work entailed. It is an essential that the Order should make a good start, since recovery after a gazette which does not strike the public mind as well chosen, must be difficult and may be impossible. . . In this new Order Departments will submit large batches of names quite unknown outside specialised circles. No general criterion or standard of criticism will exist, and a real responsibility for the selection will therefore have to rest upon the Heads of Departments who alone will be able to adjudicate among competing claims. When the Prime Minister thinks it desirable to make revisions, omissions or additions, the responsible Minister should be invited to explain his choice, otherwise the balance of his whole list may be overthrown, with serious reflex action upon the lists of other Ministers. . . Some Department must be chosen to carry on the day to day work, to maintain continuity of method, and to keep Departments in touch with each other. At first I thought the Treasury with its intimate and personal connexion with all public offices, should undertake the duty, but I now think that the Home Office is better suited for the purpose, and should become the official and permanent medium of communication. . . The task of managing this Order will be quite insuperable unless the immediate procedure is defined and a strongly equipped secretariat is appointed without delay.[13]

The Cabinet duly considered Crawford's memorandum at a meeting on 14 November, and made the following decisions:

1. The Prime Minister should be free and unfettered in adding to the list names of persons who would not be covered by the recommendations of the Departments.
2. The Home Office should act as a central office for all work connected with the Order up to the stage where the names were gazetted.
3. The chancery work should be entrusted to the Central Chancery of the Orders of Knighthood.
4. Lord Crawford, in conjunction with the Home Secretary, should draw up provisional rules for the Order to be laid before the King.
5. In due course the Prime Minister should submit Statutes for the King's approval.[14]

The decision was in essence a compromise. The Home Office would effectively administer the Order, but the Prime Minister would have final control over appointments. Crawford sent a letter to Ponsonby, dated the same day as the Cabinet meeting, in which he implicitly stated that he had tried to keep the Order out of the Prime Minister's hands, but to no avail.

He was adamant! – and I am bound to say I got no help in my suggestion that he should consult the head of Dept who would or might have made a recommendation about the same individual. That risk therefore remains – but I gave him a salutary word of warning & I hope he will be cautious.[15]

Crawford's hope proved to be a forlorn one. In giving the Prime Minister free and unfettered authority to add names to the departmental recommendations, the Cabinet had effectively abandoned any control on numbers. When the first substantive list of appointments to the Order was published in January 1918, it contained a total of 2,641 names, an unprecedented number, but criticism was directed in the main towards the large number of appointments to the first and second classes, 18 GBEs and 93 KBEs or DBEs. The number of recommendations from government departments for the second class had originally totalled 75, the extra 18 names being added personally by the Prime Minister. Crawford's 'salutary word of warning' had been in vain, and in a letter to Troup dated 7 January 1918, Ponsonby described 10 Downing Street as 'the weak spot' in collecting recommendations for the Order of the British Empire. 'We have at present imposed a limit on all Government Departments, but apparently the Prime Minister is in a position to give an unlimited number if he so pleases'.[16]

That Ponsonby firmly laid the blame at the door of Lloyd George himself is apparent from a letter he wrote to John Davies, commiserating with him in his predicament.

I cannot help feeling that you are being placed in a most difficult position as regards the OBE, as you cannot say that the numbers are limited. You are left in consequence at the mercy of Cabinet Ministers and Whips, with no alternative but to consent to their representations. I have been wondering whether, under these circumstances, you could not ask the Prime Minister to limit in some way the numbers he has at his disposal. After all he could always make an exception in any case in which he was personally interested. But it would give you some valid excuse for refusing continual additions to the list. At previous meetings of the committee on the OBE we realized the danger of having unlimited numbers, and so decided to recommend a limit.[17]

Sir Edward Troup was also cautious about a rapid increase in the size of the Order, as he confided to Ponsonby: 'The Order had a very good press today (9 January) – but I doubt if the public will welcome another as big after an interval of only five months'.[18] On 30 January 1918, he chaired a meeting to discuss the Order in the light of this first major gazette and of public reactions to its size. The meeting decided that in future gazettes, the GBE numbers would be kept small and, if possible, the numbers of KBE/DBE and CBE classes would be reduced. But those present decided not to recommend a general reduction in the number of names for the next gazette.[19]

Recommended limit or not, the appearance of the gazette of 1 January 1918 created an almost insatiable demand in the departments for an increased allocation. It was reported on 26 April 1918 that a number of departments had appealed to the King to help them in their cause. The King decided as a general rule to refer all such requests to the Home Office. 'If the distribution of this Order is to be carried out fairly throughout the United Kingdom, it is obvious that one central authority must deal with all questions relating to it.'[20]

A limit on numbers and the geographical distribution of the Order were only two parts of the problem, Ponsonby identified a third area which increased his sense of unease. On 26 June 1918 he wrote to Lord Knutsford.

The mechanism for securing recommendations is, I am afraid, anything but perfect and some of our cabinet ministers are apt to recommend people without ever taking the trouble to ascertain their antecedents.[21]

In the spring of 1919 Edward Shortt, the Home Secretary, circulated a memo-randum to his colleagues in the Cabinet informing them that recommendations for the lower three classes of the Order now amounted to some 9,000 names, and asking whether this number was so large that it ought to be substantially reduced. Lloyd George responded to the memorandum by commissioning an enquiry into the recommendations. On 8 May 1919 Lord Southborough, Chairman of the War Trade Advisory Commission and a former Civil Lord of the Admiralty, was asked to consider the number and distribution of appointments to the Order at MBE, OBE and CBE level, and to make recommendations to the Cabinet. As there were comparatively few nominations to the GBE, KBE and DBE grades, he was not asked to undertake an investigation into these appointments.

Lord South-borough's report

Southborough's report was in the form of a long letter dated 1 July 1919 to Thomas Jones, one of Lloyd George's private secretaries. He examined the question of numbers and recommendations very carefully and his report reveals no evidence, at least at government level, of anything other than the very difficult task of managing this vast new Order.

I began my investigation with a strong bias against anything like such a number as 9,000 . . . but after seeing the representatives of all the more important Departments and after visiting the Red Cross Headquarters and some other offices from which a considerable number of recommendations have come, I am converted to the conclusion that a very drastic reduction of the number of recommendations would be highly inexpedient. . . I received a great deal of evidence which convinced me that the difficulties of His Majesty's Government would be increased rather than diminished by a severe cutting down from 9,000 to, say, 4,500 or 5,000. The disappointment, complaints and allegations of want of gratitude, charges of promises made by Departments and then broken would be worse than the gibes and sneers of the Press and a section of the Public at the very large distri-bution of the Order. . . It is true that criticisms may be made and perhaps justly made on the quality and standard of the recommendations – both of those already accepted and those now before us – but as a result of my investigation, I am disposed to think that on the whole the Departments have done their best to discover the more deserving cases and to grade them in order of merit among the various Classes. The Standard of merit has no doubt been uneven: but this is a matter in which hard and fast rules cannot be laid down, and without such rules a uniform standard is impossible. When dealing with the older Orders in Peace time the most careful enquiry could be made into each case. That is impossible here. The recommendations pour in to the public Departments from County Authorities, Committees and from all sorts of War work associations, and anything like close and responsible touch between the origin of the recommendation and its final acceptance seems quite hopeless. Again the pressure upon the Departments to restrict the numbers of their recommendations has driven some of them to keep in their books the names of persons already recommended, but who have been squeezed out of successive lists, – with this result, that a number of claims to recognition have been carried over with a pledge expressed or implied that they should be put before the Prime Minister during consideration of the final War List.[22]

Southborough conducted detailed negotiations with each of the Government Departments and with the Red Cross, and reported that the figure of 9,000 could, as a result of those negotiations, be reduced to 6,500. The CBEs would total 700, the OBEs, 2,200, and the MBEs, 3,600.

If this recommendation is accepted by the Prime Minister the honours in the several Classes will be arranged according to the figures which have been prepared in consultation with the recommending authorities, and which I think will be acceptable to them, although perhaps with some reluctance. I believe that I have carried the Departments so far along the line of reduction that they will not aid or abet any outcry against what is done.[23]

Somewhat surprisingly, Southborough's most difficult interview was with the Red Cross.

The Red Cross people were very anxious that their recommendations should be accepted as they stood and I saw from my negotiations with them that not much reduction could be made with assent. There was grave risk of dissatisfaction which would have become public and widespread.[24]

Southborough sent a copy of his report to Ponsonby on 8 July, with an accompanying note which underlined the fact that poor management and an absence of clearly defined policy were hampering the development of the Order.

The whole business has been an awful grind because with the exception of yourself I could get no definition of policy. . . I really do most seriously think that His Majesty should have the whole thing overhauled before it is put on a peace footing. There are grave administrative abuses.[25]

The words, 'administrative abuses', look alarming at first sight, but they need to be read in conjunction with the report itself. Southborough admitted that perhaps standards had not been consistent, mainly because of the enormous influx of recommendations, and his report on the distribution of the Order revealed evidence only of administrative confusion, not political corruption, or the sale of honours. If the Order suffered from anything, it suffered from bad public relations, an inefficient administrative machinery, and a maverick and unpredictable Prime Minister. Southborough was grieved that, one week after submitting his report, Lloyd George had not bothered to respond to it. 'The King was much amused to hear that you had not succeeded in obtaining any answer from the Prime Minister' wrote Ponsonby, 'that unfortunately is the difficulty from which everyone suffers.'[26]

The Northcliffe Mission

During 1917, Viscount Northcliffe, the Irish-born newspaper proprietor, led a mission to the United States to create and direct an agency to bring much needed supplies to the United Kingdom. The mission was successful and Northcliffe asked that the government express its gratitude by rewarding the members of the mission with appointments in the Order of the British Empire. The recommendations were turned down. Nothing daunted, Northcliffe sent them directly to Lloyd George, who submitted them to the King. King George V suggested that any recommendations for honours for members of the Mission, should properly be directed through the Foreign Office, and cautioned the Prime Minister that it was contrary to practice to allow Missions to have decorations. Lloyd George argued that the Mission was not a Mission in the traditional sense, in that Northcliffe's stay in the United States had lasted for several months. Ponsonby reported the outcome to Theo Russell, Diplomatic Secretary to Arthur Balfour, the Foreign Secretary, in a letter dated 29 December 1917. 'He pressed the King to grant the Decorations recommended by Lord Northcliffe, and His Majesty said that, as the Prime Minister wished it, he would approve of their being given.'[27] Russell replied on the same day.

I think it perhaps wiser not to say what I feel about this whole Northcliffe incident. He had no earthly right to send in any recommendations, and they were rightly turned down by the Committee. The whole job of attempting to keep up the high standard of British decorations, for which I have worked for three years is almost despairing and I have now abandoned all hope of being able to do so. I wish someone else would have a try.[28]

Putting aside the incident of the Northcliffe Mission, Russell's comment was no more than an expression of the despair of one who was probably unable to come to terms with the principles governing the award of a new Order, an Order that was quite unlike any of its contemporary Orders. On the evidence of Lord Southborough's Report, Government Departments had done their best to find the most deserving cases, and any criticism should be directed not at the quality of the recipients but at the haphazard and variable methods of the selection procedure.

Management

On 17 May 1918, Major Berkeley Levett (later Gentleman Usher to the King 1919–31) wrote to Ponsonby recommending the names of the ladies in charge of the Free Buffets and Canteens:

who really deserve recognition. It makes it extremely hard when all the people in charge of YMCA Huts, etc. are recognized, and so far only 2 of the important Railway Free Buffets out of seven have had any recognition. Most of them are open all day and all night, and during the year 1917 served nearly six million men.[29]

The ladies concerned were: The Countess of Limerick at London Bridge Station; The Honourable Mrs Phillips-Roberts at Liverpool Street Station; Mrs Lamond Howie at the Regents Park Post Office Canteen; Miss Ada Lake at Charing Cross Station; Mrs Beryl Wilson at Waterloo Station; Mrs Elizabeth Moncrieffe at the Britannia Club, 61 Westminster Bridge Road; and Miss Marietta Feuerheerd at Euston Station.

Ponsonby did his best to help, and was successful.

I tried to find out under what Department these ladies came, and it appears that they are under General Sir Francis Lloyd, but he tells me that he has no authority to send in any recommendations. It seems to me unfair that one lot of ladies should be decorated while the other should be ignored.[30]

At its meeting on 14 November 1917, the Cabinet had decided to centre all the administrative work of collecting recommendations for the Order on the Home Office, and the unfortunate individual now responsible for this herculean task, was Sir Edward Troup, the Permanent Under Secretary of State. Ponsonby wrote to him on 4 December expressing his deepest sympathy: 'My heart is so full of pity for you at having to take over the Order of the British Empire'.[31]

Handing over

FOUR

Annoyance and Discontent

POPULAR AND OTHER REACTIONS

*People accept it, change their minds, then decline it. Some remonstrate against the
class assigned to them, claim a higher one, and if refused decline it altogether.
It is criticised, cavilled at, and even ridiculed by a certain proportion of the Press, and
an unfavourable atmosphere has been created which is disastrous to the initiation
of a new Honour.*

Lord Stamfordham to Sir Edward Troup, 29 July 1918

Anxiety and concern were very quickly followed by annoyance and discontent,
with the publication of the first full-scale list of appointments in January 1918, followed by a second list in June of the same year. The very small size of the first
'window-dressing' gazette of August 1917 quickly became apparent when it was
compared with these unprecedentedly massive lists, totalling more than 5,000
names. The January list contained 2,641 names, divided among the grades as
follows:

Grade	Numbers
Knight or Dame Grand Cross	18
Knight or Dame Commander	93
Commander	327
Officer	955
Member	1,248

The size of this and succeeding 'war' lists, which continued to appear until 1922,
caused general astonishment and some hostile criticism. The public were simply
not accustomed to the distribution of honours on such a scale and, inevitably,
there were those who thought that such an apparently profligate distribution of
the Order rendered it nearly worthless.

In his book *The Queen's Orders of Chivalry*, published in 1961, Ivan De la Bere,
wrote.

There is no doubt that appointments to the OBE and MBE classes were made on far too
lavish a scale, just as the CB (Companion of the Order of the Bath) had been awarded far
too lavishly in 1815, and there is no doubt that many of the recipients of appointments in
the Order of the British Empire had not done anything sufficiently important to deserve
an Order of any kind.

De la Bere's statement should not be accepted without challenge. During those
early years, and throughout all the war lists of 1917–22, the reputation of the
Order did suffer from a suspicion which coalesced around the belief that, because
the Order was so widely distributed, it was therefore worthless. But the Order of
the British Empire was a new Order intended for unprecedented distribution to
recognise every level of service in a major conflict. It was undoubtedly awarded
lavishly and generously, but it was not awarded carelessly or lightly.

It is easy enough to allege that an honour is 'undeserved', and to whisper insidiously that the recipient 'didn't do anything to deserve it', and this allegation was to become particularly loud and shrill at the time of the appointment of the Beatles as MBEs in 1965. Allegations of the kind made by De la Bere were noised abroad, and there is nothing so infectious as rumour. It is only too true that a story long- and often-repeated eventually acquires the respectability of common currency and finally enters the history books as fact.

Nothing whatever is to be achieved at this distance in time by an inquiry into the characters and deserving merit of the earliest recipients of the Order of the British Empire. Reading the brief citations of those awarded the Order in 1918–19, there is no evidence to believe anything other than that the overwhelming majority of awards were for faithful and dedicated service, civilian and military, paid or unpaid in a conflict that was as tragic and bloody as it was long and extensive. In that respect, the Order of the British Empire admirably fulfilled the purposes for which it was created.

The Order faced an uphill struggle in the fight to establish a place of dignity in the honours system. Unfamiliarity with the new honour and irrational suspicions about the criteria for appointment were millstones around its neck, but ignorance of the intentions which lay behind its distribution were equally to blame. It could be argued that if the government had made an announcement to the effect that the intention of the Order of the British Empire was to reward 1 per cent of the population, from all classes, for a nationwide war effort, the Order might have been saved from ridicule. The machinery governing the selection and award of honours is necessarily a confidential and secretive process, but the early publication of the general principle that governed the size and distribution of the Order might have helped to defuse criticism.

In point of fact, the intended target of 1 per cent was never reached, and a figure of 0.1 per cent was nearer the mark. The population of the United Kingdom in 1921 was approximately 46,000,000, and the membership of the Order of the British Empire was only 25,000.

Criticisms

The distribution of the Order also caused a probably predictable backlash from disappointed recipients, who had hoped either for a higher class than that which they had received, or indeed for membership of a higher Order. Ivan De la Bere accurately assessed the problems faced by the Order in 1918.

The new Order suffered from the same growing pains that had afflicted the Order of the Bath after its enlargement from a single- to a three-class Order in 1815. . . Many of those who received appointments in the first three classes were disappointed at not having received appointments in one of the more senior and exclusive Orders. One person, who was connected with the Royal Household, when he was offered the KBE, instead of the KCVO for which he had hoped, refused it, and only accepted it when he was told very plainly by the King to do so. . . To many senior officers in the armed services, the CBE was given as a sort of consolation prize, because they had not been fortunate enough to obtain a CB or a CMG, while the OBE and MBE were given in many cases to those who, if they had been more fortunate, might have received some sort of gallantry award.[1]

Comparisons were soon made, and complaints began to arrive within days of the appearance of the first gazette. One furious letter from the Lord Lieutenant of County Durham landed on the desk of the King's Private Secretary.

I am writing to you more to relieve my feelings of wrath than in any expectation of any possible help from you . . . What I feared has happened. People in the County of Durham are not only dissatisfied with the choice but with the limited number of recipients in a very populous county . . . I believe my number is only 8 – Leicestershire has, according to the Duke of Rutland, about the same number – There is no comparison between the two counties with regard to population and numbers of battalions . . . Douglas Dawson has informed me that his Majesty desires me to present the medals on his behalf 'with fitting ceremony' – Of course I shall endeavour to do so but I warn you that there will be no enthusiasm and that I shall be unable to congratulate the county on a due recognition of the service of its most useful citizens.[2]

Even Ponsonby, who had worked so hard to ensure a good start for the Order, found himself on the receiving end of a complaint. 'I was attacked yesterday by the Chairman of one of our Railways, who said that the way in which Railway Officials had been selected during the last Gazette, have given rise to a certain amount of dissatisfaction.'[3]

Further signs of discontent appeared in the summer of 1918 with a number of recipients declining the Order after their names had been gazetted. As their appointments had been formally announced in the *London Gazette*, the only course was to publish a similar statement in the *Gazette* announcing the removal of the name from the register of the Order. Sir Douglas Dawson at the Central Chancery wrote to Ponsonby on 9 July 1918 expressing his alarm that these withdrawals were becoming 'a public scandal'.[4] Ponsonby agreed, feeling that such people gained 'quite unwarranted notoriety',[5] and the King ordered that those who refused the Order after their names had been gazetted, should simply have their names removed from the records of the Order, and not have their refusals gazetted.[6]

A man appointed in the Birthday Honours List sent an angry letter dated 27 June 1918 to G. G. Whiskard, Private Secretary to the Home Secretary and acting Secretary of the Order.

I definitely decline the Order. It was supposed to be a reward for work done. It would be a punishment to me to have to accept it, and I do not see why I should be punished for what little I have done. I see that others have had their names withdrawn, and I must therefore have the right to have mine withdrawn. I did, it is true, fill in the form with my names, at my wife's wish, although I never wanted the Order myself. At that time it was impossible to foresee the way in which the Order was going to be distributed, and my wife now agrees with my refusal. . . I repeat that I positively decline the Order.[7]

Whiskard wrote to Lord Stamfordham on 16 July 1918 with details of an unfortunate encounter with a lady recipient of the MBE.

She wishes to refuse Class V because her fellow workers tell her she ought to have had Class IV. . . She talked without ceasing for 45 minutes – chiefly abuse of England and everything English.[8]

One officer in the Royal Army Medical Corps put himself at risk in the trenches by studying the shock suffered by wounded men, and was recommended for the DSO. He was furious to be appointed an OBE in a 1919 honours list and wrote immediately to Winston Churchill, Secretary of State for War, asking for his name to be removed from the roll of the Order. He seized on the fact that the music hall artist George Robey (1869–1954), had been appointed a CBE in the honours list of 1 January 1919. Robey had spent much of the war giving performances to raise funds for war charities. The officer concerned was Captain Kenneth Walker, a surgeon by training, who served in the RAMC 1915–19, and died in 1966. In his memoirs, published in 1946, he made no secret of his feelings, and of the content of his letter to Churchill. In it he stated that 'he had been awarded an OBE, that he had no use for it and that he would be ashamed to be found dead in a ditch with it. Did the Right Honourable gentleman realise that his decoration was now a music-hall joke and that George Robey was appearing in the halls in OBE trousers. He thanked the Minister of War for his good intentions, but asked only that his war services should be rewarded with one privilege, namely the privilege that his name should be removed forthwith from the roll of the Most Excellent Order of the British Empire.' Walker was summoned to a meeting with a general, whom he remembered to be scarlet with indignation, and given a severe dressing-down. The general angrily rebuked Walker for this act of near-insubordination, and said that he himself 'would have been proud to wear it'. That was the end of Walker's career in the army. 'Not only was my name expunged from the Most Excellent Order of the British Empire, but it was also removed from the Army List. I was no longer a temporary officer or a temporary gentleman, but only a citizen.'[9]

The King had indicated his concern that the names of those who refused the Order should have been gazetted before their refusal was known and then, in a most public way, ungazetted. The following words are those of Lord Stamfordham, but they would certainly have carried the King's approval.

People accept it, change their minds, then decline it. Some remonstrate against the class assigned to them, claim a higher one, and if refused decline it altogether. It is criticised, cavilled at, and even ridiculed by a certain proportion of the Press, and an unfavourable atmosphere has been created which is disastrous to the initiation of a new Honour. . . The manner in which the appointments have been made seems open to criticism: it is asserted that unsuitable candidates have been selected, while deserving cases are ignored. . . He earnestly trusts that steps may be taken to avert the unfortunate circumstances which have undoubtedly tended to bring a new Order instituted by His Majesty into disrepute.[10]

Ponsonby was as soothing as he could be and explained to the anxious Stamfordham, in a long letter dated 1 August 1918, that the hostile reaction of the press was unfortunate, but not unexpected, and based on an entire misunderstanding of the nature of the Order. Since the beginning of 1918, more than 5,000 people had received the Order, and it was undoubtedly looked on as an excessive number by those who compared it with the older Orders, to which only a few dozen appointments were made each year. The Order of the British Empire was a completely new departure in the British honours system. It was intended to be broadly based and widely distributed, and if any comparison was to be made, then it should have been made with the Legion of Honour in France, and other European Orders.

The newspapers have failed to grasp the democratic character of the new Order and that its main object is to reward good service in the lower ranks which are quite outside the older British Orders.[11]

A further criticism was that the Order had been given to people who, or whose companies had, made large profits out of the war. Cases of this kind chiefly occurred in the lists submitted by the Ministry of Munitions and the Admiralty. But it was largely in order to reward the service of persons of this class that the Ministry had originally pressed for the institution of the Order. Ponsonby's instinct was to limit the next list of the Order to no more than 1,000 names, and that from one list at least, all members of munitions firms and other contractors should be excluded 'not because they do not deserve the honour, but because the public think they should be content with their other advantages'.[12]

Ponsonby was adamant that, in the main, the Order had been fairly and carefully distributed in accordance with the principles on which it had been created.

In practically every case the honour has been given to persons who have not solicited it, and, though it was inevitable that there should be some inequalities and that some persons should be discontented, the number has been much smaller than I anticipated. . . It seems to me remarkable that out of 2,500 persons it should have been necessary only to submit three names for omission from the Order, two of them foolish persons who accepted and afterwards changed their minds.[13]

What Ponsonby did not divulge was the numbers of those who had been offered and declined the Order before the names were published in the *Gazette*. Refusals of honours are neither common nor usual, and are often motivated by personal factors, whether domestic, religious or ideological. Doubtless there were, among the refusals in 1918, many people who fell into one or other of those categories, but it is likely that there were also some refusals based on disappointment at the offered class. It is now impossible to say how many refusals fell into which category, but it is known that five individuals refused the Order in 1917, a sharp rise to 212 in 1918 was followed by a fall to 91 in 1919, and another sharp rise to 460 in 1920.

Ponsonby, in his letter to Lord Stamfordham was, as ever, the voice of balance and common sense.

The hostile criticism has been chiefly in a few leading newspapers. But the bestowal of the Order on local men known to be active in patriotic service has been welcomed in hundreds of articles in the smaller local papers. We should also remember that against the one case where there is some outcry because the recipient thinks he should have a higher place, we should set the hundred cases where the distinction has given intense gratification, but little or nothing is said.[14]

To quote De la Bere again: 'In the general estimation, to receive an OBE was not at first regarded as anything of which the recipient could feel particularly proud. There were many jeering remarks and music hall jokes about the new Order. It was said for instance that the letters OBE stood for the "Order of the Bad Egg" or the "Order for Britain's Everybody".'[15] Such comments were products of a familiar syndrome, and similar derision had greeted the generosity with which King Edward VII had distributed the Royal Victorian Order after his accession in 1901.

The 'Order for Britain's Everybody' was a description coined by contempt, but it was not wide of the mark. The Order of the British Empire was intended to be within the reach of everybody, and it most certainly was, and it still is.

Dissatisfaction   There were, of course, those who wanted an Order, but not the Order of the British Empire. A new Order takes many years to establish a reputation in public opinion, and there were those who treated it with disdain, not necessarily because it was widely given, but because it was new and of a very lowly status when compared with the older Orders. The creation of the new Order caused feelings of dissatisfaction on the part of those who might reasonably have expected to receive an appointment in one of the older Orders. Among those who pressed the point was Sir Hubert Llewellyn Smith, Permanent Secretary to the Board of Trade. Smith visited Ponsonby and told him in no uncertain terms that the Civil Service might consider a boycott of the Order.

Smith came to see me today protesting vigorously against the OBE being given to civil servants. I told him it was decided to give it to them, & that Troup and Heath concurred. On the contrary – he says Troup has changed his opinion & that as a whole he fancies the Civil Service would prefer to be left out. . . I was sceptical, as the OBE will be useful in recognising war service among numerous hardworking fellows, who have no chance of the CB. He said that an increased quota of the latter decorations should be granted, but I told him that if the Civil Service boycotts the OBE it won't be any use their asking for an extra allotment of Baths.[16]

Public complaint

After the publication of the Birthday Honours List in June 1918, twenty-five individuals, all of whom were Privy Counsellors, and all of whom were either peers or knights, sent a letter to *The Times* on 29 August, pointing out that the list covered sixty quarto pages of the *London Gazette*, and urging that the bestowal of honours should be 'protected from this sort of cheapening'. Their complaint was instantly neutralised by a Member of Parliament. 'Their indignation', he wrote:

would have impressed me more deeply if I had been ignorant of the fact that every one of the twenty-five had inherited a title or accepted one cheerfully in his own person. . . Not one of them is any less than a Privy Counsellor, while Grand Crosses have been liberally scattered amongst them.[17]

The theme was continued by Lord Crawford in a debate in the House of Lords on 13 November that year, in which he stoutly defended the Order. 'The people who had been receiving the Order of the British Empire were humble people who had been, and were, doing great work for the country. It had been his duty on more than one occasion to make recommendations to that Order, and he could not say how bitterly he resented the comments of persons of high standing and full of honours about the humble people who were receiving well-earned recognition for work of incalculable value.'[18]

On 21 August 1918, the magazine *Truth*, published a leading article that severely criticised the use of the Order to reward the armed services.

It is not surprising to find that there is a strong feeling of resentment among those who have earned the Military Cross at the low place which this honourable decoration is given in the recent Army Council Instructions which laid down the table of precedence for the various orders. All agree that the place for the MC [Military Cross] is immediately after the DSO [Distinguished Service Order], the two orders being awarded for varying degrees of gallantry in the field. To allow the fifth class of a cheap Brummagem decoration like the OBE for which any lady is eligible who leaves her home to take care of itself while she fusses about at a soldiers' canteen, is to discount the value of a decoration which can only be won by the recipient risking his life before the enemy. Again, why should the Territorial decoration be superseded by the fourth and fifth classes of this new order, which is given away by the thousand to all sorts of men and women who only began to think of their duty after the outbreak of war, and in many cases were forced by public opinion to do so? The Territorial decoration can only be earned by officers of 'proved capacity, as a reward for long and meritorious service' after a minimum period of at least twenty years active service on the force, one such decoration being worth all the OBE's put together. I trust that the Army Council Instruction will be amended in such a way as to put this mushroom order in its right place.[19]

Not content with denouncing the 'mushroom order', the author continued to voice the complaints of some of those who had been given it.

Among the many unsatisfied recipients of the OBE medal are the official photographers and cinematographists who have been working with and for our armies during the last four years. Well they may be. Their work has really been most strenuous and dangerous . . . they have shared most of the hardships and perils of the armies on active service, and it is only by luck that they survive. . . It does seem a gratuitous slight to class them for decorative purposes with girls (who) have been engaged all the time in comfortable . . . billets at home.[20]

Establishment of the military division

The article highlighted an increasing unease in service circles about the use of the Order for service personnel. From its inception on 4 June 1917, the Order was awarded to both civilian and military personnel without differentiation, and although the majority of the appointments were to civilians, many awards, especially at OBE, MBE, and BEM level, were made to members of the armed services, often for gallantry. By September 1918, active proposals had been made to divide the Order into a Civil Division and a Military Division, with the distinction between the two being reflected in the design of the insignia.

The suggestion followed a proposal by the War Office that a Military Division should be instituted for the Order of the British Empire, somewhat on the lines of the Military Division of the Order of the Bath. According to a letter from M. D. Graham of the War Office to Sir Douglas Dawson on 26 July 1920, the Military Division was created, partly to be used in place of the Distinguished Service Order, the Military Cross, and other comparable medals, and partly because:

it was highly necessary that the Naval, Military or Air Force Services which merited recognition through the medium of the Order should be dealt with by the Admiralty, War Office and Air Ministry, respectively, and have a definite connection with the Services Honours Gazette.[21]

Graham went on to make an even more revealing comment: 'Moreover, as the Military Division can be operated on by the War Office without reference to the Home Office, there was a greater facility for gazetting purposes'. On the evidence of this letter it seems likely that the establishment of the Military Division was due, at least in part, to a desire from the Service Ministries to distance themselves from the recommendations for the Civil Division which were made by the Prime Minister and the Home Office.

The War Office suggestion was conveyed informally to the King by Viscount Milner, after his appointment as Secretary of State for War, and the King provisionally assented to the proposal. Details of eligibility and changes to the insignia were worked out at a meeting, chaired by Sir Edward Troup on 8 October 1918. The Admiralty representative called for a military division for the purpose of rewarding officers employed on duties involving actual bodily danger who were not eligible for a gallantry decoration. The War Office desired it for rewarding officers who were not qualified either under the statutes for the Order of the Bath or the Order of St Michael and St George. Troup himself was opposed to including in the Division officers engaged in administrative or clerical duties which involved no risk, while civilians doing precisely similar tasks would be placed in the Civil Division. All the service representatives, together with the Ministry of Munitions and the Ministry of National Service objected on the ground of the difficulty of making such a distinction, and Troup gave way. Appointments to the civil or military divisions would in future be governed solely by the status of the recipient and not by the quality of his act or the circumstances surrounding it. The Committee further agreed that the Military Division should be established retrospectively to enable serving officers appointed since 4 June 1917 to transfer.

Those already appointed to the Order could be transferred to the Military Division on the recommendation of the First Lord of the Admiralty, the Secretary of State for War, or the Secretary of State for the Royal Air Force, as appropriate.

Whereas the military and civil divisions of the Order of the Bath are distinguished from each other by substantial differences in the insignia, this does not appear to have been considered in the case of the Order of the British Empire, presumably for financial reasons. Attention focused instead on the ribbon. The Committee vetoed the first suggestion of marking membership of the Military Division by having a design of crossed swords woven into the purple ribbon. They unanimously agreed to recommend to the King that the ribbon should be purple with two narrow white vertical stripes in the centre. The King himself overruled the recommendation on the ground that the proposed design was similar to the ribbon of the Meritorious Service Medal, and the two might be confused. 'His Majesty therefore came to the conclusion that a thin red line down the centre of the ribbon would be preferable.'[22] The Military Division was formally instituted by King George V on 27 December 1918, to date from the creation of the Order on 4 June 1917, and the *London Gazette* of 15 January 1919 contained the names of all those who were to be transferred to the new Division.

The five-class Order of the British Empire, with civil and military divisions, was now an established part of the honours system of the United Kingdom, but its very existence was the cause of rumblings of discontent which could not be ignored. This great Order was instituted to reward the nation's war effort, but the war ended on 11 November 1918, although lists of awards of the Order for war service continued to appear in the *London Gazette* for a few years afterwards. By the end of 1922 and the publication of the last war service list, the membership of the Order of the British Empire stood at 25,000 and, according to some sections of opinion, it was careering out of control.

FIVE

Retrenchment and Consolidation

THE RESTRICTION OF AWARDS

I am anxious, as soon as possible, to let the public know that even the Order of the British Empire is not so easily won as appears to be now universally considered.
Sir Douglas Dawson to J. T. Davies, 14 January 1919

The Order of the British Empire had been created to recognise the wide level of service in the war effort, and the ending of the war presented a perfect opportunity to scrutinize its future. Many were concerned at the degree of ridicule to which the Order was subjected, an attitude created as much by its comparatively free distribution as by its unprecedented size, but it was an unprecedented Order created to deal with an unprecedented situation, and it had to be of an unprecedented size. With the arrival of the armistice in November 1918 came the time to take a long and hard look at the Order and to decide exactly what its future should be.

With characteristic foresight Ponsonby had advised Sir Edward Troup a year earlier, on 23 November 1917, to think carefully about the future of the Order.

There is one question which must be decided before the end of the War, and that is for what services will the (Order) be given in peace time? Some question may arise immediately in the conclusion of peace which will commit you to a certain line without having any definite idea as to where you are going. I am most anxious that the (Order) should not develop into a reward for the disappointed, or into an inferior class of existing British decorations.[1]

No one was in any doubt that the Order should continue to exist, but something had to be done to rescue it from the contempt in which many held it. The Order had to be moved from a wartime to a peacetime footing. It had to be made clear that, now the war was over, the Order would be very different from what it had been, and the only way to accomplish this was substantially to reduce its size, by agreeing and implementing a tight control on the number of appointments and on the selection of recipients.

The Prime Minister's office At the King's command, Sir Douglas Dawson wrote to the Prime Minister's Private Secretary and to the various government departments on 18 December 1918 with proposals for a statutory limit on the size of the Order. Dawson proposed a drastic reduction from the agreed wartime figures to a maximum peacetime quota of 80 GBEs, 200 KBEs or DBEs, 400 CBEs, 800 OBEs, and 1,200 MBEs. All appointments for war service and all honorary appointments would be excluded from these figures and rank as additional members. He proposed an annual quota of a maximum of 10 per cent of the statutory limit for the next ten years, so gradually and substantially reducing the size of the Order to a level more comparable with the 'older' Orders.

Nearly a month passed by, admittedly with Christmas intervening, before

Dawson received a delaying reply from John Davies. 'The Prime Minister has been so very busy that he has not had time to consider the proposals. . . Can this matter wait over until Mr Lloyd George is a little less busy.'[2] Dawson tactfully withdrew, but fired a warning shot.

Certainly, let us leave him alone for the present. . . But I am anxious, as soon as possible, to let the public know that even the Order of the British Empire is not so easily won as appears to be now universally considered.[3]

In the meantime, Dawson confided his thoughts to Ponsonby, who agreed with him that the public should be told as soon as possible that the Order was to be limited like all Orders. 'I trust no steps in this direction will be taken without I am consulted, as I hold very strong views on the subject and I think they are sound.'[4] He differed from Dawson only in the question of numbers, proposing a further reduction of the GBEs to 50, and the KBEs or DBEs to 150, but increasing the limit of the CBEs to 600, and substantially increasing the OBEs to 2,000, and the MBEs to 3,000.

We really do not want a 1st or 2nd class, as we have so many other Decorations to give, and it is difficult to assess precisely the value of a KBE as compared with a KCB, and KCMG. . . Looking at the question entirely from the outside point of view, there seems no doubt that we do not in this country give half enough 4th and 5th classes. In all foreign countries they give an enormous number of lower classes, and although I do not propose to copy them in this respect, I think that we should increase our numbers a good deal. . . I think it would be unwise to make these 4th and 5th classes too small.[5]

Ponsonby, ever the expert on honours, had based his calculations on the premise that the DSO (Distinguished Service Order) effectively functioned as the (military) 4th Class of the Order of the Bath; and the MC (Military Cross), DSC (Distinguished Service Cross) and DFC (Distinguished Flying Cross) functioned as the (military) 5th Class. Furthermore, the ISO (Imperial Service Order), functioned as the (civil) 4th Class of the Bath. In a typically dismissive comment, Ponsonby warned Dawson that it would be a waste of time consulting government departments. 'First of all they do not understand anything about Decorations and in the second place they are guided very much by the old Orders and Decorations.'[6]

In December 1919 Dawson took alarm at a government proposal to discuss the issue of statutory limits at a conference of departments, and told Ponsonby of his fears.

This procedure is precisely what we want to avoid. The question of Statutory Numbers will be discussed by everyone representing a Department, fur will fly, and no decision come to for months. Besides so ignorant are they that they are quite capable of saying there will be no Statutory Numbers fixed, that the numbers will be those already given, roughly 30,000! Even for preserving the dignity of the Order it is necessary to fix a limit, besides as Registrar of the Order and Head of the Central Chancery I claim to be heard in this matter, for I know this proposed procedure can only end in chaos, and I will not be responsible for the Chancery being able to tackle the future work in connection with the British Empire (Order) unless some method is followed and arranged by those who understand what is involved.[7]

Ponsonby undoubtedly sympathised with Dawson, but he could see a potential clash between the Central Chancery and the Home Office, and 'I am inclined to think that the Prime Minister would support the Home Office'.[8]

Lord Stamfordham suggested to Ponsonby that the Order should now cease to be conferred. 'I hope you are considering the question whether the time is not fast approaching, if not come, for shutting down the OBE. It was I suppose created as essentially a recognition for war work. The war is over and the workers presumably have been recognized.'[9] Ponsonby replied that this was impossible: 'for the very obvious reason that we have no Decoration for women, neither have we 4th or 5th classes of any other order.'[10]

Dawson managed successfully to avert a large conference, and instead convened a small committee, with Ponsonby as chairman, which met from February to July 1920. In addition to himself as Registrar of the Order, he invited Sir Edward Troup, as Secretary of the Order and Sir Warren Fisher of the Treasury, and presented them with a detailed breakdown of departmental allocations. The committee agreed that although the new statutory limits must be sharply reduced from the war level, the relative proportions of the five classes should be similar to those originally proposed for the appointments to the Order for war service. The second class would be three times the size of the first class and the third class would be four times the size of the second class.

Grade	Numbers
GBE	100
KBE and DBE	300
CBE	1,200
OBE	4,000
MBE	6,000

The discussions of the committee raised one problem which appeared to be insurmountable in 1920 and remains insurmountable today: the virtual impossibility of keeping a record of deaths among those recipients of the fourth and fifth classes. Worthy though their service had been, it was unlikely that members of these classes would merit full scale obituaries in the national newspapers, nor was it likely that the deaths of many would be announced in the personal columns. As the insignia was not returnable on the death of the recipient.

There is no effective means of ascertaining deaths in those classes without a disproportionate expenditure of labour and money. Even in the case of Class III it is doubtful whether it will be possible to ascertain the vacancies with any accuracy.[11]

The committee concluded that although a statutory limit could be placed on the first three classes, the fourth and fifth classes could only be restricted by the imposition of an annual quota. It was also felt desirable to fix an annual quota for the first three classes to avoid filling the establishment within a few years.

It was at first reported, apparently by Dawson, that the Admiralty, the War Office and the Air Ministry would not wish to make any recommendations for the military division of the Order in peacetime and proposed that it should lie dormant until some further conflict. Whatever the reasoning behind this position, the committee suspected a motive. Although they were prepared to accept and to recommend the 'mothballing' of the military division, they issued a warning that a refusal to use the military division of the Order of the British Empire would not lead to an increase in the proportion of military appointments to the 'older' Orders, especially the Order of the Bath.[12]

The committee further recommended that consideration be given to merging the Imperial Service Order with the fourth class of the Order of the British Empire, and the creation of a small advisory committee to consider half-yearly appointments to the Order.

This last point was not liked by the Prime Minister, who saw his own authority and influence over the Order being siphoned off to an advisory committee. Dawson and Ponsonby were no doubt motivated by the best of intentions in their desire to improve the standing of the Order by standardising appointments, and by ensuring that selection was based on utter impartiality, but they were proposing a new form of selection which did not operate in any of the older Orders. After consultations with Sir Warren Fisher and Lord Stamfordham, the paragraph relating to the committee was deleted, and the remainder of the text was approved, in draft form, by the King in November 1920.

His Majesty hopes . . . that we have returned to normal conditions, and that, consequently, there is no need for special machinery to decide upon the recommendations to the King for membership of the Order of the British Empire any more than for the Order of the Bath. In all cases the responsibility for such submissions must rest with the Prime Minister.[13]

The approved document was sent to John Davies, who replied that it was impossible to implement the scheme for some while yet.

With no KCBs vacant, and with so many recommendations from Departments, especially from those which are still more or less on a war footing . . . we must find some means of rewarding those who have worked all through the war and during two years of peace but who, as yet, have had no recognition.[14]

A further delay occurred in March 1921 when Dawson produced, like a rabbit from a hat, a letter he had received from the War Council in August 1920 stating that, contrary to the impressions received by the committee, the Army Council did favour the retention of the military division.[15] Dawson excused himself by saying that he was 'waiting to place (the letter) before the next meeting of our Committee, but it never came off'.[16]

There was nothing to be done but to redraft the report, since the letter made nonsense of the paragraph that recommended mothballing the military division in peacetime. A new report would be prepared, on the civil division alone, and the future of the military division would then form the subject matter of a separate report. A committee was quickly convened to discuss military awards of the Order, at which the representatives of both the Admiralty and the Air Ministry were averse to continuing the military division in peacetime, but the Army Council was in favour. The Army won the day, on the ground that if the military division was kept open for one Service, it would have to be kept open for all three. The three Service Departments initially agreed that the Order should be open only to commissioned officers, but warrant officers were subsequently added.

The final report was drafted by Sir Warren Fisher in November 1921 and submitted by the Prime Minister for the King's approval on 6 April 1922. Fisher added a number of additional recommendations. Firstly, that all submissions for appointment should be made by the Prime Minister, and by no other Minister.

We feel it is most desirable to centralise the recommendations in this way and thus to avoid in the case of this new Order the difficulties and inequalities which not infrequently arise even in the case of the older Orders owing to the practice of spreading the right of nomination among a number of Ministers without any co-ordinating authority.[17]

Secondly, that the office of Secretary of the Order should be held by the Permanent Secretary at the Treasury and not by the Permanent Secretary at the Home Office.

There is no reason for the secretarial work of the Order to be associated with the Home Office, and there would be an obvious advantage, in view of the number of Departments concerned, in associating it with the Treasury, which is the co-ordinating Department, and of which the Prime Minister is the First Lord.[18]

Thirdly, that a committee should be established to consider the future of the Medal of the Order.

The move of the administration of the Order from the Home Office to the Treasury was not, for once, a ploy by Lloyd George to secure personal control of appointments, but merely an attempt to bring order out of comparative chaos. Writing thirty years later, in November 1952, Sir Robert Knox, quite clearly recalled the reason.

Harry Boyd (Assistant Private Secretary to the Home Secretary) was a likeable person but he and the Home Office made such an appalling mess of the appointments that arrangements for selection had to be transferred to the Prime Minister and the Treasury.[19]

Allocations   At first sight, the following tables, showing the allocation of the Order, are of no great interest, but they do show that the Order of the British Empire was very carefully distributed after 1922.

The committee spent a good deal of time discussing the details of numbers and allocation. Nobody was in any doubt that the size of the Order had to be controlled by placing a limit on numbers, but how should it be distributed? The report recommended a statutory limit to the size of the first three classes. The word 'Dominions' was a collective term used to describe Canada, Newfoundland, South Africa, Australia and New Zealand, and also India, the protectorates, colonies and mandated territories, etc.

Grade	Civil Division U.K.	Civil Division Dominions	Military Division Navy	Military Division Army	Military Division Air Force	Total
GBE	30	30	2	7	1	70
KBE/DBE	90	90	7	20	3	210
CBE	360	360	28	100	12	860

Until the establishment was full, the maximum annual quota of appointments was fixed as follows:

Grade	Civil Division U.K.	Civil Division Dominions	Military Division Navy	Military Division Army	Military Division Air Force	Total
GBE	4	4	1 in 2 yrs	1	1	11
KBE/DBE	12	12	1	3	1 in 2 yrs	29
CBE	30	30	3	12	3 in 2 yrs*	78

* but not more than 2 in 1 year

It was calculated that the full complement for the first three classes would be reached in about seven years, 'and that', wrote Sir Warren Fisher to Lord Stamfordham in June 1922, 'is a not unreasonable period'.[20] At the end of the projected period of seven years, when it was estimated that the full complement would be reached, appointments to the first three classes would be made only to fill vacancies through death.

Because of the great difficulty in maintaining an accurate estimate of vacancies in the fourth and fifth classes, these grades were limited solely by a maximum number of annual appointments. 'Here again', wrote Fisher, 'I feel that in so wide a field the number of appointments is not unduly liberal.'[21]

Grade	Civil Division U.K.	Civil Division Dominions	Military Division Navy	Military Division Army	Military Division Air Force	Total
OBE	80	80	9	36	4	209
MBE	120	120	12	50	6	308

If the full number of permissible annual appointments to any of the first three classes was not made in any year, the appointments not filled could be carried forward to future years, but in the cases of the fourth and fifth classes, the vacancies so caused should lapse.

Overseas appointments under the heading of 'Civil Division Dominions' were to be allocated as follows:

Grade	Foreign Office	India Office	Colonial Office	Total
GBE	1	1	2	4
KBE and DBE	2	2	8	12
CBE	5	5	20	30
OBE	11	13	56	80
MBE	15	19	86	120

Although an allocation in the civil division was made to the Dominions, no allocation was made in the military division. A conference at the War Office on 4 August rectified this mistake, the Service Departments agreeing to make certain surrenders from their allocations to provide for this. The total establishment for Grades 1–3 was readjusted as follows:

Grade	Navy	Army and Indian Army	Air Force	Dominions Forces	Total
GBE	2	5	1	2	10
KBE and DBE	6	15	3	6	30
CBE	24	84	10	22	140

The annual appointments to Grades 4 and 5 were to be as follows:

Grade	Navy	Army and Indian Army	Air Force	Dominions Forces	Total
OBE	6	30	3	10	49
MBE	6	40	4	18	68

It was not considered desirable to subdivide precisely the Dominions Forces quota among army, navy and air force, 'the numbers of appointments available being so small that any such subdivision would be likely to prove embarrassing to the various Departments of Defence Overseas'.[22]

The April 1922 report had recommended that all nominations to the Order should be made to the King through the Prime Minister. Fisher's supplementary report in October 1922 indicated that the services were unhappy with this procedure.

They have expressed dissatisfaction . . . on the ground that it infringes upon a privilege of long standing, whereby the Fighting Services have been permitted to submit names for the bestowal of honours direct to His Majesty.[23]

Fisher was willing to recommend that the departments should have their way but, at the same time, be reminded that they should maintain 'close and regular liaison' with the Principal Private Secretary to the Prime Minister.

It was never the intention that recommendations put forward by the First Lord of the Admiralty and the Secretaries of State for War and Air should be subject to individual criticism by the Prime Minister, but merely that measures should be taken to approximate the standards of eligibility.[24]

On 6 November 1922 Fisher warned Sir Herbert Creedy, Secretary of the War Office, that if the reputation of the Order was ever to be raised in the public esteem, the greatest care was needed, not only in establishing and maintaining a restricted size for the Order, but also in the selection of candidates.

The task of raising it from the comparative disrepute into which it sank at the end of the war will be so difficult in any event that it is essential to avoid anything which would militate against the process.[25]

It was clearly impossible to include the existing 25,000 members of the Order in the detailed calculations of 1922. If they were treated as 'ordinary' members, it would be many, many years before vacancies began to occur, and the establishment figures agreed in 1922 could be hypothetical for decades. Because of the ridicule to which the Order had been subjected, it was essential that moves should be made as soon as possible to rescue its reputation. It had to be made clear that, intentionally large though the Order of the British Empire would be when compared with its fellow Orders, still there were strict limits to its size. The Order had been created to reward a nationwide war effort, but the war was finished and it had to be reconstructed for a peacetime role. Without in any way diminishing the efforts of the 25,000 existing members of the Order, the only way forward was to put them to one side. Accordingly, all appointments to the Order made between 4 June 1917 and 28 December 1922 were deemed to be 'additional' to the new statutory limits.

With the permanent establishment of the Order of the British Empire now settled, new Statutes enshrining the recommendations of the report were issued on 29 December 1922; Ponsonby, Dawson and all who wished the Order well, heaved a sigh of relief and the Order of the British Empire put the past behind it and started again.

SIX

Stability and Popularity

THE ORDER AT HOME

*As you can imagine everyone concerned in advising since the Establishment of
the Order has had an uphill job in introducing real standards in place of the
pre-Establishment morass . . . and the British Empire Order is now really valued,
instead of being regarded with indifference.*
Sir Frederick Ponsonby to Sir John Simon, 10 November 1933

Despite the best and sometimes despairing efforts of Sir Frederick Ponsonby, the
earliest years of the history of the Order of the British Empire were marked by
many amusing stories of muddle and mistake. As he told Sir John Simon, the
Foreign Secretary, in 1933, it had been an uphill struggle to raise the reputation
of the Order in public esteem and gradually, throughout the 1920s and 1930s, the
early years were forgotten, the prestige of the Order began to rise and the number of refusals began to fall. Ennobled as Lord Sysonby in the Birthday Honours
List 1935, Ponsonby died four months later, having lived to see the Order mature
into a respected honour.

One of the great strengths of the Order was that for the first twenty years of its *Dames and*
existence, it was the only Order to which large numbers of women could be *Ladies*
admitted. The Order placed women on an equal footing with men and, for the
first time, accorded them a distinctive title of their own instead of one conferred
by marriage. Between 1917 and 1931 some 51 Dames Grand Cross and 102
Dames Commander were appointed, and by the latter year it would have been
reasonable to suppose that the title of Dame was well-established and non-
controversial, but it became something of a hardy perennial which was still being
reviewed in the 1970s.

On 26 March 1931, Robert Knox, Secretary to Sir Warren Fisher, wrote to
Major Harry Stockley at the Central Chancery of the Orders of Knighthood,
proposing that the title of Dame should be reconsidered. Knox revealed that it
had been 'under consideration here occasionally for some time past', and that
now was an opportune moment for a change to be made. Knox and Fisher both
held the view that the title 'though excellent in many ways for formal use carries
with it more than a suggestion of very great age', and their proposal amounted to
an abolition of the title by stealth. They deemed it a great disadvantage that
Dames were not allowed to be called informally 'Lady X', and that the privileges
of damehood did not include the right to be addressed as 'Your Ladyship' or to
be referred to as 'Her Ladyship'. 'As an Earl or a Marquess is known for many
purposes as "Lord A" would it not be possible while retaining the title "Dame
X.Y" as at present to permit the colloquial use where desired of the title "Lady
Y"?'[1] Any required changes to the Statutes could easily be made and could be tied
in with the proposed changes to the Empire Gallantry Medal.

Stockley's reply indicated a firm negative to any change.

This was . . . an innovation to which possibly even yet people have not become completely accustomed, in the same way as the ranks in the Air Force seemed strange at first, but these are becoming more usual as time passes. Certain ladies who have been appointed Dames and hold the style of 'Lady' from their husbands' position still retain socially the style of 'Lady', on the other hand some who hold higher rank appear to be quite upset that they are not officially styled 'Dame'. A certain Dame, who I understand, insisted on her servants calling her 'My Lady', was very proud of the title 'Dame', and would not have liked it if anyone in her own position had called her 'Lady'. This therefore cuts both ways and again as time passes any discussion on this point will probably sink gradually into oblivion. . . Possibly in time women may be created Peeresses in their own right and I would suggest that when that time comes this question could be raised again.[2]

This was not the reply that Knox had either wanted or expected, and his riposte to Stockley showed that he had a very low opinion of the title of Dame.

It is to be doubted whether the Order of the British Empire as a whole has yet quite attained the place in general estimation which one of the great Orders of Chivalry should be properly held. Where therefore the value of appointment to two of the Classes of the Order could be enhanced without offending anyone it does seem rather a pity that this addition to the Statutes should not be made, and I am sorry if you do not agree.[3]

The thought of sliding the change into the Statutes on the back of the changes to the Empire Gallantry Medal was not pursued but, nothing daunted, Fisher raised the matter again two years later.

Ladies of Grace On 26 January 1932, Sir Herbert Samuel, Leader of the Liberal Party and Home Secretary in the Coalition Government of Ramsay Macdonald, proposed extending the honours available to women by creating the title of 'Dame' as an equivalent to a Knight Bachelor, outside an Order. His argument followed the line that further opportunities for recognising the achievements of women could follow one of two alternatives, one being to enlarge the numbers of Dames of the Order of the British Empire.

But if it is thought important, as it may well be, not to lower the prestige of that Order by increasing its membership, the other suggestion, which I believe has not been put forward previously, is that the title of Dame should be conferred upon women in the same way (apart from the ceremonial) and on the same standards as the title of Knight Bachelor is conferred upon men.[4]

Samuel's proposal provided Fisher with the perfect opportunity again to attempt to dispose of the title of Dame. He consulted a number of department heads and submitted a memorandum to Macdonald on 21 March 1933. He believed that the number of women eligible for the grant of an honour which would carry a title was steadily increasing; and the institution of a new dignity was long overdue. On behalf of his fellow department heads, he proposed the creation of an honour for women equivalent to that of a Knight Bachelor, and then returned to his *idée fixe*.

We consider it unfortunate that the title Dame as a prefix was adopted for the first two classes of the Order of the British Empire. The word Dame will we consider remain in the public mind for years to come as a description of a woman of great age, a widow, or a mistress of a small school for young children. . . The title 'Lady' would in our view be more pleasant and more popular than that of Dame. If it is suggested that 'Dame' would be of greater interest historically it could equally well be urged by way of reply that every Knight should be called 'Chevalier'. We are definitely of the opinion that the title for this new Honour should be that of 'Lady' borne immediately before the surname. We suggest . . . that early opportunity should be taken to alter the style of 'Dame' used now in the first two classes of the Order of the British Empire before the Christian name to 'Lady' to be written immediately before the surname. We do not ask that any change should be made in the formal designations GBE or Dame Grand Cross and DBE or Dame Commander. We suggest that persons already members of the first or second classes of the Order should be permitted to use either kind of prefix.[5]

The substance of this memorandum was enshrined in a discussion document sent to the Committee on the Distribution of the Permanent Establishment of the Order on 10 July 1933, but Fisher's preferences were not to everyone's liking. The Secretary of the Air Ministry for one thought the title of Dame was 'fully recognised and firmly established' and 'as having a quite pleasant and dignified flavour'.[6]

It may be argued that, since it is already impossible to tell to which of a dozen or so possible categories the bearer of the prefix 'Lady' belongs, a Dame of the British Empire may as well enter the miscellany. . . Since we have inaugurated this title, which facilitates some measure of identification, it seems to me that there is everything to be said for retaining it. . . The title Dame has persisted in England as a well-recognised dignity in continuing, if infrequent use. It does not represent the reintroduction of a style dormant for centuries, as would 'Chevalier'. If the suggested substitution of 'Lady' indicates a preference for a word of old English rather than French origin, I would point out that 'Sir' equally derives from France. There is no escape from our French etymological heritage.[7]

The plan for an equivalent title to Knight Bachelor never saw the light of day. Surviving correspondence indicates a proposal to establish an honour to be known as 'Lady of Grace', and to award up to a maximum of ten in any one year. It was intended that the first appointments would be announced in the New Year Honours List 1934, but none was announced and the plan seems to have been abandoned some time in 1933.

M'Lady

In the autumn of 1965 Mrs Elizabeth Lane QC became the first woman to be appointed to the High Court bench, and the question of what title she was to have raised once more the future of the title of Dame. Judges of the High Court were, and still are, honoured with a knighthood in the grade of Knight Bachelor. There being no equivalent title for women, Mrs Lane was appointed a DBE, and the precedent has been followed with the increasing numbers of women now appointed to the High Court. The Lord Chancellor, Lord Gardiner, would in fact have preferred Mrs Justice Lane to be given a knighthood and to be accorded the title of 'Lady', as reported on 15 September 1965 by Sir George Coldstream, the Permanent Secretary of his department.

But there is no precedent. . . Moreover the Lord Chancellor is advised that to attempt to create a precedent by conferring a knighthood on Judge Elizabeth Lane would arouse ill-feeling among a number of distinguished ladies who have been created Dames of the Victorian and British Empire Orders. . . In these circumstances the Lord Chancellor suggests that the Prime Minister might like to consider recommending Judge Elizabeth Lane for a DBE on her elevation to the Bench.[8]

Nevertheless Lord Gardiner was adamant that Mrs Lane should not be addressed as 'My Lord' or 'Your Lordship', but as 'My Lady' or 'Your Ladyship'. The Prime Minister, Harold Wilson, greeted this decision with approval, as reported by Derek Mitchell, his Private Secretary, who was less than enthusiastic about the task that lay ahead.

The Prime Minister has warmly applauded the Lord Chancellor's decision. . . This has encouraged him to have the general thought that it would be a good idea to change the style and title of other Dames. . . We shall be scratching our heads about this one.[9]

The Prime Minister asked that the suitability of the title Dame, as an equivalent of a knighthood, be once more examined, and he referred the question to Sir Laurence Helsby, Head of the Home Civil Service. Helsby reported that there really was no suitable or satisfactory alternative.

Awards to many women in recognition of personal distinction and achievement have given increasing prestige to the present title. A number of those singled out in this way have been notably unlike the old idea of a Dame . . . and the public is coming to recognise that nowadays the old-fashioned overtones are found only in pantomime – and pantomime is pretty out-moded anyhow. [10]

Helsby subsequently discussed the matter with Mrs Barbara Castle, Minister of Overseas Development. The two of them put their heads together and tried to come up with a suitable alternative title, but quite without success. On 10 November 1965, he wrote again to the Prime Minister proposing, with a notable lack of enthusiasm, the possibility of using the form 'My Lady' which could be shortened to 'M'Lady', and when pronounced as such, ran quite well with most Christian names.

But I confess that I still have doubts about it, and when I tried it informally on Dame Evelyn Sharp (Permanent Secretary at the Ministry of Housing and Local Government) I got a pretty brusque denial of any merit in it. . . It is a more complex problem than at first appears . . . and the better course might be to let things remain as they are until the time comes for more drastic change.[11]

The Prime Minister was persuaded, and by 22 November 1965 'it was agreed that the whole thing should be allowed to drop'.[12]

Dames Bachelor The question was raised yet again ten years later, in June 1975. Kenneth Stowe, the Prime Minister's Principal Private Secretary, asked that consideration again be given to finding for women an alternative title to Knight Bachelor.

The scope for awards to women is restricted because there is no honour for women comparable to that of a Knight Bachelor for men. One could not think of anything less attractive than, e.g. a Dame Spinster to be awarded to women, but it may be that other more attractive possibilities could be conceived. . . There is some reason to believe that the title Dame has now passed sufficiently into common usage for it to have acquired an appropriateness which would justify keeping it.[13]

Successive generations of civil servants had tried hard to find more attractive possibilities and there was no greater likelihood of success in 1975 than there had been on any previous occasion.

Stuart Milner-Barry, head of the Ceremonial Branch of the Civil Service Department, advised against change or innovation.

The title of 'Dame' is now so well established and so generally accepted, that we should really be wasting our time in thrashing over the alternatives which have been thoroughly canvassed in the past. . . I suspect that it would cause considerable offence to existing holders, who probably have become quite attached to it, if we were now to cause an upheaval. It is after all a title of great distinction.[14]

Pointing out that 'bachelor' merely indicated a junior knight and had nothing to do with either gender or marital status, Milner-Barry half-heartedly suggested 'Dames Bachelor'.

But unless any particular advantages are foreseen by instituting a new category of honour, such as feminine Knights who are not members of an Order, there is no doubt that much the simplest course from a practical point of view would be simply to increase the DBE/KBE quota if and when we find it necessary to do so.[15]

Milner-Barry also warned Stowe of his fear that the creation of a class of Dames Bachelor would probably lead to a decline in the use of the DBE, and this fear has, to an extent, been borne out by the fate of the GBE. The class of Dames Grand Cross, once quite numerous, has now virtually ceased to exist, and at least one factor in that process has been the conferring of life peerages on women since 1958. In the years 1958–94, eighty-one women received life peerages and only three women were appointed GBEs. Only four women have held both a life peerage and the GBE, and all of them were first appointed GBE and then subsequently received life peerages.

There is nothing, it would seem, quite like a Dame, and it is now generally accepted that the DBE is the standard equivalent honour of a Knight Bachelor and is likely to remain so for the foreseeable future. Furthermore, the title of Dame, once confined to the Order of the British Empire, was adopted by other Orders as their ranks have gradually been opened to women. The Dames Commander of the Order of the British Empire (DBE) have now been joined by those of the Royal Victorian Order (DCVO) from 1937, the Order of St Michael and St George (DCMG) from 1965 and the Order of the Bath (DCB) from 1971.

As the only Order open to women, the Order of the British Empire was used extensively in the years 1917–37 to honour female members of the Royal Family, but since the admission of women to the Royal Victorian Order in 1937, the practice has virtually ceased. All the appointments were to the grade of Dame Grand Cross.

Royal Dames and Knights Grand Cross

HM Queen Mary 1917 (*wife of King George V*)

HM Queen Alexandra 1918 (*wife of King Edward VII*)

HRH Princess Louise, Duchess of Argyll 1918 (*daughter of Queen Victoria*)

HRH Princess Christian 1918 (*daughter of Queen Victoria*)

HH Princess Helena Victoria 1918 (*granddaughter of Queen Victoria*)

HH Princess Marie Louise 1919 (*granddaughter of Queen Victoria*)

HRH Princess Beatrice 1919 (*daughter of Queen Victoria*)

HM Queen Elizabeth The Queen Mother 1927 (*wife of King George VI*)

HRH The Princess Royal 1927 (*daughter of King George V*)

HRH Princess Marina, Duchess of Kent 1937
    (*daughter-in-law of King George V*)

HRH Princess Alice, Duchess of Gloucester 1937
    (*daughter-in-law of King George V*)

HRH Princess Alice, Countess of Athlone 1937
    (*granddaughter of Queen Victoria*)

The three princesses appointed in 1937 were all present at the Golden Jubilee Service of the Order in St Paul's Cathedral in 1967. After 1937 there were two further appointments of more distant members of the Royal Family.

The Marchioness of Carisbrooke 1938 (*daughter-in-law of Princess Beatrice*)

The Countess Mountbatten of Burma 1947
(*wife of Earl Mountbatten of Burma*)

Only three Royal Knights Grand Cross have been appointed.

HRH The Prince of Wales 1917 (*first Grand Master of the Order*)

HRH The Duke of Connaught 1917 (*son of Queen Victoria*)

HRH The Prince Philip, Duke of Edinburgh 1953
(*third Grand Master of the Order*)

Promotion and progression

Many appointments to the Order of the British Empire are now made to a specific grade and at the end of a long career of service, but in the past it was possible and not unusual for recipients to be promoted through several grades in the Order. No member was promoted through every grade from MBE to GBE, but many have been promoted through four grades. Several members have begun with an MBE and finished with a GBE, although all omitted at least one grade before passing on to the next higher grade.

A number of members shot up from MBE to GBE, albeit after many years. Lord Porter, a Lord of Appeal in Ordinary, was appointed an MBE for his war service in 1918, and a GBE in 1951. Viscount Esher, a prominent figure in the arts world, was similarly appointed an MBE for his war service in 1918, and a GBE in 1955. Lord MacLehose of Beoch, the long-serving Governor of Hong Kong, was appointed an MBE in 1946 and a GBE 1976. Nawab Sir Muhammad Ahmad Sa'id Khan of Chhatari, latterly President of the Executive Council of the Nizam of Hyderabad, was appointed an MBE 1918 and a GBE in 1946.

In the early years of the Order's history, when standards were still in a state of flux, a number of remarkably rapid promotions were known. Lieutenant Colonel Sir Henry Fowler (1870–1938) was appointed CBE in the first list of 4 June 1917 and rapidly promoted to KBE on 1 January 1918. Sir Charles Gordon, a Canadian, was appointed a KBE 4 June 1917 and promoted to GBE on 3 June 1918. Among the most rapid series of promotions was that of Elizabeth Harriott Kelly. She was appointed an MBE on 24 August 1917, an OBE on 7 January 1918, and a CBE on 30 March 1920, but to be dated 1 January 1920. There she rested until her final promotion, to DBE, on 1 January 1953. She was a member of the Portsmouth War Pensions Committee 1916–20, and of the Special Grants Committee, Ministry of Pensions 1917–26. At the time of her final promotion, she had been Honorary Organiser of the Portsmouth Social Service Council since 1939.

Two members of the Order were promoted from OBE to GBE via CBE and KBE. Air Chief Marshal Sir Leslie Hollinghurst was appointed an OBE in 1932, CBE in 1944, KBE in 1945 and GBE in 1952. Air Chief Marshal Sir David Lee was appointed an OBE in 1943, CBE in 1947, KBE in 1965 and GBE in 1969. Admiral Sir Peter White was appointed an MBE in 1944, omitted the grade of OBE and passed to CBE in 1960, KBE in 1976, and GBE in 1977. Dame Helen Gwynne-Vaughan, Dame Beryl Oliver, Baroness Denman and the Countess of Limerick were all promoted from CBE, through DBE, to GBE. Only one New Zealander, Major General Sir Keith Lindsay Stewart, has progressed through four grades of the Order. He was appointed MBE in 1919, OBE in 1935, CBE in 1945 and KBE in 1958.

A number of members have held both the BEM and a grade in the Order. Charles Henry Prior was awarded a BEM (Military Division) on 8 June 1944 when he was a Sergeant in the RASC. After forty years' service in the Home Office, he was appointed a CBE on 12 June 1976. Two members of the Order have held the BEM in addition to membership of the first or second class of the Order. Sir George Hart, the New Zealand hearing-aid pioneer, who was awarded the BEM in 1971, and appointed a KBE in 1973. The BEM (Civil Division) was replaced in New Zealand by the Queen's Service Medal for Public or Community Service, and not awarded after the Birthday Honours List 1977. Baroness Adrian (1899–1966) held both the BEM and the DBE, and her mother was also a DBE.

Two members (there may be others) are known to have 'progressed downwards' in the Order. Miss Ethel Mary Burnett, the only the person to receive both CBE and BEM was appointed a CBE in 1919 and was awarded the BEM in 1945. Mrs Ethne Philippa Pryor was appointed an MBE in the Civil Division in 1918 for her work as Honorary Secretary of the Prisoners of War Department, Royal Air Force Aid Committee. She was awarded the BEM (Civil Division) in January 1946 for her work as Deputy Organiser, Prisoner of War Parcels Packing Centre, in Hertfordshire.

In the earliest years of the Order's history, appointments were often made to individuals at comparatively young ages. In 1919, Robert Shaw, a naval officer who had seen action at the Battle of Jutland, and later witnessed the scuttling of the German Fleet at Scapa Flow, was appointed an MBE at the age of nineteen. Born in 1900, he died on 5 August 1995 at the age of ninety-five, having been a Member of the Order for seventy-six years. It may be that there were others who survived for longer periods, but there cannot have been many, and such records are likely to be rarely repeated.

Refusals

An honour is not to every person's liking and refusals do occur. Personal or domestic reasons are sometimes given for the refusal of an honour. Sometimes the motive is ideological, the individual concerned disagreeing with the principle of an honours system or with the way in which honours are distributed. Others believe, wrongly, that the acceptance of an honour will compromise their independence and inhibit their freedom of speech; the novelist and poet, Rudyard Kipling, refused the Order of Merit for those very reasons. Some recipients have felt impelled in interviews to assure those listening that, by their acceptance, they have 'not joined the Establishment'. Religious reasons are occasionally given, where the rules of a particular denomination forbid the joining of any other organisation, including an Order. Some people are disappointed at the offered grade and decline in the hope or the expectation that a higher grade will be offered at a later date. Then there are those who decline an honour from a genuine sense of unworthiness.

In the early days of inefficient management, appointments to the Order were gazetted, only for some recipients to ask subsequently for their names to be removed. The current practice is for recipients to be discreetly asked well in advance of publication whether they wish to accept a particular honour, and this is the point at which a refusal may be made. The measure of the stature of the Order of the British Empire is in the very few people who now refuse the Order compared with the large numbers in 1918–20. In those three years, 761 individuals declined appointments, making an average of 126 refusals at each honours list. At the time of writing, approximately 1,000 new names are added to the Order in each Honours List, compared with an average of 15 refusals.

Refusals of the Order of the British Empire are mostly at MBE, OBE and CBE levels, numbering approximately 2,000 in the years 1917–94. Of that number, approximately half declined the Order in the first five years of its existence. Refusals at KBE and DBE level are much more rare, with a total of 23 in the years 1917–94, of which five were from overseas. Refusals at GBE level are rarer still, only seven being known.

No discussion of the subject of the refusals would be complete without a post-script on the subsequent feelings of regret felt by some of those who decline an honour. As the result of years of hard work and careful selection, the Order of the British Empire had acquired a high reputation by the early 1950s, and some of those who had refused the honour in the early years had begun to regret their decision. In October 1920 one individual was offered the OBE but never returned the form of acceptance. In accordance with what may have been the practice at the time, because of the floods of refusals, this was noted as a refusal. In 1952, the same individual returned the form, pleading the excuse of sickness and family bereavement. 'If he made no reply', observed Sir Robert Knox, 'the excuse . . . seems to have lasted him for 32 years; a longish time to think out an answer to a letter, even though it came from a Government Department.'[16]

Forfeiture   Appointment to the Order of the British Empire, as to every other Order, is normally for life, but there is no right to hold an honour for life, and appointments are reviewed and sometimes cancelled when a recipient has been convicted of a criminal offence.

Forfeiture of honours was a rare occurrence before 1917 because of the very limited number of people who held an honour. With the substantial increase in honours, caused by the very large membership of the Order of the British Empire forfeiture, though still infrequent, was not as rare as it had been. It occurs only as the result of clear and firm evidence and never as the result of rumour or accusation. In April 1936 Sir Warren Fisher outlined the criteria governing forfeiture.

The view we have taken is that appointments should usually be cancelled on conviction by a competent Court of an offence for which there had been a sentence to a term of imprisonment of something more than a nominal period, or a substantial fine has been imposed, and the offence has involved moral turpitude. Most of the cancellations have been for embezzlement, theft or some such other offence.[17]

The task of deciding on cancellation is neither pleasant nor enviable, and it can be a distressing experience for the individual to be removed from the Order. Forfeiture is only recommended after careful consideration, and with due regard to the maintenance of the reputation of the Order. A member of the Order convicted of a criminal offence has, albeit unintentionally, brought the name of the Order into disrepute, and his or her continued membership must be seriously questioned.

One category of honour, the recognition of acts of gallantry, is usually excluded. Conviction of a criminal offence does not impair the quality of the act of gallantry which led to the award; and it is thought that forfeiture of a gallantry award would not normally be regarded by public opinion as either necessary or right.

The normal procedure is for each case to be individually considered and for an appropriate submission to be made to the Queen recommending cancellation. The recipient is informed that his appointment in the Order has been cancelled, and a notice to that effect is published in the *London Gazette*. There have in fact been very few cancellations; 17 MBEs, 3 OBEs and 1 CBE were removed from the roll of the Order in the years 1917–63. Among the more notable cancellations was that of the spy Harold Adrian Russell (Kim) Philby who was appointed an OBE in 1946. His appointment was cancelled in 1965.

A cancellation need not be permanent and, very occasionally, a recipient has had his appointment re-instated. Mir Shakar Khan was appointed an MBE in 1919 and removed from the Order in 1921. His appointment was restored in 1931 in recognition of 'the special services which he recently rendered in the extermination of a notorious gang of outlaws in Baluchistan'.[18]

Forfeiture of profession

An alternative example of forfeiture occurred in the case of Sir Robert Hyde (1878–1967) who chose to accept appointment as a KBE and, as a result, forfeit his profession. Hyde was ordained a priest of the Church of England in 1903. After serving in parishes in the east end of London, and a period as a hospital chaplain, he was employed by the Ministry of Munitions to oversee the welfare of boys working in industry. From that experience, and encouraged by Archbishop Cosmo Gordon Lang of Canterbury, he founded the Industrial Welfare Society in 1918, an organisation intended to take the initiative outside government and function as a catalyst for changing the conditions of the workplace.

In 1949 he was offered and accepted a KBE and expressed a strong wish to be allowed to receive the accolade and to use the prefix 'Sir' as a way of honouring the Society. He was summoned to a meeting with Archbishop Geoffrey Fisher of Canterbury and told that if he wished to receive the accolade he must renounce Holy Orders, and the archbishop's views were tendered to King George VI by the Home Office. Accordingly Hyde sought and was granted release from his Orders, but the experience caused him great sadness and distress, and his entry in *Who's Who* noted that he had been 'compelled' to renounce them. The title of his autobiography, *Industry was my parish*, says much about the way in which he happily combined his two vocations.

Resignation

Occasionally members of the Order have indicated a wish to resign their appointments, sometimes for religious reasons, and sometimes for personal reasons. In 1936 a recipient of the MBE applied to resign his membership of the Order as 'owing to private circumstances, he is unable to maintain the honour and dignity which Membership conveys'.[19] There is, however, no machinery by which resignation can be made. Members may drop all outward signs of the honour by ceasing to use the postnominal letters and by ceasing to wear, and even returning, the insignia, but unless the appointment is cancelled by forfeiture, they remain members of the Order until death. Many others, although proud to be members of the Order, choose not to use postnominal letters.

The Beatles

Some attempted resignations from the Order occurred in June 1965 when four young musicians from Liverpool were appointed MBEs. George Harrison, John Lennon, Paul McCartney and Ringo Starr, formed the group known as 'The Beatles' that burst on to the British and subsequently the international musical scene in 1962, beginning a revolution that changed the face of popular music. In many ways they encapsulated the mood and the spirit of the early 1960s. With the long-ish hair affected by the youth of the age, but well groomed and neatly attired, and singing songs about love and freedom, they avoided the dishevelled appearance and radical messages of other contemporary groups and achieved a wide appeal across the generations.

It would be simple enough to state that the appointment of the Beatles caused an uproar and that innumerable members of the Order sent back their insignia in disgust, and that that was the end of the matter. In fact the events of June 1965 were much more complex and brought to the surface a widely varied mixture of attitudes towards honours in general and towards the Order of the British Empire in particular. Many of the letters and leading articles which appeared in the newspapers in the days following the awards betrayed an ignorance of the functioning of the honours system and produced a series of reactions that were initiated by emotion rather than logic. Many of these were trite and made disparaging comments about hair styles and youth; 'disgust' was a word often used. On 16 June 1965, the *Daily Sketch* seized the opportunity to ridicule the Order of the British Empire with a laughably inaccurate leader.

For years now the distribution of such awards has been so prolific, so haphazard and, to all intents and purposes, so without method, that the whole system is being debased. The outcry which has greeted the award of the MBE to the Beatles is not the beginning but the end of a sad decline in a long-standing muddle over medals. . . But while it was distributed sparingly – as at first it was – it fulfilled its purpose with dignity. Today various degrees of this Order are distributed at a rate of 3,000 a year.

On the same day, *The Sun* called for the scrapping of the honours system and delivered an attack on the Prime Minister: 'If Mr Wilson thought that an MBE for the Beatles would catch the fancy of young people, my guess is that he has miscalculated'. The appointments even made headlines in the overseas press. An editorial in the *Philadelphia Inquirer* reported the honouring of the Beatles as 'a dismaying demonstration of inexcusably poor judgement on the part of Labour Government politicians who engineered this travesty in the name of the Queen'.

On 17 June 1965 *The Times* published two letters critical of the awards, and reported that the Prime Minister had received scores rather than hundreds of letters, in the ratio of 2:1 against the awards. The *Daily Express* received nearly 1,000 letters, 468 in favour of the award and 446 against.

Objections to the appointments of the Beatles coalesced around a number of attitudes. There were those who simply disliked their style of music; there were those who felt they were too young to receive an honour; there were those who felt that the Beatles received a more than sufficient financial reward and should not receive an honour; there were those who felt that more deserving cases and categories had been overlooked; there were those who felt that they had not done anything to deserve it; there were those who were convinced that the whole honours system was failing, and the appointment of the Beatles proved it; there were those who thought it a political gimmick, observing a certain coincidence of geography between the Prime Minister of the day and the Beatles; and there were those who were simply jealous.

A former RAF officer announced that he would sell his MBE and use the funds to pay off a mortgage on a pensioners' club. Another former RAF officer announced that he had packed up his MBE and sent it back to the Queen. A former Liberal member of the Canadian Parliament similarly announced that he would return his MBE. And so grew the legend that a deluge of insignia was returned by members of the Order of the British Empire, disgusted at the use to which their Order had been put. The complaints were familiar: disapproval of the culture represented by the Beatles; the lowering of standards for honours; resentment from those who had been awarded the Order in respect of gallantry. One recipient complained that all they had done was 'to sing, romp and make millions in the United States'.[20]

All these comments need to be set in perspective. The Order of the British Empire had a total membership of approximately 85,000 in 1965, of whom only 22 returned their insignia; 18 MBEs, 2 OBEs, 1 CBE and 1 BEM were sent back in protest, and another OBE was returned by the widow of the recipient. Each piece of returned insignia was stored safely and the letter acknowledging receipt stated that it would be kept until such time as the recipient wished it to be returned; 6 recipients did subsequently ask for their insignia to be returned.

Comments were not entirely negative. A letter to the *Daily Express* on 15 June.

Thousands of long-faced moaners have got the needle with the Beatles over the MBE award. There is only one conclusion: jealousy. As an old-timer, I salute the award because the kids thoroughly deserve it.

On the same day Labour Members of Parliament representing Merseyside constituencies tabled a motion in the House of Commons welcoming the award of the MBE to each of the four Beatles.

That this House recognises the great good and happiness that the Beatles have provided to millions throughout the world and furthermore being the first English group that has captured the American market and brought in its wake great commercial advantage and dollar earnings to this country, strongly appreciates the action of Her Majesty in awarding the Beatles the MBE.

The words 'commercial advantage and dollar earnings' lay at the heart of the matter. The work of the Beatles put British pop artists on the map, with the result that the overseas earnings of other artists had risen very substantially, though no accurate figure could be given, and credit for these earnings can fairly be attributed, in part at least, to the Beatles themselves. Whether or not one liked their music, there was no disputing the fact that foreign currency earnings arising from their activities from all sources had, by that time, amounted to several million pounds. It was a pity that the publication of each of their names in the Birthday Honours List was followed by the words 'Member of the Beatles' whereas 'for services to export' would have been a better citation. John Lennon, interviewed by Peter Grosvenor of the *Daily Express* in the issue for 16 June, said as much.

I can understand a few people saying they don't think much to it. But for people actually to send their MBEs back to the Queen. . . Well, there must be something wrong with them. I mean to take it that seriously. Anyway I don't reckon we got it for being rock 'n' roll singers. On that basis we'd have got the OBE and the Stones would have got the MBE. I reckon we got it for exports, and the citation ought to have said that to clear up the misunderstandings. Look, if someone had got an award for exporting millions of dollars' worth of fertiliser or machine tools everyone would have applauded. So why should they knock us?

Whatever the rights or wrongs and likes or dislikes of the affair, let the last comment rest with the British High Commission in Ottawa. The High Commission reported to the Foreign Office in London that the awards had stirred up a good deal of interest, both for and against. 'These awards made the 1965 Birthday Honours List the most talked of list in Canada for many a year.'[21]

Nomination and selection

The appointment of the Beatles left some people wondering about the process by which names are included in the Honours Lists, with a suspicion that it was haphazard.

There is in fact nothing haphazard about the nomination and selection of names for honours. Names can be submitted by both government departments on behalf of their ministers and by the general public. Every name submitted for the Order of the British Empire or for any other honour is treated seriously and subjected to scrutiny by a network of specialist committees. The committees embrace most walks of life including science, medicine, sport, industry, commerce, agriculture, the police, the health service, local government and all the voluntary organisations. The most diverting, in terms of content and name is the Maecenas committee which selects recipients from the world of the arts, literature and learning (Maecenas, who died in 8 BC, was a Roman statesman and patron of Horace and Virgil). Membership of the committees is not necessarily internal to the civil service; distinguished experts in their field predominate on many of the committees. When the nominations have been sifted and reduced, the selected names are sent to 10 Downing Street for the Prime Minister to consider, and to accept or reject such names as he chooses. The Prime Minister is free to add further names to the list, with the proviso that all such names are examined by the Political Honours Scrutiny Committee. The Defence Secretary and the Foreign Secretary submit their own lists. Commonwealth realms submit their lists directly to the Sovereign.

Honours for political service are examined by the Political Honours Scrutiny Committee. This committee was established by Order in Council on 10 January 1923, and its duties and membership have been regulated by successive Orders in Council. It was created as a result of a report by the Royal Commission on Honours set up in the aftermath of the abuse of honours during Lloyd George's premiership. The debates in Parliament during June and July 1922 specifically focused on the question of honours being granted in connection with contributions to party funds, and the principal task of the committee is to ensure that the sale of honours which occurred under Lloyd George is never repeated.

The committee consists of three Privy Councillors from across the political spectrum. Since 1962 the members have invariably been peers, but need not be so. The Prime Minister submits certain particulars to the committee about persons proposed to be recommended for honour for their political services, and the committee makes such enquiries as it thinks fit and reports accordingly.

Publication of names

Appointments to the Order of the British Empire are usually announced in the twice-yearly published honours lists. The Birthday Honours List is published on the Sovereign's Official Birthday, usually the second or third Saturday in June. The New Year Honours List, was traditionally published on New Year's Day until 1974. From 1974, New Year's Day became a public holiday and the Newspaper Publishers' Association decided to make it a non-publication day. Because of a desire to maintain the tradition, the Honours List was made available to the press on 31 December 1973, but embargoed until 23.59 hours on 1 January 1974. The List appeared in the national daily newspapers on 2 January, but the ploy of lifting the embargo at one minute to midnight on New Year's Day enabled the issue of the *London Gazette* that contained the List, to be dated

1 January. In 1977 New Year's Day fell on a Saturday, which would have meant publication on Sunday in Sunday newspapers. Because of the tradition of publishing the List first in *The Times* and the other national daily papers, publication was brought forward to 31 December, and so it has remained. If New Year's Eve falls on a Sunday, publication is brought forward again to 30 December.

Appointments can be, and occasionally are, made at other times during the course of the year, sometimes related to specific events, or to the armed forces in relation to a specific campaign, or to an individual in respect of an official appointment. Occasionally a recipient is engaged in work of a confidential nature, and the award of an honour may be thought to draw attention to the work. In such cases awards are made and recorded but not published, though they may be at a future date.

In 1917 Sir Frederick Ponsonby had thought that a membership of 3,500 would be quite sufficient; his colleagues disagreed and proposed 6,000. By 1921 the figure had risen to 25,000 and by 1960 to 90,000. The group that met at Buckingham Palace on 1 May 1917 and decided on the figure of 6,000 would be astounded to know that the present size of the Order is approximately 100,000, the membership of the third class alone being 9,000. *Control of numbers*

The size of the membership has been regularly increased, but only to meet a perceived need and only after careful consideration. The decision rests with the Queen, who is advised by the Committee on the Grant of Honours, Decorations and Medals. Membership comprises the Queen's Private Secretary, and senior representatives of the Armed Services, the Home Civil Service, the Diplomatic Service and the Prime Minister's office. Its function is to review generally the honours system, including a decision on whether the quota of available honours should be increased or decreased.

Although the quinquennial establishment figures are never exceeded, numbers of additional appointments have been made in connection with special occasions. As with the appointments of 1917–22, these appointments are all noted in the Statutes to be additional to the establishment, and the death of a recipient does not create a vacancy to be filled. *Additional appointments*

The following occasions are listed in the Statutes of the Order: The disturbances in Waziristan in the North West Frontier Province of India in 1924; the Silver Jubilee of King George V in 1935; the Coronation of King George VI in 1937; the Second World War 1939–45; specified operations in South East Asia including the Netherlands East Indies in 1945–6; minesweeping, mine or bomb clearance 'arising out of, and subsequent to, the cessation of hostilities in the Second World War, or in recognition of gallantry at any time subsequent to the cessation of hostilities in the Second World War'; the events in 'Palestine and the adjoining waters' leading to the creation of the State of Israel in 1945–8; the communist insurgency in Malaya in 1948–60; the Korean War in 1950–3; the Mau Mau rising in Kenya 1952–6; the Coronation of Queen Elizabeth II in 1953; the disturbances leading to the independence of Cyprus in 1956–9; the Suez Canal Crisis in 1956; the Arabian Peninsula in 1957–60; the conflict between Yemeni and British Forces in the Radfan Area of South Arabia in 1964; the Indonesian incursions into Borneo in 1962–6; the disturbances leading to the independence of South Yemen 1964–7; the involvement of Australian troops in the Vietnam

War in 1967–72; the Investiture of Prince Charles as Prince of Wales in 1969; the troubles in Northern Ireland from 1971; the Silver Jubilee of Queen Elizabeth II in 1977; the Falklands War in 1982; and the Gulf War in 1990–1.

In the service
of the nation

Not until the 1950s did the editor of *The Times* feel able to state that he thought a particular Honours List was 'dull'. The said editor was then summoned to a meeting with Sir Edward Bridges, Head of the Home Civil Service, and told that good deeds were often dull, but that the conferred honour represented recognition of a lifetime of service.

On the publication of the New Year and Birthday Honours Lists in the newspapers, there is a natural and widespread tendency to look first at the photographs and then through the list of the higher honours for the names of 'celebrities', for 'sensational' awards, and for the names of people that one knows; and if none are found, then the List is dismissed as uninteresting.

The great majority of names in each Honours List are unknown to the great majority of the population, and appointments to the Order of the British Empire make up the bulk of each List. Many of the appointments at MBE and OBE level are for local service and unlikely ever to be known outside their locality, but to describe them as dull, uninteresting or even unknown, is to ignore a lifetime of conscientious service and the very real pleasure that the Order brings, not only to the recipient, but to the locality or the institution in which he or she works. The appointment of an MBE is recorded in a minute typeface on the inside page of a national newspaper; but it may be headline news on the front page of the local newspaper; and the stories of the celebratory 'surprise' party with the specially baked cake proudly bearing a representation of the MBE insignia in coloured icing, say a great deal about the pleasure that it brings to families, friends and colleagues.

There is a good chance that everyone in the United Kingdom will know someone, or know of someone who is an MBE or an OBE, and they will know roughly what those letters stand for, unlike any other honour. In November 1915 Sir Frederick Ponsonby had written 'Some form of recognition must be devised for all classes and indeed for a considerable proportion of the population'. Looking back over the history of the Order of the British Empire, there is no doubt that it has become what its founders intended it to be – an Order for the nation and the nation's Order.

SEVEN

Foreign and Commonwealth

THE ORDER OVERSEAS

I have been trying to think out some method of restricting the numbers of the Order of the British Empire to be given to the Allied Countries, but it is not easy to find any guiding principle. I have come to the conclusion that the best plan would be to fix a scale and try to adhere to it.

Sir Frederick Ponsonby to The Honourable Theophilus Russell, 25 May 1917

As a product of the First World War, the Order of the British Empire was distributed not only in the United Kingdom and the Dominions, but also among the victorious Allies. News of the impending creation of the Order had circulated around the United Kingdom embassies and legations in Europe, and by 21 May 1917 recommendations were already beginning to flow in. Theophilus Russell, Diplomatic Secretary to the Foreign Secretary, alerted Ponsonby to the need for the immediate imposition of a quota of some kind.

It is . . . essential that we should discuss the question of restricting recommendations for the new Order. At present our people abroad are absolutely shameless in this respect, and if they are allowed to continue, the whole value of the Order will decline. If I could be told that we might have a limited number for the Foreign Office we could manage here to fix the amount for each Allied Country and thus stop this hurricane of recommendations.[1]

Calculations

Allocations to the Allies were a little easier than allocations to government departments, but Ponsonby admitted to Russell that 'it is not easy to find any guiding principle'.[2] He drew up a scale based on the general principle that all the Allies would eventually receive half the number of Decorations given to British subjects. 'That is a possible hypothesis, although not necessarily one that will carry conviction in disappointed Embassies and Legations.'[3] On the basis of the numbers agreed by the committee in May 1917, he calculated the numbers available for distribution:

GBE	50
KBE/DBE	150
CBE	300
OBE	1,000
MBE	1,500

The Allied Countries in question were France, Russia, the United States, Italy, Belgium, Portugal, Romania, Serbia and Montenegro, but there were still unknown factors.

I am assuming that, first, America will be allowed to accept Decorations, and secondly, that the Russians will still be treated on an equality with the French. If America, Russia and Portugal do not accept any Decorations, all the better, but it is necessary to bring them into the calculations.[4]

Ponsonby envisaged treating France, Russia and the United States as equals, with Italy receiving one-half of the numbers allotted to them, and the other countries having either one-fifth or one-tenth. These calculations gave the following percentage share:

	%
France	20
Russia	20
United States	20
Italy	10
Belgium	4
Portugal	4
Romania	4
Serbia	4
Montenegro	2
Reserved for future Allies	12

These percentage allocations produced the following distribution:

Country	GBE	KBE/DBE	CBE	OBE	MBE
France	10	30	60	200	300
Russia	10	30	60	200	300
United States	10	30	60	200	300
Italy	5	15	30	100	150
Belgium	2	6	12	40	60
Portugal	2	6	12	40	60
Romania	2	6	12	40	60
Serbia	2	6	12	40	60
Montenegro	1	3	6	20	30
Future Allies	6	18	36	120	180
Total	50	150	300	1,000	1,500

For all his careful calculations, Ponsonby knew that strict enforcement of such quotas was unlikely to work.

The binomial theorem is a mere jest to this and although I feel it is folly to attempt to distribute Decorations on arithmetical calculations, the above might possibly form a basis for the distribution. . . France will never be satisfied with so few, but if you can say that the numbers are restricted without giving exact figures, it may help put a restraint on recommendations.[5]

In fact, his arithmetic was accepted and mostly observed, although the Bolshevik Revolution put an end to any question of awarding decorations to Russians. Eleven French were appointed GBEs in 1918–20, one more than Ponsonby's calculation, but the first appointment was Sir Basil Zaharoff, the armaments contractor. Although a French national, he was born in Turkey of Greek parents, and could conceivably be excluded from the French quota. Three Americans were awarded the GBE, among them Henry Morgenthau (1856–1946), the diplomat who had looked after the diplomatic interests of the Allies during the War. Although Portugal was allotted only two GBEs by Ponsonby, the removal of Russia from the equation allowed the appointment of five Portuguese in 1917–20. Two Belgians, four Italians and a solitary Montenegrin were appointed, but no nominations at GBE level were made from Serbia or Romania.

Having calculated the mathematical distribution of the Order among the Allies, a more detailed machinery was put in place to ensure that nominations received were of a comparable standard from country to country. On 3 December 1917 Ponsonby informed Sir Edmund Wyldbore-Smith at the Board of Trade, that the British ambassador or minister to the Allied country concerned would have charge of recommendations from the country to which he was accredited, the Foreign Office merely exercising sufficient supervision to ensure that a similar standard was maintained in each country. Although their names would be recorded, the appointments of foreign nationals would not be gazetted, and could be made throughout the year.[6]

The precise details of the machinery for recommending foreign nationals for the Order emerged from a meeting to discuss the awards to French officers and to civilian officials, held in Sir Frederick Ponsonby's room at Buckingham Palace on 19 July 1918. Apart from Ponsonby, those in attendance included the Earl of Derby (British Ambassador in Paris), Theophilus Russell of the Foreign Office, Lieutenant General Sir Francis Davies of the War Office and Rear Admiral A. F. Everett of the Admiralty. The meeting quickly produced a draft governing the award of the Order to foreign nationals in general.

Machinery of recommendation

All recommendations were to be forwarded to the Foreign Office for transmission to the ambassador of the country concerned. The ambassador was to be responsible for the distribution of the different classes of the Order in the country to which he was accredited; that is he would ensure that officers and civilians recommended were not proposed for a grade to which their rank or position did not entitle them. He would have the right to omit any name he considered undesirable, and to transfer intended recipients from one class to another. He would consult the government to which he was accredited and ask whether the classes were correct, and whether any of the persons recommended, holding military rank, would be more appropriately rewarded with a military decoration. He would scrutinise the lists to see that the total number of recommendations did not exceed the agreed limit. As the Order was to be used primarily to recognise services of a civilian character, the recipient's civil status was to be taken as an indication of the class of the Order for which he was eligible. The military rank of an officer or soldier performing civilian duties was to be ignored, if such duties were held to qualify him for the Order. After consulting the foreign governments as to the classes and character of the decoration to be awarded, the ambassadors were to forward their lists to the Foreign Office for submission to the King. When the King's approval of the recommendations had been received, the insignia would be forwarded to the embassy abroad by the Foreign Office for distribution.[7]

All such foreign appointments are regarded as 'honorary' appointments and are not counted against the size of the establishment of the various classes recorded in the Statutes. If a foreign national, who is an honorary member of the Order, is subsequently naturalised as a subject of the Crown, he or she may take the rank of an Additional member of the Order.

After the end of World War I and the completion of the war service lists, the Order of the British Empire might not have been used again for foreign nationals. Since the reign of King Edward VII, the Royal Victorian Order had become the customary award to be distributed during state visits. King Edward had given

State Visits

it freely, some thought too freely, on his many visits to Europe and it was well established as the normative decoration for such occasions.

The Order of the British Empire had been used, in the immediate aftermath of the War, as the honour for distribution on the occasion of 'guest of government' visits rather than state visits, and there were also instances of the Order being given in connection with Missions to the United Kingdom. This practice was extended in October 1921 when Ponsonby proposed that the Order might be used in connection with the impending visit of the Prince of Wales (later King Edward VIII and Duke of Windsor) to Japan. The visit of the Prince returned a visit made by the Japanese Crown Prince (later Emperor Hirohito) in May 1921, and Ponsonby reminded Sir Warren Fisher, Permanent Secretary to the Treasury, that it would be impossible for the Prince to use the Victorian Order on his visit.

Owing to the visit of the Crown Prince of Japan to this country, it may practically be said that all the leading Court officials in Japan have been decorated with the Victorian Order, and in the ordinary course of events it would be necessary to give presents in lieu of Decorations, but as this would cost a considerable sum and since there is little likelihood of the Treasury increasing the grant of money to the Prince of Wales, I have suggested that in cases where the Victorian Order can no longer be bestowed, the British Empire Order should be given.[8]

His proposal was not well received by the Foreign Secretary, Lord Curzon.

He is rather alarmed at the idea that when, on the occasion of a Royal visit to our country the Victorian Order has been given, the same recipients will receive other British Orders on a return visit from our Royalties. This seems quite a new theory and one which it would be well not to have established. Otherwise we shall find ourselves landed in never-ending difficulties.[9]

At the heart of Curzon's objections lay a fear that such an exchange of decorations would ultimately lead to demands for the Order of the Bath and the Order of St Michael and St George. 'We are safe against such demands now by pointing to the rule that only the Victorian Order, specially created to meet the circumstances, is conferred on these occasions.'[10] Curzon concluded by suggesting that an effort should be made to obtain an additional Treasury grant for presents.

Ponsonby duly estimated the required sum to be £3,000 but the Treasury, in the shape of Sir Warren Fisher, was adamant that Parliament, having already voted £25,000 for the tour, was unlikely to agree to a further £3,000.

The Foreign Office take an exaggerated view of the matter, for after all the value of the Order is affected very little by the number or character of the honorary appointments. . . What counts is the standard which is set in the home appointments. And I do not feel very apprehensive that the distribution of a few OBEs to Japanese officials would lead to any irresistible demands for the Bath, and Michael and George, which can properly be regarded as domestic orders whereas the British Empire – as its name implies – is suitable for the wider field.[11]

Ponsonby's suggestion was adopted, and the Order of the British Empire was given by the Prince of Wales on his visit to Japan.

The Order is now often used in State Visits, although to a lesser extent than the Royal Victorian Order. The customary procedure is that before a state visit takes place, an advance party will consider whether or not decorations are to be exchanged, and in what numbers and at what level. There are no hard and fast rules, but those holding offices within the household of the Head of State of the country concerned, may receive the Victorian Order. Those further removed from the personal staff of the Head of State, may receive the Order of the British Empire, and senior officers in the armed forces of foreign countries will usually receive the Order because, unlike the Victorian Order, it has a military division.

During the First World War, there lived at Farnborough Hill in Hampshire a sur- *Distinguished*
vivor of the second French Empire which had collapsed more than forty years ear- *expatriates*
lier – Eugénie, the last Empress of France. Emperor Napoleon III and Empress Eugénie had been welcomed to England in 1870 by Queen Victoria, and after the Emperor's death, the two widows had been devoted friends. After the Queen's death in 1901, the Empress remained on friendly terms successively with King Edward VII and King George V. At the outbreak of the war she had turned one wing of her house into a hospital for injured servicemen. The hospital was a small establishment, but the Empress maintained it for five years entirely from her own resources, spending something like £30 per month per patient, as well as buying the latest equipment needed by the resident surgeon. The hospital was not shut until the discharge of the last patient in September 1919. The Empress's generosity had not gone unnoticed, and in March 1919 the Prince of Wales and the Duke of York called at Farnborough Hill to invest the Empress with the insignia of a Dame Grand Cross of the Order of the British Empire. The Empress was greatly touched.

Sire, I thank Your Majesty for the GBE which the Prince of Wales gave me in Your Majesty's name. I owe this much more to the kindness of Your Majesty than to any merit of my own, and I appreciate this token of friendship very much. The charming young Prince who presented it has doubled the pleasure for me. Please believe in the sentiments of sincere affection with which I am, Your Majesty's most devoted Eugénie.[12]

The Empress enjoyed the honour for a little more than a year, dying on 11 July 1920 at the age of ninety-four.

Another exiled sovereign was not so fortunate. After a reign of two years, King Manoel II left Portugal after an uprising in 1910 and spent the remaining twenty-two years of his life in England. The king and his wife, Queen Augusta, lived quietly in Twickenham. In March 1918 Sir Arthur Stanley, Chairman of the Joint War Committee of the British Red Cross Society and the Order of St John, pressed for the King to receive recognition for his war work.

He really has done very good work and if he were a British subject I should probably have put him forward for the OBE or the CBE on this next occasion. I am afraid, however, that politics may stand in the way of his being given anything as I suppose you could not give less than the GBE to a King even although he is so little of a King and this our 'oldest allies' might object to.[13]

After some discussion Ponsonby replied that there might indeed be some difficult questions and criticism in the press, and it should best be postponed until a later date. King Manoel never received the GBE, and died in 1932 at the age of forty-two, but as he had been appointed a Knight of the Garter in 1909, while still King of Portugal, he had already received the highest Order in the United Kingdom.

More than seventy years later, another distinguished expatriate was to receive the Grand Cross of the Order at an age even more advanced than that of Empress Eugénie. Count Edward Raczynski, who had first visited England on holiday in 1906, studied at the London School of Economics before the First World War, married the daughter of a British MP, and in 1922–6 was Secretary at the Polish Legation in London. He returned to London in 1934, this time as Polish

Ambassador and, with the establishment of the communist government in 1945, he remained in exile in London and became a leading member of the Polish émigré community. The Polish Government, which had escaped to London in 1939 in the face of the German invasion, continued to exist after 1945, regarding itself as the legitimate government of Poland. A succession of Presidents-in-Exile was maintained until the collapse of communism, and Count Raczynski held the office 1979–86. By the time that freedom returned to Poland, the Count was in his late nineties and too old to contemplate returning home. He continued to live in London and celebrated his one-hundredth birthday with a party at the Polish Embassy in Portland Place on 19 December 1991. To commemorate the occasion and to celebrate a long and distinguished life, as much lived in and committed to the United Kingdom as to Poland, Mark Lennox Boyd MP (Parliamentary Under Secretary of State at the Foreign and Commonwealth Office) presented the Count with the insignia of a GBE. The Count had already lost his sight, but was able carefully to feel the insignia and to appreciate the honour given to him. He died on 30 July 1993.

Forfeiture In time of war, consideration is always given to the forfeiture of United Kingdom honours held by nationals of enemy countries, and in the issue of the *London Gazette* for 23 August 1940 a notice, dated 20 August, recorded the King's command to remove from the lists of honorary members of the Orders of Chivalry, and from the rolls of foreign holders of British decorations and medals, the names of 'all persons therein who are of German or Italian nationality'. A similar notice, dated 26 February 1942, appeared in the issue of the *Gazette* for the following day, cancelling awards to citizens of Bulgaria, Finland, Hungary, Japan, Romania and Siam. The best known removal from the roll of the Order of the British Empire during the Second World War was a man whose name has become a synonym for treachery, Major Vidkun Quisling. Quisling was appointed a CBE on 22 November 1929 in recognition of services rendered to His Majesty's Government in connection with the protection of British interests in the Soviet Union while he was serving on the staff of the Norwegian Legation in Moscow. After the German invasion of Norway on 8–9 April 1940, Quisling headed a puppet government under German occupation, and his CBE was cancelled and annulled by royal warrant dated 22 May.

Empire to From its inception, the Order of the British Empire was intended to be the Order
Commonwealth *for* the British Empire, and from 1917 until the 1960s it certainly performed that role. Australia, New Zealand, South Africa, India and the dependent territories, each made recommendations in the bi-annual honours lists. Canada effectively ceased to participate in the United Kingdom honours system in 1919, apart from a brief period in 1933–5, and again in 1944 and 1946 as a means of honouring Canadian soldiers who had fought in the Second World War. South Africa similarly ceased to participate in 1925 after the election of the government of James Herzog. The government of Jan Smuts (1939–48) submitted recommendations for war service, but the formation of a government by the Nationalist Party after the general election in June 1948 marked the beginning of the end of recommendations from South Africa. In December 1948 the South African government requested that all references to the Union of South Africa and to South African citizens be deleted from the Statutes of the Order of the British Empire, and the

end of South Africa's participation in the Order came on 29 August 1952 when the High Commission in London delivered a formal note to the Commonwealth Relations Office.

It is considered that since it is now generally agreed that the word 'Empire' is not a correct description of the Commonwealth and can, at most, only relate to the United Kingdom and Colonies, it would be inappropriate for the Union to participate in an award which bears no indication that it is also intended for the recognition of services rendered to a particular member of the Commonwealth other than the United Kingdom.[14]

In 1947 the newly independent states of India and Pakistan, ceased to make recommendations for United Kingdom honours and began the process of creating their own honours systems. They were followed on the path to independence by Burma and Sri Lanka in 1948, Ghana and Malaya in 1957, Nigeria in 1960, Cyprus, Sierra Leone and Tanzania in 1961, Jamaica, Trinidad and Tobago, and Uganda in 1962, Kenya in 1963, Malawi, Malta and Zambia in 1964, The Gambia, The Maldives and Singapore in 1965, Barbados, Botswana, Guyana and Lesotho in 1966, Mauritius and Swaziland in 1968, Fiji, Tonga and Western Samoa in 1970, Bahamas in 1973, Grenada in 1974, Papua New Guinea in 1975, Seychelles in 1976, Dominica, Solomon Islands and Tuvalu in 1978, Kiribati, St Lucia, and St Vincent and the Grenadines in 1979, Vanuatu and Zimbabwe in 1980, Antigua and Barbuda, and Belize in 1981, and Brunei in 1984. By the mid-1980s, there was hardly anything left of the Empire which had given the Order its name in 1917.

Although the pattern and timing varied from country to country, the move towards the creation of an indigenous honours system became the norm throughout most of the former British Empire, and the submission of names to London for appointment to the Order of the British Empire, began to fade away. Some Commonwealth nations ceased to make recommendations for United Kingdom honours on independence, whereas others continued to make recommendations long after independence. Mauritius, for example, became independent in 1968, but continued to use the United Kingdom honours system until republican status was adopted in 1992. Fiji, which became independent in 1970, submitted recommendations until its Commonwealth membership lapsed after the overthrow of the government and the adoption of republican status in 1987. Although New Zealand, and a number of Caribbean and Pacific nations continue to submit recommendations, the Commonwealth as a whole has largely withdrawn from using the honours of the United Kingdom. The establishment of the Order of Australia in 1975 and the Queen's Service Order in New Zealand in 1975 and the Order of New Zealand in 1987, in particular, have diminished the use of the Order of the British Empire in these historic parts of the Empire in which it had once been widely used.

Australia and the Australian Associations

In the late 1970s a series of local 'Associations' of the Order of the British Empire were formed in Australia. On 7 August 1975, Major General Peter Gillett, Registrar of the Order, was visited at the Central Chancery of the Orders of Knighthood in London by two Australian members of the Order. Councillor James McGregor-Dowsett, OBE, a former Mayor of Geelong, and Lieutenant Colonel Henry Jackson, MBE. They brought with them a cheque for £2,157.48, raised by members of the Order throughout Australia, chiefly by the enthusiasm of McGregor-Dowsett. He had organised a dinner for Australian recipients of the Order at Geelong on 20 December 1974, with about fifty members being present. One person remembered it with affection. 'It was an excellent evening. There was no suggestion or thought of setting up any new organisation. But everyone went away thoroughly happy and resolved to meet again.'[15] A second dinner, on 22 May 1975, attended by 231 recipients, spontaneously raised the sum which was now being presented to the Order. The sum was used specifically to install a sound-link between the Chapel of the Order and the main body of the Cathedral.

McGregor-Dowsett was born in 1899 at Launceston in Tasmania and joined the Royal Australian Naval Reserve in 1916. Serving in the New Guinea Civil Service in 1921–6, he left to join the Edie Creek Gold Rush. He then ran a cocoa plantation on the coast of New Britain and, in 1939, joined the New Guinea Volunteer Rifles and saw service in the Middle East. He spent thirty years on Geelong City Council, serving two terms as Mayor. Promoted to CBE in 1976, he died on 13 February 1990.

In addition to the cheque, McGregor-Dowsett also informed General Gillett of his proposal to establish a local chapter or association of the Order in his native Victoria, and to meet on an annual basis. The proposal had to be treated with a degree of caution since it was made at a time of some political sensitivity. The 1972 federal general election had been won by the Labour Party, which had been in opposition since 1949. The new government, headed by Gough Whitlam, introduced a number of changes reflecting its desire to 'Australianize' the monarchy. Among the changes was a decision to cease making recommendations for United Kingdom honours and, instead, to institute a purely Australian honours system, with the Order of Australia at its head. Three years of confusion followed. While the federal government pursued its committed policy, a number of the Australian state governments continued to make recommendations through the Foreign Office in London, as they had every right to do, and it was against this background that the Australian Associations were born towards the end of 1975.

The election of a conservative federal government in 1975 ensured a temporary period of revival of awards and a new influx of members to the Associations, but it came to an end with the return to power of a Labour Government in 1983. The federal government made a policy decision not to submit any further recommendations for United Kingdom honours, but to increase the use of the Order of Australia, and to extend the Australian honours system. The last Australian federal government honours list appeared in the New Year Honours List in 1983, although the conservative-led state governments of Queensland and Tasmania continued to submit lists until 1989. This recognised anomaly was due to the wording of the Commonwealth of Australia Act of 1900 which allowed the State governments to retain all the powers, including submissions for honours, which they had previously enjoyed as Colonies of the United Kingdom, except where a surrender of power to the federal government was explicitly set out in the Constitution.

Although recommendations from Australia ceased in 1989, a unique, unprecedented and, in the opinion of some, quite unnecessary formal notice of closure was inserted in the revised statutes of 1995. Under the terms of the curiously-worded Statute 21, the Sovereign acceded to the 'expressed desire' of the Prime Minister of Australia, and the Premiers of each of the Australian states to 'cease from the submission of recommendations' for appointment to the Order. Presumably the intention of Statute 21 is to bind morally all future Australian governments, but no such statute has ever been thought necessary in the case of other Commonwealth nations, and statutes can always be revised or repealed.

The Australian Associations quickly became social and informal gatherings of recipients, and although there was a common desire to promote loyalty to the Crown, they generally eschewed any overt 'political' or 'campaigning' standpoints. Given the distance between Australia and London, and the lengthy and expensive journey involved in attending the services at St Paul's Cathedral, the greatest use of the Associations was to enable Australian members of the Order of the British Empire to meet on a regular basis in their own country. The associations have also provided the useful service of maintaining registers of Australian recipients of the Order, and notifying the Central Chancery of deaths.

The Victorian Association was formally constituted on 24 May 1976 and held its first service at St Paul's Cathedral in Melbourne on 22 May 1977. In addition to an annual meeting and dinner, an annual service takes place: in 1978, at St Patrick's Roman Catholic Cathedral, in 1979 at Wesley Church, and in 1980 at the Scots Presbyterian Church. In recent years it has been held at St James's Old Cathedral, King Street, Melbourne, the preachers coming by rotation from different denominations. By 1980 membership of the Association stood at 1,116, and in 1983 the Association was able to make a gift of £1,000 to the Chapel of the Order. In 1977 the Association established Silver Jubilee Scholarships which were awarded on an annual basis to schoolchildren. In 1990 there were 367 applicants from 143 schools.

The New South Wales Association was also formed in 1976, and membership stood at 700 in 1978. It holds a social outing each year in February or March, an annual meeting and luncheon, and an annual service in St Andrew's Cathedral, Sydney, all in May, and an annual dinner in November. In recent years the Association has opened membership to spouses of deceased members, members of the Royal Victorian Order, Knights Bachelor, Companions of the Distinguished Service Order, Companions of the Imperial Service Order, and recipients of the Royal Red Cross. The Association had more than 600 members in 1995.

The Western Australia Association was formed in 1976. Membership stood at 300 in 1978, approximately 430 in 1981 and about 230 in 1995. The Association meets twice yearly, in May for an annual commemorative dinner and a dedication service at St George's Cathedral, Perth, and in December for a Christmas luncheon.

The Queensland Association was formed in October 1977. The initial membership of 98 had risen to 287 by the end of 1978. The Association holds receptions in March and September, and a church service and dinner in May each year. In 1984 the Association made a donation to provide the Chapel of the Order with baptismal cards, and in 1994 a grant to the Salvation Army Drought Relief Fund.

The South Australia Association was formed in February 1978 with a membership of approximately 250. In 1978, the Association presented a drinking fountain to the City of Adelaide to mark the bicentenary of the arrival of Captain Cook in Australia.

The Australian Capital Territory Association was formed in 1979 at the suggestion of the Grand Master, to complement the state associations. An informal social gathering is usually held in February each year, followed by an annual service of dedication, held each year at the Anzac Memorial Chapel of St Paul at the Royal Military College, Duntroon, and a dinner in October. Membership initially stood at 22, and reached a peak of 250, but stands in 1995 at 212. The Association's annual service on 25 May 1980 was honoured with the presence of The Queen and The Duke of Edinburgh. The service was attended by representatives of all the State Associations.

The first meeting to establish a Tasmanian Association took place in May 1976. Only 30 people attended and, because of lack of enthusiasm, the matter lapsed. A renewed and successful effort was made in August 1978. The Association had a membership of 300 at its peak, but this had reduced to 161 members by 1993 and was preparing to 'diminish with dignity' in the words of its Secretary. The Association holds an annual dinner and an annual service of dedication.

With declining memberships, the Australian Associations will inevitably cease to exist in the form in which they were founded, but they have many years of existence ahead of them, and a number have taken the decision to create a broader membership. Their future may well lie in the formation of joint associations with recipients of the Order of Australia, a symbolic joining of the old and the new.

A role model   The use of the Order of the British Empire in the Commonwealth over recent years has been clearly marked by decline, but this process should not be taken as a reason to dismiss the Order by reason of redundancy. For many years the University of London functioned as a parent body, validating the degree courses of many newly-created and developing university colleges throughout the Empire, until they were ready and able to achieve university status in their own right and award their own degrees. In the same way, the Order of the British Empire provided a useful and respected way of honouring the citizens of nations that were not yet ready to introduce their own honours. The desire of the Commonwealth nations to institute their own honours is a positive statement about the development of those nations, not an implicit and negative criticism of the Order of the British Empire, despite its, some would say anachronistic, name.

Change of name   The transformation of the British Empire into the Commonwealth of Nations was a process which took place over a long period of time, and led to many other changes in the nomenclature of related institutions and events. Historically, the Empire was run by the Colonial Office, but the title of the department had really ceased to be appropriate for the independent states of Canada, Australia, New Zealand and South Africa, and in 1925 the Dominions Office was established to conduct relations with those countries. The Dominions Office was renamed the Commonwealth Relations Office on 7 July 1947, and further renamed the Commonwealth Affairs Office on 1 August 1966, before being merged with the Foreign Office on 17 October 1968. The Colonial Office began to share its ministers with the Commonwealth Relations Office in 1962. It was brought under the jurisdiction of the Commonwealth Affairs Office on 1 August 1966, and formally abolished on 7 January 1967.

The Colonial Conferences of 1902 and 1907 were succeeded by the Imperial Conferences of 1911–37, and then by the first Commonwealth Prime Ministers' Meeting in 1944. The 'British Empire Games', held in 1930, 1934, 1938 and 1950, were followed by the 'British Empire and Commonwealth Games' of 1955, 1958, 1962 and 1966, the 'British Commonwealth Games' of 1970 and 1974, and then by the 'Commonwealth Games' from 1978. On 7 May 1958, the Royal Empire Society changed its name to the Royal Commonwealth Society, and on 18 December 1958, the United Kingdom Government announced simultaneously in the House of Lords and the House of Commons that the name of 'Empire Day' would be changed to 'Commonwealth Day' forthwith.

By 1960 the very name 'British Empire' was beginning to acquire an embarrassing air of obsolescence, and the title, 'Order of the British Empire', was sounding redolent of an age that was passing. Respect for an imperial honour was giving way to expressions of exasperation, ridicule, mirth and cynicism. As so many other similarly named organisations and events were beginning to change, was it not also time for the Order to change? Many of the comments about the 'obsolete' title of the Order date from the period of the 1960s when the British Empire ceased to exist and the Commonwealth of Nations came into being, and many people thought it valid and entirely appropriate to ask the question 'When will the Order of the British Empire have its name changed?'

Before looking at the consideration that was given to this issue in 1962–4 and again in 1966, it should be noted that many of the questions and comments about the title of the Order began from the premise that it was anachronistic and that a change *had* to be made, and that the question to ask was not 'Why should it be made?', but 'Why has it not already been made?' and 'When is it going to be made?' These questions were contemporary and relevant to the 1960s. They were the product of a time when the United Kingdom was shedding one role and assuming another, a time when any allusion to the country's imperial past was a reminder of something that many people were trying to forget. The South African government had already dismissed the Order in 1952 because of the words 'British Empire'. From about 1960, letters began to appear in newspapers after the publication of honours lists, all saying roughly the same thing; 'Why do we still have an Order of the British Empire when there is no longer a British Empire?' The issue was also the subject of a number of parliamentary questions throughout the 1960s and 1970s, some thoughtful and some polemical, but all underpinned by the belief that the Order of the British Empire had to be changed or abolished.

Change contemplated

Towards the end of 1962, Duncan Sandys, Secretary of State for Commonwealth Relations, asked for serious consideration to be given to the possibility of changing the title of the Order. The issue had been discussed within the Commonwealth Relations Office, and a number of suggestions had emerged, all based on the premise that the Order of the British Empire was increasingly untenable under its present title. Possibilities, all involving an alteration of the title, included the Order of the Commonwealth Star, the Order of King George V, the Order of the British Commonwealth, the Order of the Commonwealth, the Order of Liberation, the Order of Queen Elizabeth II, or the Order of Free Peoples; and the change of the motto from 'For God and the Empire' to 'For God and the Commonwealth'.[16]

In considering what, if any, changes should be made, that veteran honours specialist and Ceremonial Officer, Sir Robert Knox, looked at all sides of the question in 1963, and was careful not to begin with the premise that a change had to be made. He looked at the state of the Commonwealth and asked two questions.

Firstly, was there any discernible demand for a change of name from the Commonwealth nations, and secondly, would any benefit accrue either to the Order or to the Commonwealth were such a change to be implemented? And in each case, the answer was 'no'.

By 1963, India, Pakistan, Ghana, Malaya, Ceylon, Cyprus and Tanzania, had all become independent and, with the exception of Ceylon, all were republics, and none of them made recommendations for United Kingdom honours. Most of them had instituted their own honours systems and, wrote Knox, 'it is evident that no change in the description of the Order of the British Empire would be likely to have the slightest effect on honours policy in those territories'.[17] While Australia, the Australian States, New Zealand, Sierra Leone, Jamaica, Trinidad and Tobago, Uganda, Rhodesia and Nyasaland all continued to use the Order, 'there has been no pressure at all from them that any change should be made in the description of the Order'.[18]

Knox additionally noted the gradual drift towards republican status in the newly independent states and the institution of separate honours systems.

The view may be taken that there would be great objections to the creation of a new Order, that there are already too many different Orders . . . and that to institute a new Order would not be justifiable at the present time, particularly when the creation of Republics in the Commonwealth reduces the field for the grant of British awards. It would be difficult to set up a new five-class Order which would be eagerly sought after and deeply valued by the recipients, from its inception, and it is very doubtful whether it would be wise to recommend that the attempt should be made.[19]

In December 1963, Christopher Eastwood, Assistant Under Secretary of State at the Colonial Office wrote to Sir Neil Pritchard, Deputy Under Secretary of State at the Commonwealth Relations Office advising against a change of name, remarking that an Order with an obsolete title was not without precedent, and should not lightly be abandoned to accommodate contemporary changes.

It may have an increasingly antique flavour, but to some there may be attractions in that. After all, the Order of the Bath has long survived the discarding of ablution from the ceremony of installation.[20]

During 1964 the Colonial Office consulted a number of colonial governors about possible reaction in their territories to a potential change of name, while the Commonwealth Relations Office did the same with United Kingdom High Commissioners in those Commonwealth countries of which Queen Elizabeth II was still head of state. The unanimous response was that there was no discernible demand for change.

In Canada such a change was not seen to be of any practical importance or concern in view of the general policy of not making recommendations for the award of United Kingdom honours. The High Commissioner in Australia reported that there was no feeling that either the Order or its title, in their present form, had outlived their usefulness, and a similar opinion emerged from New Zealand. The High Commissioner to Sierra Leone reported a few private comments about the title, but there was no evidence that these had had an influence on the Government recommending and individuals accepting the Order. In Southern Rhodesia, the majority of Europeans had a nostalgic regard for the days of the Empire and would regard a change as regrettable. Similarly, in Trinidad and Tobago there was no evidence to suppose that the title influenced the Trinidad Government in recommending, or individuals in accepting, appointments in the Order. Nor was there any sign in Jamaica of any local feeling about the title. 'A recent press article poured scorn upon a system of awards for services to the British Empire, "which is not only foreign but also extinct",'[21] but a subsequent article in another paper justified the retention of the title, on the ground that, if titles and honours were to have glamour and romance, they must be associated with the past and not with the present, and quoted the Order of the Garter and the Order of St Michael and St George as honoured examples. The author observed that the title 'British Empire' 'evokes a perfume of Clive at Plassey and Wolfe at Quebec'.[22]

Writing in December 1964, Sir Robert Black, recently retired as Governor of Hong Kong, urged caution before taking action.

We are still in a period of transition, and the Commonwealth ties are so slender and delicate that it might prove unrealistic and the object of contumely if we changed the form of an order which has acquired a measure of age (46 years) and, in consequence, a degree of tradition.[23]

The question of a change of name was considered again in 1966, but the conclusions of 1962–4 remained valid.

The harder one looks at the Order of the British Empire the clearer it becomes that its name could only have been changed in the 12–18 months period before its creation was formally announced in August 1917. Various names had been suggested at the time, and among the proposals was one to style it 'Order of the Commonwealth'. Sir Graham Greene, Secretary to the Ministry of Munitions had implied as much to Ponsonby on 21 May 1917.

Too late to change

If anything is to be done, it would be better that the actual designation of the Order should be changed. Apparently there is a good deal of sympathy for Smuts's [Prime Minister of South Africa] view of the composition of the British Empire as a Commonwealth of Nations, and I should not be sorry to see the term 'Commonwealth' introduced far more generally than it is at present.[24]

If any change was to have been made, it should have been made then, in 1917; fifty years later was too late.

The discussions and investigations of 1962–4 concluded that the Order was not really at a disadvantage through bearing the name of a defunct institution, and that as the Empire disappeared into the sands of time, the less difficulty there would be in retaining the name. It may have been a mistake to call the new Order when it was founded in 1917 by the name of an existing institution, but fifty years later there were no signs of local prejudice in the Commonwealth against the title. To some it might have been an embarrassing reminder of a past that they themselves wished to forget, but they were far outnumbered by the many, not least the many recipients, whose regard for the Order was high enough for them to accept it.

Changing the name of the Order to 'The Order of the Commonwealth' was an attractive proposal, but would such a name have passed the test of time? In the naming of an honour one needs to take a very long-term view, and a period of fifty years is comparatively short. In choosing a name that evokes an existing institution, the possibility of controversy, and of political difficulties and sensitivity, would inevitably arise and a completely innocuous name, if such could be found, would need to be chosen.

The test of time

If there had been any evidence that the name of the Order of the British Empire was unpopular either at home or abroad, to the point of a widespread dissatisfaction, a change might have been justified, but there was no evidence in support of such a contention. Such a change could only be considered if there was evidence that the designation 'Order of the British Empire' was offensive to a substantial number of potential recipients, and there was never any evidence for this. It could rightly be said that the few refusals of the Order in and since the 1960s compare very favourably with the many refusals in the 1920s.

The Order was still widely used throughout the Commonwealth in 1966, and any attempt to change the name by seeking and gaining the general support of the Commonwealth governments for a new name, would almost certainly have opened a long, divisive and probably inconclusive debate. If the title was to go, the new title had to be something that would last and not require a further change in thirty or fifty years' time. There were overwhelming arguments for being cautious about subjecting the title of the Order to scrupulous logic and for leaving the Order as it was. Such a conclusion was reached by the Committee on the Grant of Honours, Decorations and Medals, when it reported on 7 October 1966. 'Our conclusion is that this is a case for leaving well alone, and we recommend that the present arrangements should not be disturbed.'[25] The Order was due to celebrate the fiftieth anniversary of its foundation in 1967 and, as another observed, it would surely be very sad, and would occasion a great deal of misunderstanding, if it had to be admitted that the 50th Anniversary Service was in effect to be the funeral service of the Order.[26]

During the 1960s, the title of the Order of the British Empire was thought by some to be an embarrassment, a relic of an age that had passed; but the succeeding age has itself passed, and the name of the Order has gradually achieved the status of a charming and honoured historical survival. The further the British Empire recedes into the past, the less embarrassed people will feel in referring to it. The title of the Order will soon have no more meaning than the title of the Order of the Bath with its reference to the obsolete medieval rite of purification before admission to knighthood.

Of doubtful legality — Changing the name of the Order was suggested as though it could be done by the stroke of a pen, but the research of 1962–4 showed that, although it could be done, it would be legally dubious to do so, and the ramifications of doing it militated against such a change. The Letters Patent of 1917 declared that the Order should be 'called and known forever hereafter' as The Order of the British Empire. The first Statute reiterates the title and states that the Order shall be known 'by no other designation'. Although both Letters Patent and Statutes could in theory be amended, to do so would be to overrule the most explicit intentions and instructions of the founders. To change both the name and, inevitably, the insignia, would change the Order beyond recognition and effectively create a new Order.

If the name of the Order of the British Empire is, in the future, again thought to be an embarrassment, it would be better to bring the Order to a close and institute a new Order to take its place, though that in itself would begin a new set of problems. The existing members would suddenly find themselves members of a devalued and dying Order, which might, by virtue of being declared obsolete, become the object of ridicule and amusement. The Order is the most widely used of the United Kingdom honours, and it has the largest membership. To substitute a new Order – which would probably take a generation to establish itself in public esteem – would be quite possible, but the resulting upheaval would be out of all proportion to any possible benefits.

In the investigations of 1962–4, and since that time, no evidence has been produced to show that the Order of the British Empire has outlived its usefulness, and that a new Order is either needed or desired to replace it.

In medieval Europe, two authorities were considered to be paramount in honour and possessed of a semi-divine authority – the spiritual authority of the Pope, and the temporal authority of the Holy Roman Emperor. The final European court of appeal rested with the authority of the Pope in Rome, and it was the Pope's prerogative to anoint and crown the Holy Roman Emperor who was ex officio the principal sovereign in Europe. All the European sovereigns accorded the Emperor a primacy, at least of honour if not of jurisdiction.

'This realm . . . is an Empire'

This medieval order began to wane before the onslaught of the religious and political upheavals of the 16th century. After his failure to secure a papal dispensation for his divorce from Catherine of Aragon, King Henry VIII secured the passage of a number of significant pieces of legislation through the English Parliament in the mid-1530s, all of which were designed to show that both he, and England, were jurisdictionally autonomous. The 'Act in Restraint of Appeals', passed by Parliament in 1534, stated in a famous phrase that 'this realm of England is an Empire'. The Act was intended to prevent appeals to any court outside England, and the assertion implied that the King of England was of equal authority with, and in no way inferior to, the Holy Roman Emperor.

If there should be any future debate about the title of the Order of the British Empire, it might be remembered that there is an historic meaning to the word 'empire', which has nothing whatever to do with the possession of overseas territories. The clear intention of those who drafted the act of 1534 was to define England as an empire, and by so doing, to proclaim that it was independent of any authority other than that of its King.

EIGHT

The Robes and Insignia of the Order: I

THE OLD PATTERN

The King said that after all he did not like the ribbon the Queen had chosen.
This is a rather delicate matter as it is the Queen's favourite colour.
Sir Frederick Ponsonby to Sir Douglas Dawson, 7 September 1916

Ponsonby was adamant that the design of the insignia should remain the responsibility of the King, and be kept away from the hands of the government and the civil service. With the King's permission, he enlisted the aid of Prince Louis of Battenberg, a cousin of the King and grandson of Queen Victoria. Prince Louis had enjoyed a distinguished career in the Royal Navy until a wave of anti-German hysteria swept the country at the outbreak of the War and forced him to resign as First Sea Lord in 1914. Since that date he had lived in virtual retirement in his house at East Cowes on the Isle of Wight. There, in July 1916, he received a letter from Ponsonby which damned the civil service as much as it flattered him.

The Order of the British Empire is slowly progressing and the report of the Committee appointed to enquire into the advisability of instituting this new Decoration is now before the Cabinet. I hardly think, however, they are a competent body to deal with a matter of this sort, as none of them have the slightest knowledge of Orders, or Decorations. The Clapham Parish Council would have done equally well for the consideration of a new Decoration. I have now made it clear that the designs must be left entirely in the King's hands and His Majesty thinks he cannot do better than consult you in the matter.[1]

While Ponsonby, Troup and Bonham Carter were busying themselves with their report to the Cabinet, debate about the manufacture of the insignia of the new Order was already beginning at a lower level between the Privy Purse Office and the Lord Chamberlain's Office. The consensus was that, as the insignia of the new Order would need to be manufactured in large numbers, and quickly, Garrard, the Crown Jewellers, was the obvious choice. The company was well accustomed to making insignia, being already responsible for the Orders of the Garter, the Thistle, the Bath, the Star of India, St Michael and St George, the Indian Empire, and the Distinguished Service Order.

Ponsonby commissioned Miss Elinor Hallé to design the insignia. Daughter of Sir Charles Hallé, founder of the Hallé Orchestra, Elinor Hallé was a noted sculptress, enamellist and medallist in her day, and she exhibited at the Royal Academy on a number of occasions between 1892 and 1914. Among her works were a bronze medal of Cardinal Newman in 1887, and one of Countess Feodora Gleichen in 1914. Forrer's *Biographical Dictionary of Medallists*, published in 1904, records that 'she first made her mark at the Grosvenor Gallery in 1884 with a low-relief of "Music"'. She later abandoned the field of sculpture for medal-designing and enamelling. She became a member of the Society of Medallists, at the exhibitions of which 'she has exhibited some nice works'. She was well known to

Ponsonby who had commissioned her to design the collar of the Royal Victorian Order in 1911.

Ponsonby warmly commended her to Prince Louis on 12 July as 'one of the leading metal workers of this country'.[2] He wrote in a similar vein to Dawson on 15 August: 'She has not only got a great name in England, but succeeded in winning an open competition for a Burgermeister's Chain at Munich, beating all other European artists'.[3] Ponsonby had seen her by 12 July 1916 and commissioned her to prepare designs with due economy in mind.

I pointed out to her that while we had no wish to imitate German methods and produce gimcrack Orders, it might be possible to reduce the cost by omitting the enamel work. Miss Hallé told me that she considered the present charges for British Decorations were preposterous. It would be quite a simple matter to cut these down. I told her to make enquiries in Birmingham where all these things were actually made and ascertain for me what approximately would be the cost of such Decorations, if ordered in large quantities.[4]

Ponsonby reported to Prince Louis that the Prime Minister 'was somewhat taken aback'[5] to hear that the usual cost of British Orders was £50 for the Grand Cross, £20–25 for a second class, and £6–7 for a third class.

First designs

Miss Hallé initially submitted two designs for the star, which are described in correspondence as 'A' and 'B' but Ponsonby liked neither of them. He described them as 'not very happy, in fact, I am sure none of them will do. I have explained to her that it is advisable not to have the spiky ends of the Star sticking out.'[6] Prince Louis disagreed and liked star 'A'. 'Most original and I see no objection to the 4 projecting points; ordinary Stars have more; to keep them inside the circumference would spoil the design.'[7] He thought that it would do for both the first and the second classes. For the first class the star could be gold or silver-gilt, and for the second class, it could be silver. 'In both cases the background must be enamelled (light blue for choice) to show off the Star, but that is not a difficult and costly pattern, especially if the 8 gold wavy points are omitted.'[8]

Ponsonby was dissatisfied with the prospect of using the same star for both classes, and asked Miss Hallé to produce a further design, star 'C', with eight points, which could be used for the first class. 'It differs from every other English Star and would therefore be suitable.'[9] Either star 'A' or star 'B' could then be used as the star of the second class. Prince Louis agreed.

There must be a certain similarity between the Stars of Grand Cross and Knight Commander . . . but the latter Star must show its inferiority to the former, by being less elaborate, having fewer points etc. . . . I still consider that A and B are entirely original in design compared with existing British and Foreign Orders. B is perhaps too elaborate with its Swords and Palms (tho' a pretty piece). As an alternative to using A: (1st class Gold, 2nd Class silver) I would suggest making the Kt Comdr Star of 4 points instead of the 8 for Grd Cross; it should also be smaller in diameter.[10]

Ponsonby showed all three designs to the King and Queen, who both liked star 'C'. The King disliked stars 'A' and 'B' on the ground that they were 'too artistic and the public might not like them'.[11] Queen Mary expressed a liking for star 'A' and supported Prince Louis's argument that it was quite different from any other star then in existence. The King agreed to meet Miss Hallé and show her all the British and foreign stars he had in his collection. 'She is now engaged in more designs for these Stars.'[12] In the absence of further information, it seems that the stars for the first and second classes, which came into use in 1917, were roughly based on designs 'C' and 'A'.

Miss Hallé admitted to Ponsonby that 'every conceivable form has already been used and that it is practically impossible to design a Star which does not form part of an existing Order in Europe',[13] but this was of little avail. Ponsonby thought that her design for the badge was 'too ornate and not sufficiently strong',[14] and he sent it to Prince Louis on 12 July 'in the hope that you may perhaps be able to design something yourself'. In fact Prince Louis was generally pleased with her designs which he thought 'very good and decidedly original'.[15] Miss Hallé's design for the badge was a cross surmounted by a crown with a globe suspended from the bottom of the cross. The central medallion bore a seated figure of Britannia in profile with a lion at her feet, that Prince Louis likened to 'the stuffed animals in a museum'.[16] He suggested that the globe 'would drop off very soon and had better be omitted'.[17] Prince Louis also suggested abandoning Britannia in favour of a coloured enamel representation of the national flag. 'It flies in every one of the King's Dominions.'[18] This suggestion was subsequently vetoed by the King who thought that it was 'unsuitable as an emblem for the whole British Empire'.[19]

Ponsonby and Dawson had the designs vetted for heraldic accuracy by the College of Arms, and because of the absence in Scotland of Sir Alfred Scott-Gatty, Garter King of Arms, the task fell to Henry Farnham Burke, Norroy King of Arms. Burke replied on 22 September, criticising the size of Miss Hallé's sketch, which was 'so enormous that it was impossible to appreciate what the cross would be like in a small size as worn on the breast'.[20] She had also included a wreath, which 'has always been reserved in British orders for military services, and is therefore not applicable to civilians'; a lion, 'meaningless from an heraldic point of view'; the Royal crest, which 'had already been made use of in the Victoria Cross'; and allegorical representations of 'Peace' and 'War' that 'would be so small that they would be quite undecipherable'.[21]

The Motto   Miss Hallé had also produced a motto rendered in a form of Latin which Dawson dismissed as 'rather crude'[22]. She had proposed *Imperium Brittanicum*, admitting that she was 'not very sure of my Latin', or 'Order of the British Empire' in English. 'Or is there any short motto which would apply to the circumstances? "Unity is strength" seems more to the point as applying to the help the Colonies have given us. We might put it in Latin if it would look better.'[23] Dawson proposed 'For God and Empire' and Miss Hallé produced new designs, but included the definite article and altered it to read 'For God and the Empire':

not only because it filled the space better, but because it struck me afterwards that 'the Empire' means our Empire as it exists, while 'for God and Empire' might be taken to mean aspirations towards a universal Empire, which might ruffle the feelings of other nations, but I daresay I am wrong. . .[24]

Although Dawson disagreed with Miss Hallé and felt that the definite article should be omitted, he gave no reasons, and was overruled by Prince Louis of Battenberg, and also by the King, who admitted that it was 'a very difficult point to decide',[25] but preferred English to Latin. Miss Hallé's original design showed the motto on a white enamel background. Queen Mary suggested a light transparent grey, but the colour eventually selected was a dark crimson.

These early designs for the insignia are the work of Elinor Hallé
and probably date from the second half of 1916

II   The Medal of the Order, 1917–37

1. The Medal of the Order 1917–22, Civil Division

2. The Medal of the Order for   3. The Medal of the Order for
Meritorious Service 1922–37, Civil Division   Meritorious Service 1922–37, Military Division

4. The Medal of the Order for Gallantry 1922–37, Military Division

Scale 1:2

MBE: The Badge of a Member of the Order, 1917–37

1. Woman, Civil Division   2. Woman, Military Division

3. Man, Civil Division   4. Man, Military Division

1. belonged to Evelyn Lucy Rehm who was appointed an MBE in 1920 and died in 1978. The case of issue contains the note 'To be returned at once after my death to my Queen at Buckingham Palace'. 2. bears the London hallmark for 1919–20. 3. belonged to Sydney Thomas Walter Harrison, appointed an MBE in 1920, and was returned after his death in 1976.

Scale 1:2

IV   OBE: The Badge of an Officer of the Order, 1917–37

1. Woman, Military Division   2. Woman, Civil Division

3. Man, Military Division   4. Man, Civil Division

1. belonged to Dr Adeline Roberts, appointed an OBE in 1919, and was returned after her death in 1955.

Scale 1:2

CBE: The Badge of a Commander of the Order, 1917–37   V

1. Man, Military Division   2. Man, Civil Division

3. Woman, Civil Division

1. belonged to Colonel W. H. Cunningham, appointed a CBE in 1935. He was promoted to KBE in 1955, and died, as Major General Sir William Cunningham, in 1959.

Scale 1:2

VI   DBE: The Badge and Star of a Dame Commander of the Order, 1917–37,
Civil Division

This badge and star belonged to Dame Margaret Oudendyk who was appointed an Honorary Dame Commander on 15 December 1918 when her husband was Dutch Minister at St Petersburg. As a diplomatic representative of a neutral country, he and his wife were able to render service to a number of British subjects imprisoned in Moscow after the Russian Revolution. Dame Margaret acquired British nationality in 1949 and was reclassified as an additional Dame Commander with effect from 1 January 1949. She died on 1 November 1971 at the age of ninety-five

Scale 1:2

KBE: The Badge and Star of a Knight Commander of the Order, 1917–37 VII

1. The star

2. The badge suspended from
a ribbon of the Military Division

3. The badge suspended from
a ribbon of the Civil Division

Scale 1:2

VIII   GBE: The Insignia of a Dame Grand Cross of the Order, 1917–37

1. The star and broad ribbon of the Civil Division

2. The collar and the badge

GBE: The Insignia of a Knight Grand Cross of the Order, 1917–37   IX

1. The star and broad ribbon of the Civil Division

2. The collar and the badge

The star and badge belonged to Admiral Sir William Kelly (1873–1952). He was appointed a GBE in 1934 and exchanged this insignia for the new pattern in 1937.

| X | GBE: A Diamond Star and Badge
of a Knight Grand Cross | GBE: The Diamond Star
of the Princess Royal |

A set made by Spink c. 1930. The pieces are made of gold, silver and enamel. The badge is set with blue sapphires within a diamond border; the crown and ring being set with diamonds, two emeralds and a ruby. The star is set with brilliant cut diamonds. The reverse is inscribed 'Spink and Son, London, By Appointment'.

Scale 1:1

This star, containing over 350 brilliant-cut diamonds, was made by Hennell for HRH the Princess Royal (Princess Mary, Countess of Harewood), who was appointed a Dame Grand Cross of the Order in 1927.

GBE: The Knights and Dames Grand Cross

1. The mantle, collar and badge
of a Knight Grand Cross from 1937
Worn by Sir Alexander Graham, GBE

2. The mantle, collar and badge
of a Dame Grand Cross from 1937
Worn by Dame Mary Donaldson, GBE

3. The mantle, hat, collar and badge
of a Knight Grand Cross 1917–37

4. The mantle, hat, collar and badge
of a Dame Grand Cross 1917–37

XII   BEM: The Medal of the Order from 1937

1. Woman, Civil Division   2. Woman, Military Division

3. The Emblem for Gallantry when the ribbon alone is worn

4. Man, Civil Division   5. Man, Military Division

6. Man, Civil Division (with the Emblem for Gallantry)

Scale 1:2

MBE: The Badge of a Member of the Order from 1937   XIII

1. Woman, Civil Division   2. Woman, Military Division

3. Man, Civil Division   4. Man, Military Division

Scale 1:2

XIV   OBE: The Badge of an Officer of the Order from 1937

1. Woman, Civil Division   2. Woman, Military Division

3. Man, Civil Division   4. Man, Military Division

Scale 1:2

CBE: The Badge of a Commander of the Order from 1937   XV

1. Man, Civil Division   2. Man, Military Division

3. Woman, Civil Division   4. Woman, Military Division

1. and 2. are suspended from miniature width ribbons.

Scale 1:2

XVI   DBE: The Badge and Star of a Dame Commander of the Order from 1937

1. The badge suspended from   2. The badge suspended from
a ribbon of the Civil Division   a ribbon of the Military Division

3. The star

Scale 1:2

KBE: The Badge and Star of a Knight Commander of the Order from 1937   XVII

1. The badge suspended from a miniature
width ribbon of the Civil Division

2. The badge suspended from a miniature
width ribbon of the Military Division

3. The star

Scale 1:2

XVIII   GBE: The Insignia of a Dame Grand Cross of the Order from 1937

1. The star and broad ribbon of the Civil Division

2. The collar and the badge

Scale 1:2

GBE: The Insignia of a Knight Grand Cross of the Order from 1937   XIX

1. The star and broad ribbon of the Civil Division

2. The collar and the badge

The Badges of the Grand Master and the Officials

1. The Grand Master

2. The Prelate   3. The King of Arms

4. The Registrar   5. The Secretary

6. The Gentleman Usher of the Purple Rod

7. The Dean   8. The Prelate Emeritus

Scale 1:2   9. The Sub-Dean

The Crown and Rods

1. The Purple Rod
of the Gentleman Usher

2. The Crown
of the King of Arms

3. The Rod
of the King of Arms

XXII   The altar plate of the Chapel of the Order, made by Meadowcroft and Sarll,
was dedicated in 1963

XXIII   *Opposite above*   The Chapel of the Order, looking towards the east

             Opposite below   The Chapel of the Order, looking towards the west,
showing the 1993 screen and chairs

XXIV   The Grand Master and Officials of the Order in the Blue Drawing Room
at Buckingham Palace on 26 July 1995

From left to right: The Dean, the Very Reverend Eric Evans; the Registrar, Lieutenant Colonel Anthony
Mather; the Prelate, the Right Reverend and Right Honourable David Hope; the Grand Master, HRH The
Prince Philip, Duke of Edinburgh; the King of Arms, Admiral Sir Anthony Morton; the Secretary, Sir Robin
Butler; the Gentleman Usher of the Purple Rod, Commander and Alderman Sir Robin Gillett, Bt. Behind
the Grand Master and Officials can be seen a portrait of Queen Mary, second Grand Master of the Order.

Although it was agreed that Britannia should appear at the centre of the Badge and Star of the Order, the stuffed lion was dropped. Prince Louis pointed out that on the royal arms, the lion stood for Scotland, while England was represented by three leopards.

The crowned lion on the Royal Crown is really the King's Crest. If represented without the Crown on its head, or the one on which it stands, we are back again at the stuffed specimen of the Museum.[26]

So the despised stuffed lion was abandoned, and Britannia was shown holding a trident in her right hand, seated on a shell throne next to a shield bearing the national flag, her left arm extended and pointing across the sea beneath a blazing sun.

The King initially favoured his image appearing on the obverse of the Medal of the Order but gave way and agreed to Britannia when confronted with the combined opposition of Prince Louis, Ponsonby and Dawson who saw the medal as an integral part of the Order. Ponsonby suggested that, in the interests of economy, the Badge of the third class should be enamelled, that of the fourth class should be gilt, and that of the fifth class should be plain silver.

This would undoubtedly be a great economy, but I think we should be careful in effecting any economy on this Decoration as it is the only one to which women are admitted. If they gain the impression that we are trying to economise on them, there might be trouble.[27]

The suggestion was adopted and the OBE and the MBE acquired their respective gold and silver appearances which have continued to the present day.

The Ribbon

The choice of colour for the ribbon produced a much more lively correspondence. Prince Louis suggested a striking design, combining the crimson of the Order of the Bath with the pale blue of the Order of the Star of India. The ribbon would be crimson, with two narrow light blue stripes set a little way in from the edge.

It is true that this combination exists in the Serbian Order of [the] White Eagle, but the red, I believe, is scarlet, which is a sufficient distinction, besides being watered, like all foreign ribbons. The defunct Hanoverian Order of Ernest Augustus had the same combination of Colours, but here again the red was scarlet. – In the Hessian Order of Phillip the light blue is an Edge, not a stripe near the Edge.[28]

Queen Mary preferred a dusky shade of pink, and sent a sample of silk to Sir Frederick Ponsonby with the accompanying comment: 'What about this as a colour for the new Order? The King is sure to say that it will get dirty but does that matter.'[29] The Queen also selected a shade of grey for the enamel on the cross. In fact neither suggestion was adopted. The King objected to Prince Louis's proposal on the ground that every shade of red and blue had already been used, and in any case he opposed a ribbon of many colours, and the Queen's belief that the King would object to pink on the ground that it would get dirty, especially in London, proved to be correct.

Dawson preferred the colour purple for the ribbon, and sent a number of samples to Prince Louis, together with an example of the violet ribbon of the French medal *Palmes Universitaires*.

The palme is more purple than I thought and would I fear clash with the one I like best. Again how would the purple go with the dark crimson centre. Perhaps after all the 'fraise écrasé' [crushed strawberry] the Queen prefers would go best with the crimson centre.[30]

Prince Louis was in no doubt at all: 'Purple is incomparably finer and more regal, or rather imperial, than that horrid pink, suggesting a Siamese decoration'.[31] The King agreed with Prince Louis, believing that purple was:

more dignified and regal. The King has therefore selected the red purple, a sample of which you send. It should not be watered silk and if kept to this colour exactly, there should be no danger of its being confused with the Palmes.[32]

As Ponsonby told Dawson, 'the King said that after all he did not like the ribbon the Queen had chosen. This is a rather delicate matter as it is the Queen's favourite colour.'[33] So Queen Mary was overruled, and had to wait for twenty years until, in 1936, she was given the opportunity, and the authority, to alter the colours of the Order of the British Empire to her favourite pink and grey, that she had wanted in 1916.

The Manufacturers

Miss Hallé took a possessive interest in the manufacture of the central medallion depicting Britannia, as it was the one aspect of the insignia that was, artistically, her personal creation.

The die should be made under my supervision, otherwise the die striker would make a hash of the modelling . . . would it not be best to employ Pinches – the only man over here who can make decent dies, and let him supply Garrard or whatever jeweller is employed, with the finished medals . . . ?[34]

Prince Louis agreed.

Speaking as one who has studied & collected medals for half a lifetime, I endorse emphatically all Miss Hallé says. Die-sinking is a rare art among us. Pinches stands fairly high on top, but even he must work under the artist's supervision.[35]

As the King had expressed the wish that the Order should be ready as soon as possible, Dawson decided that putting the manufacture out to tender would cause unnecessary delays.

I think we have now got a design, devoid of unnecessary ornament, which should not be expensive, but which should at the same time be of thoroughly good material and workmanship. The die for the medallion in the centre will of course be struck by Messrs Pinches, but with regard to the rest of the Insignia, I propose to send for Mr Pearson, of Garrards, thoroughly impress upon him that the Insignia is to be made as cheaply as possible, combined with good workmanship, and ask him to give me estimates for all Classes.[36]

The King was reported to be 'much opposed' to Garrard and would have preferred Collingwood,[37] but relented on being told that the former was the only company who could possibly produce such large numbers of insignia in the short time available. Mr Pearson did his best, but at the end of January 1917, he reported that the shortage of steel, gold and labour was causing delays, and he did not expect to be able to produce samples for the King's inspection until March.

The King and Queen saw the insignia early in March and, with some minor criticisms, 'were very much pleased'.[38] The King initially thought that the Grand Cross Star was too big for women, but dropped his objections when the Queen pointed out that it was no bigger than the Garter Stars worn by herself and Queen Alexandra.[39] The King was particularly pleased with the Star of the Second Class, which he thought 'extremely neat, but as you may remember, His Majesty always likes small Stars'.[40] The King wisely suggested that a memorandum on the procedure for wearing insignia should be placed in the box of each class. 'This is most important as regards the Ladies' Decorations, as he is convinced they would invariably wear the badge in the wrong place.'[41] Ostensibly a display of masculine prejudice, it was only a practical suggestion to smooth the path of a major innovation; and he was supported by Queen Mary. Dawson duly proposed a tastefully delicate distinction between instructions for a Knight Grand Cross, and for a Dame Grand Cross: For gentlemen (used in all other Orders): 'The Riband is worn over the right shoulder, the Badge resting on the left hip'. 'The Star should be affixed to the left breast'. For ladies: 'The Riband is worn over the right shoulder, the Badge resting just below the waist'. 'The Star to be worn on the left side.' Ponsonby thought this a little too vague, and proposed the addition of the words 'not higher than six inches above the waist'. 'In cases where ladies have no other decorations they may easily wear the Star on the shoulder.' Both Ponsonby and Prince Louis were strongly against lady members of the second and third classes wearing the badge from a ribbon around the neck. It had to be worn from a bow on the left shoulder. The broad ribands of the first class measured 3¾ inches wide for Knights Grand Cross, and 2¼ inches for Dames Grand Cross.

One suggestion by the King caused a good deal of anxiety to Garrard. He asked for the ribbon of the fourth and fifth classes to be increased to 1½ inches in width, to match the width of the CB (Companion of the Order of the Bath) ribbon. Back came the worried reply.

Would it be possible for the first few issues of these Classes to be made with the ribbon in its present width and in later cases with the size His Majesty desires? It took the ribbon people at Coventry about sixteen weeks to produce the quantity we at present hold (289 yards), and we are fearful it might interpose some delay in the delivery of the amount we anticipate by the end of April.[42]

The King was understanding and Garrard was so authorised.

Ponsonby had not forgotten the efforts of Miss Hallé in designing the insignia of the Order, and pressed her case in March 1918 to Sir Edward Wallington, Private Secretary to Queen Mary.

Will you ask the Queen whether it would be possible for Her Majesty to recommend Miss Hallé for the Order of the British Empire? The only reason that I am anxious she should receive it is that she was the artist who designed the Order. I am not sufficiently conversant with her work to know whether there is any chance of her being recommended for the Order, but as she works under Queen Mary's Guild, it is possible that a recommendation from Her Majesty may be necessary.[43]

Miss Hallé was duly appointed a CBE on 5 June 1918 and died on 18 May 1926 at the age of seventy.

From 1917 until 1924 the stars of the Knights and Dames Grand Cross were of identical size. In the latter year King George V, who, reported Ponsonby, 'had been looking at Lady Willingdon's Star',[44] ordered that they should be reduced in size, on the ground that he believed them to be too big and heavy for ladies to wear, and that 'no dress could hold it properly'.[45] The matter was first brought to the attention of Sir George Crichton, the Secretary of the Central Chancery, by the Master of the Household on 15 July, and a design had been approved by the King by the end of August. The new star was the same length from top to bottom as that for the Dame Commanders, the remainder of the star being drawn in proportion to the original star for Dames Grand Cross. The centre medallion was the

Alteration of the Stars of the Dames Grand Cross 1924

same size as for Dames Commanders. Garrard manufactured 30 stars of the new size at a cost of £3 10s each. The old Dames' stars were simply absorbed into stock to be used in future by Knights. Crichton proposed to write to the Dames Grand Cross, asking them to return their old stars for ones of the new pattern. All those ladies who were in possession of stars made from diamonds in the large size could of course retain them, 'though possibly they may wish to have them made up in the smaller size'.[46]

The institution of Collars for Knights and Dames Grand Cross 1923–9

There is no evidence that the provision of a collar for Knights and Dames Grand Cross was considered in 1916–17. Prince Louis wrote to Ponsonby on 13 July 1916, assuming that there would be no collar, 'it would add enormously to the cost.'[47] Ponsonby agreed with him, though apparently for another reason. In his reply, dated 18 July 1916, he wrote: 'There would be no Collar attached to this Order, as we have at present quite enough Collars'.[48] Almost certainly the exigencies of a wartime economy would have made a collar seem an expensive and unnecessary luxury.

The first evidence of a serious debate about the institution of a collar is a letter dated 13 February 1923 from Ralph Harwood, Deputy Treasurer to the King, to Sir Warren Fisher, Head of the Home Civil Service and Secretary of the Order.

If you do agree to consider a proposal to start a British Empire 'Collar', a Committee will presumably be set up to consider the design. It *might* be well to have a Treasury man on it, with a view to keeping the cost down to a reasonable amount. At any rate you might think over that aspect of it.[49]

The advice was well given. A preliminary estimate of 124 collars at £45 produced the sum of £5,580. Fisher was quite agreeable to the idea.

As Secretary of the Order I have considered the question with some care, and I am satisfied that there is everything to be said for bringing the Order of the British Empire into line with the other Orders of Chivalry in this respect. I shall therefore be glad if you will submit to the King my recommendation to that effect and take His Majesty's commands on the subject.[50]

But he warned Lord Cromer, the Lord Chamberlain, that the inevitable substantial increase in the budget of the Lord Chamberlain's Office might attract criticism in the House of Commons, 'particularly at a time like the present of such widespread want and poverty',[51] and suggested the purchase of a small number of collars each year to spread the cost. 'I am satisfied that enough money can be found in 1924–5 for nine or ten Collars.'[52]

In November or December 1923, Sir Douglas Dawson showed Cromer the draft of a letter that he proposed to send to Fisher.

I can testify that the design of Collars was not lost sight of in the early days. The idea was turned down . . . partly on the grounds of economy, partly because of the difficulty of associating a Collar with an Order to which women would be appointed. It should be borne in mind that, with a Collar, the demand for a Mantle is sure to follow. . . It is a subject I have long had at heart and been interested in. Perhaps one day when time offers you would let me come and discuss it with you.[53]

Cromer expressed his approval in principle, and agreed that the matter should be raised with Fisher. Fisher himself was in agreement and suggested that Dawson send a short memorandum to the King explaining the position and asking for permission to go ahead.

Whether Dawson did in fact consult the King is uncertain because no further work was done until the end of the following year. Fisher wrote to Cromer on 27 November 1924 asking for an update on progress, and received an apologetic letter from Cromer the next day stating that very little had been done due to the illness of Dawson.

I am therefore only able to send you a provisional reply to say that the matter will be submitted to the King, whose wishes I will certainly communicate to you as soon as I am acquainted with their nature.[54]

The King was consulted by Ponsonby on behalf of the Lord Chamberlain and, although not enthusiastic, had given his approval in principle by 13 December.

He presumes, however, that in due time he would be informed of the steps that were taken to pay for this new Collar, and he hoped you would ensure that no Collar was produced without his having first seen the design.[55]

Lord Cromer also reported to Fisher that the King was 'averse from any ideas of Collars being worn by ladies who are Dames Grand Cross'.[56] The dangers of denying collars to Dames Grand Cross raised the spectre of the debates of 1917 around precedence and the title of 'Dame'.

It will presumably follow that they will not have Stalls or Banners when a Chapel is established, or take part in the Services for the Order. As the Order was created partly to enable women to be admitted to an Order of Chivalry, their exclusion from its ceremonial side would probably be criticised. The Dames themselves would certainly feel aggrieved.[57]

Fisher's suggestion that the cost of the collars might be spread over several years, with a piecemeal manufacture and issue of perhaps ten each year, was vetoed by both Dawson and Cromer. 'It would take seven years before you would be ready to carry out the new departure, and announcement of the intention . . . before you are ready, would only encourage clamour for further delivery.'[58] Fisher then proposed to incorporate a sum for the purpose of providing collars in the Estimate for the Lord Chamberlain's department for 1925–6, without increasing its total of that for the preceding year.

Preliminary designs for the new collar had been prepared by Garrard at the end of 1923, 'to show what could be produced for £40 or less',[59] and a quotation for £37 was supplied on 29 June 1925. Objections had been raised to the commissioning of an artist to produce a special design, on the ground that a fee, likely to be £100 or more, would be charged, and that a lengthy delay would result. It would also have been difficult to find someone who had sufficient technical knowledge to design a collar which would cost a pre-determined amount.

The question of the design of a collar was referred to the Royal Mint Advisory Committee. The Committee was dissatisfied with the four alternative designs submitted by Garrard's and entrusted the work to George Kruger-Gray at their meeting on 3 February 1925. Kruger-Gray was one of the most prolific coin and medal designers of the first half of the twentieth century. He received many commissions from the Royal Mint, and his knowledge was such that he could more than hold his own in discussions with the heralds at the College of Arms. From a technical point of view, he was admirable, his crisp modelling lending itself well to reduction to coin or medal size. Among his many commissions, were the designs of the crown, half-crown, florin, sixpenny and threepenny pieces in 1927, and later the reverse of the 1937 Coronation crown. Born George Edward Kruger in Jersey in 1880, he was trained at the Royal College of Art, from where he graduated in 1904. During the First World War he served in the 2nd Artists Rifles. In 1918 he married Audrey Gordon Gray and added her surname to his own. He was appointed a CBE in 1938 and died on 2 May 1943. His final design for the collar was approved by the Committee on 13 May 1925. The design was sent to Garter King of Arms, who expressed his entire satisfaction with it, and then to Fisher, as Secretary of the Order, to be put up officially for the King's commands. 'I may say that it has already been shown to His Majesty informally by Sir Frederick Ponsonby, and he has expressed himself as very pleased with it.'[60]

Unfortunately, due either to uncertainty or to misinterpretation, the Mint Advisory Committee then proceeded to authorise manufacture to begin. Fisher's opinion that the place of manufacture of the collar had yet to be decided,[61] caused consternation on the part of Colonel (later Sir Robert) Johnson, Deputy Master of the Mint (1922–38).

From the very first it has been understood that the artist who prepared the designs should also supervise manufacture, the whole point being (and nobody is stronger about it than Ponsonby himself), that good workmanship on objects of this nature is best secured by allowing the artist-craftsman actually to manufacture with his own hands, and not merely prepare drawings or models, the quality of which may be absolutely murdered . . . by careless and mercantile execution at the hands of some under-paid employee of a wholesale jewellery firm. . . The artist was definitely commissioned to commence manufacturing the links of the chain. This he has done, and has already, therefore, put in nearly six weeks' good work on them. . . All public work connected with Seals, Coins, Medals or Decorations must go to the Mint and nowhere else.[62]

Beneath the imperious tone of his letter, Johnson may have been expressing a personal anxiety that he had authorised the start of work on the collars without formal approval from the Lord Chamberlain's department, but from another angle, he probably genuinely believed right to be on his side. The Royal Mint Advisory Committee on Taste, to give it its full title, was established at his suggestion in June 1922 to remedy the malaise from which English medal designing was suffering, and to advise on all matters connected with the design of coins, medals, seals and decorations. After a short exchange of correspondence between the two men, the matter was smoothed over, and the Mint was formally authorised to supervise the manufacture. A specimen collar was formally approved by the King in February 1926, and 80 collars for Knights Grand Cross were delivered to the Central Chancery in February 1927.

The collar of a Knight Grand Cross is 1½ inches wide, and 48 inches long, the same length as a collar of the Order of St Michael and St George. This compares with 65 inches for the collars of the Orders of the Garter and the Bath; 63 inches for those of the Orders of the Star of India, the Indian Empire, and the Royal Victorian Order; and 37 inches for those of the Orders of the Thistle and St Patrick. The collar is manufactured in silver gilt, and formed of six medallions bearing the Royal Arms and six medallions bearing the Cypher of King George V alternately, linked together with cables on which is superimposed a crown between two stylised sea-lions. The artist originally proposed that the arms of England, Scotland and Ireland should be shown separately on separate medallions, but this suggestion, for various reasons, was not adopted by the advisory committee. The collars are of silver-gilt and were supplied in purple leather cases.

Work on collars for the forty Dames Grand Cross was delayed until the autumn of 1928, all parties being anxious not to incur any extra expenditure until payment for the Knights' collars had been completed. The King authorised the collar of a Dame Grand Cross to be of a 'similar but lighter pattern',[63] and, although identical in design, it is about ⅝ of the size of a Knight's collar.[64] A Dame's collar was submitted to Queen Mary in April 1929 for her approval, and forty collars were delivered to the Central Chancery by November that year.

There is no reference to the provision of either a mantle or a hat in the correspondence of 1916 and 1917, but without a collar, there would have been no question of providing either article.

The institution of the mantle and the hat

With the institution of the collar in 1928–9, attention turned to the design of mantles and hats. Kruger-Gray had expressed the wish to design the mantle as well as the collar 'on the ground that recent mantles have been cut wrongly & and have incorrect hoods'.[65] Whether he played any part in the design of the mantles is uncertain, but unlikely. A Treasury note suggested that there was no need to pay an artist to produce a design when copying the cut of a mantle of an existing Order would be sufficient:

Is it not the case that the Mantle is embroidered with the Badge of the Order? If so there would be little scope for the artist, since the Badge already exists, unless he proposed to alter the Badge. Colonel Johnson's desire to modify the Insignia of the Order was negatived by the King in 1922.[66]

The old pattern mantle was of purple satin lined with white silk, fastened with a cordon of white silk with two purple and silver tassels, and with an embroidered representation of the Star of a Knight Grand Cross on the left side. The institution of the mantle was decreed by an additional statute dated 25 June 1929.

The old pattern hat was of purple velvet lined with white silk. The hat was not formally instituted by the additional statute in 1929, nor is it mentioned in the revised statutes of 1934. The black hats worn by the Knights Grand Cross of the Order of the Bath were, similarly, not mentioned in the Statutes of that Order. As hats were not intended to be worn other than at outdoor processions, it is unlikely that they were ever worn ceremonially. In a letter to the Treasury dated 25 July 1929, Major Stockley of the Central Chancery remarked:

You will perhaps note that at some date we shall have to provide . . . a sealed pattern Mantle and Hat for the Knights and Dames, but these I think we can safely leave until there is a possibility of an occasion rising when they may be required.[67]

Although at least one purple mantle and a purple hat are known to have been made, they would not have been manufactured in any great quantity, and probably very few were made. The only ceremonial occasions on which they would have been worn were the Silver Jubilee Thanksgiving Service of King George V in 1935, and the Coronation of King George VI in 1937.

The old pattern mantles and hats had a very short lifespan. The death of King George V in January 1936 was followed by the appointment of Queen Mary to be Grand Master of the Order two months later, and the Queen lost no time in signalling her desire to see a radical change.

NINE

The Robes and Insignia of the Order: 2

THE NEW PATTERN

Sir Warren Fisher has heard from various sources that Queen Mary who has very graciously agreed to become Grand Master of the Order of the British Empire, does not much like the colour of the ribbon. . . What Her Majesty's views may be Sir Warren cannot presume to guess. . .

Robert Knox to Gerald Chichester, 21 March 1936

On the accession of King Edward VIII in January 1936, a committee was established to consider what changes should be made in the insignia of the Orders of Chivalry, in decorations and in medals, as a result of the change of reign, and to make recommendations. This committee is constituted at the beginning of each new reign and considers such questions as the change of the effigy of the monarch, the change of a royal cypher, and occasionally a change of name.

The committee reported on 12 May 1936, and its most far-reaching recommendation was the wide series of changes that it proposed to make in the appearance of the Order of the British Empire.

By far the most effective method of commemorating the last Reign in relation to the Orders of Knighthood and the Decorations and Medals, is to connect His late Majesty's name permanently with the whole Order. . . Since 1910 there have been revolutionary changes in the constitution of the Empire, and it is appropriate that an Order with this title selected for commemorative purposes should be connected with the period during which the self-governing Dominions first acquired their present status. The Order was created when the War was at its height, and will serve as a reminder of the events of the Reign. We therefore wish to recommend that the Order of the British Empire should be selected as a medium for the commemoration of the Reign of King George V.[1]

The committee made these recommendations, all of which were adopted.

Firstly, no change should be made to the collar, or to the motto of the Order 'For God and the Empire', which would remain in gold on a dark red background.

Secondly, although the general shape of the badge should remain unchanged, the figure of Britannia should be abandoned and replaced with the crowned effigy of King George V or, subject to the Queen's approval, the crowned effigies of King George V and Queen Mary, as on the King's Silver Jubilee Medal of 1935.

Thirdly, as with the badge, the figure of Britannia on the stars of the Knights and Dames, should be abandoned and replaced by the crowned effigy of King George V or, again subject to the Queen's approval, the crowned effigies of King George V and Queen Mary. The committee also noted that the overall appearance of the stars was unsatisfactory and should be changed.

In our view, the Stars of the Order do not, in appearance, compare very favourably with those of the other Orders, and we recommend that this opportunity should be taken to consider whether it may be possible to improve them in this respect. It has taken many years of uphill work by those concerned to bring the Order to its present high place in general regard, and anything even of this nature which may tend to diminish its importance may as well be rectified.[2]

Although the general outline of the stars remained unchanged, the rays were now to be chipped instead of fluted. The new design had been approved by King Edward VIII and Queen Mary by 18 May 1936.

Fourthly, and curiously, since it was being dropped from every other piece of insignia, the committee recommended that the effigy of Britannia should remain on the medals of the Order, for Gallantry and for Meritorious Service, but that the inscription 'Instituted by King George V' should be added somewhere on the medals.

The committee concluded by recommending that members of the Order could retain their existing insignia if they so desired, or they could exchange it for the new pattern at their own expense.

In recent years, manufacture of the insignia has been put out to tender and the work is undertaken by a number of companies. Very slight differences in the colour of the enamel and the shade of the ribbon can sometimes be detected but, as there is no sealed pattern of the ribbon and the insignia, this is inevitable.

The committee made no recommendation with regard to the colour of the ribbon, but this was in fact the most visible and the most memorable of the changes of 1936. Within two months of his accession, King Edward VIII decided to appoint his mother, Queen Mary, to be his successor as Grand Master of the Order, and the Queen was not long in sending out a signal that the colour of the ribbon of the Order must be changed. She had never liked the purple chosen in 1916, and twenty years of usage had done nothing to diminish her dislike. To her mind it looked dull against uniforms and clashed horribly with the pastel shades of ladies' evening dresses.

From purple to pink

Sir Warren Fisher was quickly apprised of Queen Mary's intentions 'from various sources',[3] and began work on the selection of a new colour. After 'considerable thought',[4] he proposed a shade of violet, with the continuing central red stripe for the military division. In fact his proposal, if implemented, would have caused a change that was hardly noticeable, and he intended it to be that way. He had considered a number of other options, including oyster grey, powder blue, old gold, auburn, and rose pink which he found 'not unpleasing',[5] but preferred violet or light mauve.

It has this great advantage, that there would be a connection with the colour of the present Ribbon used since the foundation of the Order. A sudden change say to orange would not perhaps be so justifiable, and it would be possible to announce with regard to this merely that it had been found advisable to lighten the colour of the ribbon.[6]

Fisher was a very senior civil servant, and one presumes that his 'considerable thought' would have involved reading the files relating to the history of the Order and the choice of colour in 1916. Although Knox courteously stated in his letter of 21 March: 'What Her Majesty's views may be, Sir Warren cannot presume to guess', it could be that Fisher was well aware of Queen Mary's predilection for rose pink, and endeavoured to pre-empt the Queen, and thereby avoid too radical a change, by suggesting a colour of his own. His letter, to Gerald Chichester, the Queen's Assistant Private Secretary, was answered, almost by return of post, leaving him in no doubt that his choice was firmly vetoed. The Queen 'does not very much like this shade', and asked if 'you will be so good as to send a further selection of shades of ribbon for Queen Mary to choose from, and Her Majesty will then consult the King about this question'.[7]

Summoned to a meeting with the Queen on 24 March, Fisher had to send his abject apologies because of an already committed diary, but he was shrewd enough to sense that the cause of violet, mauve or purple, of whatever hue, was definitely lost. Realising which way the wind was blowing, he took refuge in a letter congratulating Queen Mary on her appointment as Grand Master and added 'it is a very happy consequence that the ugly ribbon of the Order will be altered'.[8] Although Queen Mary 'much appreciated' this comment, his proposal for violet was indeed lost. 'I am afraid,' wrote Gerald Chichester, 'that the Queen does not very much like this shade, but Her Majesty quite realizes how difficult it is to find something suitable for both men and women.'[9] Fisher had an audience with Queen Mary on 31 March, and was given the parameters of colour within which to work, and asked to submit specimens for her approval.

Rumours that a change of colour was on the way had begun to appear in the press from the middle of April, and Robert Knox, on Fisher's behalf, submitted six specimen patterns to the Queen on the 18th of the month. His accompanying letter was written with all the composed and polished deference of one whose task was to do nothing more than agree to implement the details of a policy already decided. 'If I may say so I think that the colours which the Queen has picked out have been chosen with the unerring taste with which Her Majesty is always credited.'[10] His first set of examples were variations on the theme of a red ribbon with grey-blue edges. The edging, far more blue than grey, had been selected by Knox in an attempt to match the blue field of the badge of the Order. The second set of examples were of an identical pattern, except that the red was of a pastel shade and closer to the rose pink desired by the Queen. 'I do not think it is as Royal looking or so effective', Knox wrote cautiously. The third set continued the red in pastel shade, but moved the blue stripes slightly in from the edges. 'It is not I think sufficiently unlike B to prove of use.' The fourth set was a variant of the first set, with a thin red stripe imposed on the blue edging. Although it was quite suitable for use on the Grand Cross ribbon, when added to the narrower ribbons of the fourth and fifth classes, 'the line does little more at a short distance than to make the light blue edges appear a trifle unclean'. The fifth set was of identical pattern with the fourth set, although the red stripe on the blue edging was made wider. The sixth and final set of specimens proposed two further narrow blue stripes, set some way in from the blue edging, for the civil division; and a single central blue stripe for the military division. Knox was sure that this final set would 'carry out the Queen's wishes almost entirely, and at the same time enable the ribbon to be picked out at once'.[11]

Knox's efforts were quite in vain. None of the sets of examples was approved, either by the Queen or by the King. Queen Mary showed them together, one presumes, with her own favoured colours, to her son King Edward VIII, and by 18 May 1936, the King had approved the rose pink and pearl grey colours that the Queen had so much wanted in 1916.

Samples of the ribbon were distributed around government departments at the end of July, and were generally well received. The only discordant note came in a reply from Sir Robert Johnson, the Deputy Master of the Mint, who stated bluntly that he thought the colour was 'awful'.[12] The circular included a notification that the introduction of the new colour ribbon would be delayed until 1937 to accompany the new pattern insignia.

> It is proposed to introduce these for the Investitures after the Coronation. If they were to be brought into use following the Honours List of the 1st February [1937], it would be quite obvious that the alterations had not been instituted by King George VI. It is clearly desirable that the change should be connected with the reign of the present King.[13]

The colours selected by Queen Mary are still in use today. The ribbons are rose pink edged with pearl grey, with the addition of a vertical pearl grey stripe in the centre of the ribbon to denote membership of the Military Division. *Ribbons and ribbon widths*

The broad ribbon of a Knight Grand Cross is 4 inches wide and the broad ribbon of a Dame Grand Cross is 2¼ inches wide. The Statutes prescribe that the neck ribbons of Knights Commander and Commanders shall be 1¾ inches wide, and although these ribbons are provided with the insignia, and the recipient is invested with the badge suspended from this width of ribbon, it should never be used again outside the ranks of the armed forces. With day dress and with evening dress, the badge worn by these three grades is always suspended from a ribbon of miniature width, the full width being worn only with No. 2 and No. 4 dress in the Army. The ribbon of Officers and Members is 1½ inches wide.

In the colour changes of 1937, Queen Mary decreed one further change. The ribbon of the Military Division was to be distinguished by the central grey stripe, but Queen Mary specifically requested that this should not apply to Military Dames Grand Cross, as she did not wish any Dame Grand Cross to wear a ribbon that was different from her own. This exception to the rule proved to be hardly necessary because of its very limited application. There have only ever been three Military Dames Grand Cross of the Order, all appointed in 1918–19, and although all three were still alive in 1937, they were fully entitled to continue wearing the old pattern ribbon with the central vertical red stripe. Dame Sidney Jane Browne (GBE 1919) had been Matron-in-Chief of the Territorial Force Nursing Service, and Dame Ethel Hope Becher (GBE 1918) and Dame Emma Maud McCarthy (GBE 1918) had both been Matron-in-Chief of Queen Alexandra's Imperial Military Nursing Service. No further Military Dames Grand Cross have ever been appointed.

Queen Mary's ruling was enshrined in the new Statutes of 1937 and remained in force until 1970, but it was never put to the test. Sir Robert Knox was aware of this anomaly, but it remained in the Statutes until after his death. During the consolidation of the Statutes in 1969–70, the draft of December 1969 still observed Queen Mary's wishes, but the published version of April 1970 brought the Military Dames Grand Cross into line with their male counterparts.

The old mantles of purple satin, lined with white silk, fastened with a cordon of white silk with two purple and silver tassels, were abandoned, and replaced by new mantles of rose pink satin lined with pearl grey silk, fastened with a cordon of pearl grey silk with two rose pink and silver tassels, with a representation of the new star on the left side. The old pattern hats of purple velvet for the Knights and Dames Grand Cross were changed to black velvet to match the hats of the Knights Grand Cross of the Bath, but whether any new black hats were made is uncertain. The hats are not, and never have been, prescribed by the Statutes, and *New mantles* none has ever been worn or carried at services of the Order. During the planning of the first Service in May 1960, a decision was made in February of that year, that the Knights and Dames Grand Cross would have no official hat.

Although a few mantles were probably in existence between 1937 and 1959, there cannot have been many, as there would have been no occasion for them to have been worn apart from the Coronation of Queen Elizabeth II in 1953. One mantle at least was prominently displayed on that occasion. The familiar picture of the smiling Queen Salote Tupou III of Tonga, attired in the mantle and collar of the Order of the British Empire, has remained one of the enduring memories of that Coronation Day. In July 1958, the Officials of the Order decided to establish a stock of sixty mantles, a figure subsequently increased to eighty in May 1959. The mantles were made in 1959–60 by Toye and have been used at successive services since 1960, being renovated as and when required.

Public reaction The reaction to the change of design and colour was, inevitably, mixed. One honorary recipient of the OBE noted the changes and asked if he might be promoted! 'As I have just celebrated my 80th birthday, perhaps H.M. would approve of my promotion to a higher class.'[14] There were those, including the Maharajahs of Bikaner and Kapurthala who asked, almost immediately, to be issued with the new pattern insignia. At the other end of the spectrum were those who were attached to their insignia for historic or sentimental reasons and were concerned that they might have to part with it. The following letter from Major John Benthall is representative.

There is one thing I should so much like to be allowed to do & that is to keep the old CBE just as it is, that King George V gave me in 1919. He was always very good to me & knew me from a boy shortly after I left Harrow in 1887 when we played racquets together. . . I value that as when he gave it me he stopped the whole Investiture for about 10 minutes while he asked after all we had been doing in Sheffield.[15]

Aesthetic reactions were equally mixed. One retired admiral stated that he had 'never liked' Britannia and purple and was glad to see it go. One recipient in 1953 complained that it was bad enough to be using stocks of the medal so old that Queen Elizabeth II's grandparents were still shown; but it was far worse that the ribbon was so old that it had faded from purple to pink. The complainant thought that this was carrying economy too far.[16] Another recipient, in 1966, complained that:

the Award received is of George VI (*sic*) vintage with a somewhat faded ribbon, and I would therefore like to enquire whether, in the 14th year of the reign of Queen Elizabeth the Second, this is in order.[17]

Many people appointed to the Order before the changes of 1936 continued to wear their old pattern insignia and were perfectly at liberty to do so. In February 1967, Miss Kathleen Thomas of South Australia, who had been appointed an OBE as far back as 1 January 1918 noted the changes to the insignia and the ribbon, and asked if it was still in order for her to wear the old pattern insignia that she had been given nearly half a century earlier.

It had taken twenty years for Queen Mary to secure her desired and now very familiar rose pink and pearl grey colours for the Order of the British Empire, but the memory of the old insignia clearly lived on for many years afterwards.

TEN

The Robes and Insignia of the Order: 3

THE OFFICIALS

*The Gentleman Usher of the Order has hitherto been known as 'Purple Rod' and it is
suggested that this should be carried on.*

Major Harry Stockley to the Lord Chamberlain, 5 October 1936

The Order of the British Empire has a Grand Master, who is a member of the
Royal Family, and a number of ceremonial officials: a Prelate, a King of Arms, a
Registrar, a Secretary, a Dean, and a Gentleman Usher of the Purple Rod.
Provision is also made for conferring the titles of Prelate Emeritus and Sub-Dean.
The Officials usually meet on one or more occasions in each year to discuss all
aspects of the Order, and all of them will attend services of the Order in St Paul's
Cathedral. Only two of them – the Registrar and the Secretary – are assigned
specific duties by the Statutes.

The Registrar shall 'record all proceedings connected with the Order in a register to be appropriated for that purpose and shall . . . prepare all Warrants and
other Instruments to be passed under the Seal of the Order and engross the
same'. The Registrar is also required, 'when so commanded', to summon the
Knights Grand Cross to attend the Sovereign at all Investitures of the Order. It is
not known whether this clause was ever operative, but it is unlikely that separate
investitures of the Order of the British Empire were ever held. The only duty
assigned to the Secretary is to 'collect and tabulate the names' of those persons
admitted to the Order or awarded the Medal.

The Statutes specify that all the Officials hold office 'during good behaviour'.
In February 1934 King George V placed a limitation on this by ordering compul-
sory retirement at 75. The decision was simply the extension of a practice already
operative for Officers of the the King's Household and subsequently extended to
the Order of the Bath, and then to the Order of St Michael and St George and
the Order of the British Empire. The age limit was thought desirable 'in the interests of the Officers themselves as much as of the service of the Order'.[1] The ruling was to apply to future appointments, but all Officers currently in post were
exempt.

The Insignia

The badge of the Prelate, the badge and rod of the King of Arms, the badge of
the Registrar, the badge of the Secretary and the badge and rod of the Gentleman
Usher, are thought to have been made by Garrard in 1919–20 and were not
altered in 1936. Consequently, they still present the striking purple and gold
appearance of the first pattern of insignia. The badges were originally suspended
from purple ribbons on the grounds of expense. The present 18-carat gold chains
were introduced in 1929, their introduction being contemporary with the manufacture of the collars of the Knights and Dames Grand Cross.[2] With no change

in either his rod or his badge, it was felt that there was no need to change the title of the Usher, and he remains to this day the Gentleman Usher of the Purple Rod.

The badge of the Grand Master was made in 1954 for the Duke of Edinburgh on his appointment as Grand Master.

The badges of the Dean, the Prelate Emeritus and the Sub-Dean were made in 1957. Sketches and estimates were submitted by Garrard, Spink, and Collingwood in 1957, and the designs by Spink were chosen.

The mantles and hats

The first suggestion that the Officials of the Order be provided with mantles and hats occurred in 1929, during the debate on the provision of and payment for collars for the Knights and Dames Grand Cross. Major Stockley, then Secretary of the Central Chancery, took the view that there was no immediate hurry, and that manufacture could wait until such time as they were needed.[3] The Treasury indicated that funds could be found, and the mantles were provided in 1930 at a cost of £21 10s each. They were of white satin lined with purple silk, fastened by cordons of white silk with two tassels of purple and gold, and with purple velvet hats. As with the hats of the Knights and Dames Grand Cross, there was no mention of the Officials' hats in any amending statute after 1929. None of these old pattern mantles or hats appears to survive.

The changes of 1936 introduced mantles of pearl grey satin lined with rose pink silk, except for the Prelate, fastened by cordons of pearl grey silk with two tassels of rose pink and gold. Pink hats were at first suggested, but the more sensible suggestion of black was adopted. Whether any new black hats were in fact made for the Officials is uncertain. The design of the mantle badges was left unchanged.

The present robes and insignia of the Sovereign, Grand Master and the Officials are as follows.

The Sovereign

The Sovereign has no distinctive badge, but a mantle of unusual style that was made in 1960 for the first service of the Order. The mantle is in the style of a modified kirtle with flowing cape and train. At the Queen's direction, it was designed from sketches by students at the Royal College of Art, after discussions with Robin Darwin, the Principal, and Professor Anthony Blunt, Surveyor of the Queen's Pictures. The mantle star, of a smaller size than those of the GBEs, was designed after consultation with Professor R. Y. Gooden of the School of Silversmiths and Jewellery. The cost of the design was £15 15s, the sum being shared among the students.[4] The mantle was made by Ede & Ravenscroft at a cost of £271 19s. It was also suggested that the Queen should, additionally, wear a black velvet hat with a plume of pearl grey, but this idea was dropped in favour of a tiara.

The Grand Master

The Order has had three Grand Masters. The appointment of the Prince of Wales in 1917 was intended to give the new Order as much prestige as possible. On his accession to the throne in 1936, the novel suggestion was made that Queen Mary should succeed him. The suggestion was originally made by Sir Robert Knox on 27 February 1936 in a memorandum to Sir Warren Fisher. Knox made the valid observation that, although the appointment of a woman would be a new departure, the Order of the British Empire had admitted women jointly with men since its inception.[5] The suggestion was supported by Fisher and by Lord Wigram, The

King's Private Secretary, and an appropriate submission was made by Fisher to Stanley Baldwin, the Prime Minister.

The appointment of Her Majesty Queen Mary would give the greatest satisfaction to the whole Order and I recommend that a submission should be made to the king accordingly if you see fit. I understand from His Majesty that both he and Queen Mary would be pleased if a recommendation were to be made to this effect.[6]

The same procedure was followed by Sir Robert Knox, Sir Alan Lascelles and Sir Winston Churchill on the appointment of the Duke of Edinburgh in 1953.[7]

The Statutes do not assign a distinctive mantle to the Grand Master, who wears the mantle of a Knight Grand Cross. The mantle worn by His Royal Highness the Duke of Edinburgh was made by Ede & Ravenscroft in 1957–8 at a cost of £104 6s 5d.

The badge of the Grand Master is of an unusual design, using the badge of the first three classes of the Order as its base. There are green enamelled laurel leaves between the arms of the cross, clear of the central medallion, and the medallion itself is surrounded by a platinum chain representing 'Unity'. The surmounting hinged crown is enamelled in its 'proper' colours, the arches being set with pearls and the bands with rubies and emeralds. On the reverse of the badge is the royal cypher GRI set within a circular frame. There are no hallmarks, but it was made in 1954 by Collingwood of Conduit Street, London, the design being personally selected by the Duke of Edinburgh. The badge measures 2½ inches wide by 3⅓ inches to the height of the crown, and is worn by the present Grand Master from a military ribbon. The badges of the Grand Master and all the Officials are worn outside the collar of their mantles.

The Prelate

The office of Prelate has been held since the foundation of the Order by successive Bishops of London, but it is not held ex officio, and each Bishop of London has been formally appointed Prelate of the Order, rather than simply inheriting the office as an appurtenance to his see. The original selection of the Bishop of London was almost certainly made on the ground of his being the bishop of the capital city of the Empire. In 1945 Bishop Geoffrey Fisher resigned the office of Prelate on his departure to be Archbishop of Canterbury, and some thought was given to breaking the link with London and appointing either Bishop Haigh of Winchester or Bishop Herbert of Norwich, but the position of London at the heart of the Empire remained a cogent reason for the appointment of its bishop as Prelate. On the departure of Bishop Wand in 1955, plans for St Paul's Cathedral to be used as the Chapel of the Order were well advanced, and there was no suggestion that the new Prelate should be anyone other than Bishop Wand's successor. When Bishop Montgomery Campbell retired in 1961, some thought was given to appointing a bishop with Commonwealth experience and connections but as his successor, Bishop Stopford, fulfilled those criteria the office remained with the see of London for a further period. On the appointment of Bishop Ellison in 1973, the views of the other officials of the Order were canvassed, but by the time of Bishop Leonard in 1981 and Bishop Hope in 1991, it was generally accepted that the office of Prelate would be held by the Bishop of London 'of the day', and the bishop is now customarily invited to serve as Prelate.

The Statutes prescribe that the Prelate shall wear the mantle of a Knight Grand Cross, although in recent years, with the approval of the other Officials, the

Prelate has tended to wear a cope and mitre at services of the Order. The badge is circular and surmounted by a crown, and measures 2 by 3 inches to the height of the crown. The central medallion depicting the old pattern badge of the Order set in a field of purple enamel, and surrounded by the motto of the Order in gold set in a circle of red enamel. The reverse is plain. The badge is worn on 'great and solemn occasions', from a gold chain of two strands, and on other occasions from a ribbon of the civil division. The badge is not hallmarked, but is thought to have been made by Garrard in 1919–20.

The King of Arms   The office of King of Arms is not held ex officio. The first King of Arms was General Sir Arthur Paget and since his death in 1928, the office has passed to a senior officer of each of the armed services in turn.

The King of Arms wears a mantle of pearl grey satin lined with rose pink silk. On the right side is a shield of purple silk charged with a gold representation of the original badge, surrounded by the motto of the Order embroidered on a purple silk background. Unlike the original badge of the members of the Order, the medallion depicts a swan at the feet of Britannia. The badge depicts a gold representation of Britannia impaling the Royal Arms, surrounded by the motto of the order in gold set in a circle of red enamel. The badge is gold and enamel but is not hallmarked. It is thought to have been made by Garrard in 1919–20. The reverse is plain. The badge is circular and surmounted by a crown, and measures 2 inches in diameter and 3 inches to the height of the crown. The badge is worn on 'great and solemn occasions' from a gold chain of four strands, and on other occasions, since 1957, from a ribbon of the civil division.

The rod of the King of Arms depicts at its summit, the Royal Arms impaled by a gold representation of Britannia on a purple field on the two larger squares, and Britannia alone on the two smaller squares, all surmounted by a crown enamelled in its proper colours. The rod is 28 inches high and was made by Garrard. It is gold and bears the London hallmark of 1919–20, and the maker's mark SG.

The crown of the King of Arms, worn only at coronations, is of the style of all such crowns. Sixteen acanthus leaves spring from a rim on which is inscribed the first verse of Psalm 51 MISERERE MEI DEUS SECUNDUM MAGNAM MISERICORDIAM TUAM (Have mercy upon me O God according to your great mercy). Underneath the ermine of the cap are inscribed the words BRITISH EMPIRE KING OF ARMS THE PROPERTY OF THE STATE. The crown is silver gilt and bears the London hallmark for 1936–7.

The Registrar   The office of Registrar is held ex officio by the Secretary of the Central Chancery of the Orders of Knighthood.

The mantle of the Registrar is identical to that of the King of Arms. The badge is similar to that of the Prelate, except that the central medallion shows the cross of the Order, enamelled in light blue, set in a field enamelled in purple. The cross itself is charged with a closed book of red enamel with gold ornamentation. The reverse is plain. The badge measures 2 by 3 inches to the height of the crown. There are no hallmarks but the badge is thought to have been made by Garrard in 1919–20. The badge is worn on 'great and solemn occasions' from a gold chain of four strands, and on other occasions, since 1957, from a ribbon of the civil division.

The office of Secretary was at first held by the Permanent Secretary of the Home Office and subsequently, ex officio by the Head of the Home Civil Service.

The Secretary

The mantle of the Secretary is similar to that of the King of Arms. The badge is similar to that of the Prelate, except that the central medallion depicts the old pattern badge of the Order set in a field of purple enamel, with two crossed quill pens in pearl enamel saltirewise between the arms of the cross. The reverse is plain. There are no hallmarks but the badge is thought to have been made by Garrard in 1930. The original badge was stolen from the home of Sir Warren Fisher at Marylebone, London, in February 1930. The badge measures 2 by 3 inches to the height of the crown. The badge is of 18-carat gold, and is worn on 'great and solemn occasions' from a gold chain of four strands, and on other occasions, since 1957, from a ribbon of the civil division.

The office of Dean was created in 1957, consequent upon the creation of the chapel of the Order in the crypt of St Paul's Cathedral. The Dean of the cathedral has been ex officio Dean of the Order since that date.

The Dean

The Dean wears a mantle of pearl grey satin with a lining of rose pink silk. The present mantle was made in 1957–8 by Ede & Ravenscroft. The badge is similar to that of the Prelate, except that the central medallion shows the cross of the Order on a background of rose pink enamel surmounted by crossed swords (an allusion to the coat of arms of the Diocese of London) and the letter 'D' in gold on the upper arm of the cross. There are no hallmarks, but the badge is of 18-carat gold and was made by Spink in 1957. The badge is normally worn by the Dean from a ribbon of the civil division, although the Statutes make provision for a gold chain on 'great and solemn occasions'.

The office of Gentleman Usher is not held ex officio; all the holders have however been Knights Grand Cross. The first Usher of the Purple Rod was Sir Frederic Kenyon, Director of the British Museum. At that time, probably more so than today, museum directors ranked as senior civil servants and heads of departments, and the appointment of the director of the national museum was probably intended to reflect those members of the Order appointed for their achievement or eminence in the arts. Sir Frederic was an eminent scholar, the recipient of a number of honorary degrees and a Fellow of the British Academy.

The Gentleman Usher of the Purple Rod

In frail health, and at the age of eighty-seven, he expressed a wish to retire in August 1950, but was asked to stay on as no duties would be required of him. After the death of King George VI, with a coronation in prospect, he again sought permission to retire in February 1952. The search for a successor was virtually complete when Sir Frederic died, still in office, in August 1952.

It was agreed that, with the office of King of Arms being held by a senior officer from one of the armed services, the appointment of a civilian was appropriate, and the choice settled on Sir Ernest Gowers, former Chairman of the Board of Inland Revenue. Sir Ernest remained in office until the passing of his eightieth birthday when he asked to be allowed to retire. He was succeeded by Sir Malcolm Trustram Eve, later Lord Silsoe, and then by two former Lord Mayors of London, Sir Robert Bellinger and Sir Robin Gillett.

The Gentleman Usher wears a mantle similar to that of the King of Arms. His badge is similar to that of the King of Arms, except that the central medallion shows a representation of Britannia in gold, with a gold sea, set against a sky of purple enamel with a blazing gold sun. The reverse is plain. There are no hall-marks but the badge is thought to have been made by Garrard in 1919–20. The badge measures 2 by 3 inches to the height of the crown. The badge is worn on 'great and solemn occasions' from a gold chain of four strands, and on other occasions, since 1957, from a ribbon of the civil division.

The rod of the Usher was made by Garrard. The stem is of wood, varnished purple, with gold ornamentation. The upper piece is of 18-carat gold and shows an escrol bearing the motto of the Order surmounted by a representation of Britannia. The centre and lower pieces are silver gilt. All three sections bear the London hallmark for 1919–20 and the maker's mark SG.

Prelate Emeritus

Among the Orders of Chivalry, the title of Prelate Emeritus is peculiar to the Order of the British Empire, and was created in 1957 specifically for Bishop William Wand. The bishop had played a substantial role in the work of the committee that established the Chapel of the Order in St Paul's Cathedral. After his retirement as Bishop of London in 1956 he was, unusually, appointed to a residentiary canonry in the cathedral, and the title of Prelate Emeritus was created in 1957 and conferred on him. The use of the title was discussed by the Chapel Committee at its meeting in 1976, and it was agreed that as Bishop Wand had been appointed for special reasons, there appeared to be no case for continuing the title after his death. He died in 1977, and the title has not been conferred since that date.

A Prelate Emeritus wears a mantle identical to that of the King of Arms. The present mantle was made by Ede & Ravenscroft in 1957–8. The badge of a Prelate Emeritus is similar to that of the Prelate, except that the central medallion depicts the new pattern badge of the Order on a field of rose pink enamel. The badge is of 18-carat gold and measures 2 by 3 inches to the height of the crown. There are no hallmarks, but the badge was made by Spink in 1957, and the reverse is engraved SPINK, LONDON. The badge is worn on 'great and solemn occasions' from a gold chain of four strands, and on other occasions, since 1957, from a ribbon of the civil division.

Sub-Dean

Similarly, the title of Sub-Dean, created in 1957, is, like that of Prelate Emeritus, peculiar to the Order of the British Empire. It seems that the office was created mainly to relieve the workload of Dean Matthews who was 'much occupied with his writings on theological subjects'.[8] The first Sub-Dean was the Archdeacon of London, who was an ex officio Canon of St Paul's Cathedral. On his departure in 1961 to be Dean of Winchester, the appointment passed to Canon Frederic Hood, another residentiary canon of the cathedral. It was felt that the workload of the new archdeacon would preclude his taking an active role in the affairs of the Order. When Canon Hood resigned as a Canon Residentiary of the cathedral in 1969, he was allowed to remain as Sub-Dean of the Order until he resigned in 1971. The Chapel Committee took the view that the appointment of Sub-Dean was an ad hoc appointment, and that no successor need be appointed. The committee discussed the title again in 1976 and came to the conclusion that there was no urgent need for an appointment, and that consideration of a successor should be deferred for the time being. Some thought was given to making an appointment from a Commonwealth country in 1980–1 but the proposal found little favour.

After a gap of twenty-five years, the Dean's increasing workload led to the appointment of the Venerable George Cassidy, Archdeacon of London, as Sub-Dean.

The Sub-Dean wears a mantle identical to that of the King of Arms, and the present mantle was made by Ede & Ravenscroft in 1957–8. The badge is similar to that of the Prelate Emeritus, except that the central medallion shows a blue enamelled cross on a field of rose pink enamel. There are no hallmarks, but the badge was made by Spink of 18-carat gold in 1957, and the reverse is engraved SPINK, LONDON. The badge measures 2 by 3 inches to the height of the crown. The badge is worn on 'great and solemn occasions' from a gold chain of four strands, and on other occasions from a ribbon of the civil division.

Canon Hood enquired in May 1962 as to what constituted 'great and solemn occasions'. After consultations with the Officers of all the other Orders, the Chapel Committee decided that the Badge should be worn from a gold chain whenever members of the Royal Family were present. On all other occasions, it should be worn pendant from a ribbon.

ELEVEN

The Robes and Insignia of the Order: 4

THE MEDAL OF THE ORDER
AND THE EMBLEM FOR GALLANTRY

*If the medal is restricted to acts of gallantry during air raids and explosions
in factories, for what services will it be given in Peace time when such occasions will
not arise?*

Sir Frederick Ponsonby, June 1918

From its creation, the Order had an associated Medal, eventually styled 'The British Empire Medal', much like the Royal Victorian Order, also a five-class Order with a Medal. The British Empire Medal has fallen into desuetude in the United Kingdom since 1993, as a result of a review of the honours system, but recommendations continue to be made by certain Commonwealth realms. The cessation of recommendations in the United Kingdom was welcomed by some as the end of a sociological anachronism, and deplored by others as an unfortunate mistake based on a lack of understanding of the intricacies of the subject of honours.

The medal has not been abolished and a description of it remains incorporated in the Statutes of the Order, but it has had a complicated history, and the medal in its last manifestation was a very different medal from the one instituted in 1917.

The Medal of the Order 1917–22

The Medal was the broad base of the Order, and was intended to reward large numbers of workers, especially those employed in the munitions industries. Writing on 1 May 1917, Ponsonby urged the institution of a medal to reward the kind of grit determination at factory level, which was so important a part of the war effort.

The medal is a very difficult subject, because we have applications from all over the place asking for a medal of some sort. If there is a man in the Dominions or Colonies who does perform wonderful services you have nothing to give him. It is the same here in England; unless a man saves somebody's life he cannot get a medal. There is no civil medal of any sort to give a man of that class; so I think a medal is really very much needed.[1]

The intention to reward service in the munitions industries was prompted by a statement by Field Marshal Lord Kitchener in the House of Lords in the Spring of 1915.

His Majesty has approved that where service in this great work of supplying munitions of war, has been thoroughly, loyally and continuously rendered, the award of a medal will be granted on the successful termination of the war.[2]

The statement led to the establishment of a Munitions Medals Committee, under the chairmanship of Sir George Younger, which met from 1916 to 1918.

Ponsonby doubted that effective machinery for implementing Kitchener's pledge could be established. Apart from the difficulties of manufacturing several million medals, the term 'munitions worker' was incapable of any satisfactory definition, 'and no permanent government office would undertake the distribution of 9 million medals to persons scattered about the United Kingdom',[3] especially after the Ministry of Munitions had ceased to exist. There was a thought that perhaps the medal might be issued in silver and bronze and, in the latter form only, used to reward munitions workers who had served for a certain length of time, but shopfloor reactions ended any plans for a widespread distribution of the medal of whatever manufacture.

Guided by Ponsonby, the Medal Committee concluded that it would be desirable to fulfil Kitchener's pledge, but it would not be justifiable to do so by the imposition of an unnecessarily burdensome amount of work on existing government offices, or the creation of a new office specifically for the purpose of distributing a new 'munitions medal'. Given the creation of the new Order of the British Empire to reward war service, the Medal of that Order would serve perfectly well and there was no need for a separate medal for the munitions industry.

No doubt acting with the best and most democratic of intentions, the War Cabinet decided that the medal should be given in the proportion of one for every one hundred workers and that the workers themselves should be allowed to nominate their fellow workers for awards. The decision was reported by Ponsonby to the Ministry of Munitions on 23 May 1917.

I have now heard . . . that the proposal to allow the men to nominate the recipients of the Medal has been approved, You may, therefore, proceed upon the lines of 1 per cent being given.[4]

The first Statutes of the Order, published on 24 August 1917, provided for:

a circular medal in silver, having on the obverse a representation of Britannia within the circle and motto of the Order and on the reverse Our Royal and Imperial Cypher, and shall be worn on the left side suspended by a ring to a purple riband of one inch and one sixteenth of an inch in width.

The mounting of the medal was the same for men and women, i.e. no bow for women.

There is no different mounting to the Military Medal & war Medals which are given to Nurses, etc, and it is not thought necessary to go to the additional expense of a bow mounting in case of the Medal of the OBE.[5]

These small medals were not engraved with the name of the recipient, and a total of 2,014 were issued between August 1917 and January 1923.

The first list of recipients, published on 25 August 1917, was accompanied by a preliminary notice outlining the general criteria for award.

The Medal of the Order . . . will be awarded for services of special merit rendered to the Empire by men and women in manual and other work done for the war. Such service will include acts of great courage, self-sacrifice or high example; of initiative or perseverance; of skill, resource or invention. It is hoped that in some industries arrangements may be made under which weight can be given to recommendations made by the workers themselves of men and women most deserving to receive this Honour.[6]

It was recognised that the method of selection by the workers themselves could not be generally applied, e.g. for service in the War Office and the merchant navy, but in any case, considerable difficulties soon emerged.

In October 1917 a circular letter was sent out to employers requesting them to submit the names of any workers who had distinguished themselves on any of the grounds specified in the preliminary notice, and instructing them to give full consideration to any recommendations that might be put forward by workers themselves. The result was a display of deep hostility, and the following extracts indicate the intensity of feeling:

. . . Practically impossible to select a certain number for special recommendation without doing an injustice and causing heart-burnings.

. . . Impossible to pick any particular men or women for special recognition . . . the matter would lead to very great discontent amongst the employees.

. . . That this meeting of Shop Stewards deprecates the selection of individual men for distinction where all have done their best, and expresses the opinion that an autograph letter addressed to the employees of Ruston, Proctor & Co., Ltd., and signed by the Prime Minister or some other high authority would be highly appreciated and would adequately meet the case.

. . . We have applied to the men themselves to select representatives which by practically unanimous voting they have declined to do. The majority opinion is represented by a large number of voting papers to us marked 'To Hell with Medals, Get on With the War.' Under these circumstances and as an expression, which we send to you with all respect, is altogether admirable, we have no alternative but to return your list unfilled.

. . . That this meeting of Shop Stewards and Representatives entirely dissociate themselves from the proposed distribution to workpeople of Medals of the British Empire Order.

. . . Our workmen have passed a resolution to the effect that they do not desire to participate in the awards, the reason given being that the men feel that such a distinction would be invidious.

. . . We are of the opinion that as all have done their best as the opportunity has been given them and ability allowed, we collectively are not able to nominate any particular persons for the honour in question, and to make a distinction as to the degree of merit as to the services rendered would only result in bad feeling and jealousy, which does not now exist.[7]

In many cases employers took the same view as their workforce and refused to make any recommendations on the ground that it was impossible to select certain workers without doing an injustice to many others and causing envy and disappointment. Only a very small proportion of companies replied at all.

In the light of these reactions, any thought of a widespread distribution of the medal to workforces had to be abandoned, and almost immediately the medal of the Order was converted into a civilian gallantry medal. A list of nearly 376 people (including 100 women), who had performed 'acts of great courage or self-sacrifice', was published in January 1918. It attracted a good deal of attention and was favourably commented on in the press.

No criticism of the fact that it was limited to special acts of this kind has reached the Home Office and the limitation has certainly tended to enhance the value of the medal in public estimation.[8]

The following citations are examples of the January 1918 list:

> Violet Annie Davis: *For courage in remaining at her post at the telephone during a severe explosion. Age fifteen.*

Michael McGrath: *For courage in ascending a furnace under conditions so dangerous that all others had refused to do so.*

Ella Trout: *While fishing, accompanied only by a boy of ten, she saw that a steamer had been torpedoed and was sinking. Though fully realising the danger she ran from enemy submarines, she pulled rapidly to the wreck, and succeeded in rescuing a drowning sailor.*

As the *Daily Express* observed on 9 January, 'Such little-great deeds as these keep warm the heart of humanity. For the hope of the world may be in the heroism of the humble.'

The large numbers of medals to be awarded, probably combined with the fact that many of the recipients would be unable to afford the time and the cost of a journey to London, brought forth a decision from the King, reported by Sir Douglas Dawson on 27 November 1918, that Lords Lieutenant of Counties should present the medals to the recipients, on his behalf.

At its meeting on 24 April 1918, the War Cabinet confirmed that the British Empire Medal would be awarded for 'acts of courage and self-sacrifice or specially distinguished service' rendered during the war. *For courage and for service*

Further considerations arose in June 1918 when the Foreign Office submitted a list of Italian civilians, and the India Office proposed to use it for rewarding services in connection with recruiting in India. This was a departure from the criteria and it worried Ponsonby.

The question therefore arises whether it is possible to give the medal on one principle at home and on another totally different principle abroad and in India. You have been forced to give it at home as a sort of third-class Albert Medal and if it is to retain this character it cannot well be used abroad to reward services rendered by civilians on the railways and in connection with the food supply, nor can it be given in India in connection with recruiting. The difficulty then arises what medal or decoration can be given in such cases. We have at present nothing that can be given. It therefore amounts to this: a civilian bravery medal is no use abroad and a medal for ordinary service of a civilian character is no use at home. If the medal is restricted to acts of gallantry during air raids and explosions in factories, for what services will it be given in Peace time when such occasions will not arise?[9]

Presaging a decision to be made in 1922, he wrote to Troup on 26 June 1918 giving his opinion that there should be two medals, one a gallantry medal, and the other, the 'ordinary' medal of the Order. 'The gallantry medal could be distinguished on the ribbon by a line of light blue.'[10]

Although a Military version of the Medal was established in December 1918, the War Office, for one, made very little use of it. In July 1920 M. D. Graham of the War Office confirmed this fact to Sir Douglas Dawson.

The basic reason for having any Military Division of the Medal at all was merely to have a form of award available for members of enrolled Women's Corps not eligible for a class of the Order.[11]

By the summer of 1921, awards of the medal for war services were largely complete, and Ponsonby's concerns were echoed in June of that year by Lord Stamfordham, who brought to the attention of Lloyd George's Private Secretary, *After the War*

John Davies, the example of a park keeper in Richmond Park who had displayed great gallantry when attacked and fired upon by two men.

The Home Office rule is that he is not qualified for the British Empire Medal. So let it be, if this is according to any definite regulations, but, as I pointed out before, the Medal has been given abroad and in the Colonies for services other than those rendered in the War.[12]

With the imminent completion of the war service honours lists, serious consideration of the future of the medal was needed, as awards of the medal for services otherwise than in connection with the war were outside the rule laid down by the Cabinet in April 1918.

The committee set up to examine the future of the Order in 1921–2 recommended that the medal, like the Order, should be made a permanent institution. In consideration of the Cabinet decision of 1918, it should continue to be given for acts of gallantry, but it should also be given to those who had rendered meritorious service. In the latter respect, and unlike the Imperial Service Medal, it would not be given automatically (though subject to standard of conduct) after a certain period of service. The 1922 Statutes stated that military awards of the medal for meritorious service, should only go to those persons 'subordinate to those who are eligible for the Military Division of the various classes of this Order'.[13] No such restriction was placed on those to be awarded the medal for gallantry.

The recommendation was submitted to the Prime Minister in November 1921 and approved by the King in April 1922, but subsequent debate concluded that for a medal to be awarded in two quite different fields, not one, but two new medals should be instituted.

An identical decoration for two forms of service so widely different as those in question would create a difficulty that had not been foreseen. It was felt that the award of a medal for meritorious service would tend to depreciate its value in cases in which it was bestowed for gallantry, and that past recipients who were awarded it on that ground would tend to prize the decoration less highly in the future.[14]

Lord Stamfordham proposed that there should be a slight difference either in the ribbon or in the design of the medals to distinguish between the two areas of award. The proposal was referred to the Standing Committee on Medals, chaired by the Deputy Master of the Mint, in July 1922.

The committee recommended that the two medals should be distinguished by different clasps and by different wording, and especially that the design of the existing medal should be altered. The members of the committee were 'strongly of the opinion' that the existing design was unsatisfactory.

The Committee think the existing medal too bad to perpetuate, and they are in favour of scrapping it and substituting a larger and better one, and finding the bullion for these anyway by melting down the existing stock of 4,000 unissued medals.[15]

The committee decided to commission an artist to prepare a new design, though keeping the elements of the old design, i.e. Britannia with her trident beneath a blazing sun. The committee also recommended that the ring should be replaced by a straight clasp, ornamented with laurel leaves for gallantry and oak leaves for meritorious service, and that the size of the new medals should approximate to that of 'other existing medals with which it is likely to be worn'. The committee further recommended that the medals should in future be manufactured at the Royal Mint and not by Pinches, to 'ensure a consistently high standard both of workmanship and material'.[16] The committee also went beyond its brief and recommended that a new design of the medal should become the model for the insignia of the Order. This recommendation was rejected by the King, in October 1922, who felt, with good reason, that a change to the insignia of the Order so soon after its foundation was neither wise nor necessary.[17]

By the revised Statutes, dated 29 December 1922, the medal of 1917 was super-seded by two new medals, officially known as the Medal of the Order for Gallantry, and the Medal of the Order for Meritorious Service. Recommen-dations for both medals were to be examined by a committee consisting of the Permanent Secretary to the Treasury, the Private Secretary to the King, and the Private Secretary to the Prime Minister. The Permanent Secretaries to the Admiralty, the War Office and the Air Ministry would be added to the commit-tee when recommendations from the services were considered. No statutory lim-its were set to the numbers of each medal to be awarded, but Sir Warren Fisher, Head of the Home Civil Service, took the view that the demand for gallantry medals would be 'considerably less'[18] than the demand for meritorious medals.

Two Medals

The post-1922 medals were larger and more stylish versions of the 1917–22 medal. They were designed by J. Langford Jones who received a fee of £100 for his work. Jones, who was active until about 1946, was one of a relatively small group of freelance artists who received commissions from the Royal Mint during the inter-war years. His design, which remains in use, depicts Britannia, now sit-ting erect, and moved to the centre of the design. The shell throne was aban-doned, the trident was moved to the perpendicular position, and the Union flag shield was now largely concealed.

Although a member of the Mint Committee, Ponsonby was never entirely in sympathy with the two new medals. His opposition was based mostly on well-founded objections to a scheme which he believed to have too many inherent flaws, and partly perhaps on pique. The committee had reached its unanimous decision to establish two new medals at a meeting on 29 July 1922, a meeting from which Ponsonby was unavoidably absent because of illness. As an un-doubted, if somewhat opinionated, authority on the subject of honours, he was always quick to observe the flaws and weaknesses of ill-thought out decisions, and point them out to those responsible. He had no objection in principle to the con-cept of a gallantry medal but he did object to it being made a part of the Order of the British Empire, and his arguments were proved correct in the long term. The Order itself, he argued, was not a gallantry decoration 'and therefore it is perfectly wrong to make the medal of a different character'. An entirely new gallantry medal would be preferable to 'distorting the regulations' for the medal of the Order, and he described the almost indistinguishable designs of the two different medals of the Order as being 'quite ineffectual'.[19]

He was still complaining about the medals in November 1922 when he warned Fisher that the size of the lettering on the medals, and the difference between the laurel leaf and the oak leaf was so small that the public would be unable to dis-tinguish between the two. The committee, he said, had 'got into difficulties' over the question of design, and technical questions of this sort really should have been dealt with by the Central Chancery. 'If you agree with this contention, I think the Deputy Master of the Mint should be told to put up to the Central Chancery all the difficult points that had arisen.'[20] The Deputy Master, Sir Robert Johnson, was irritated with Ponsonby for finding fault with the decision of the Mint Committee, and enlisted the aid of Lord Stamfordham, the King's Private Secretary. Correspondence dragged on until February 1923 when Stamfordham gave his approval to the new medals, and Johnson sent a letter, half-serious and half-humorous to Ponsonby.

> In future . . . I hope we shall be able to avoid a procedure which has resulted in my sweating about with a bag like a little commercial traveller. The blessed design has actually been to the palace three times, and Stamfordham's room is only a few yards from yours. . . Meanwhile no great harm has been done except to the soles of my boots.[21]

Ponsonby was not accustomed to defeat on the question of honours, and the fact that his opinion had been rejected continued to rankle. In May 1925 he wrote to Sir Warren Fisher.

> I quite understand that there are now two distinct medals, but will you let me know whether they should both be alluded to as the British Empire Medal, or if it is necessary to put anything in brackets; presumably they differ either in ribbon or design; but this I am not interested in, it is merely the name of the medal.[22]

Fisher patiently and courteously told Ponsonby what he must have already known, that the official titles were 'The Medal of the British Empire Order (for Gallantry)' and 'The Medal of the British Empire Order (for Meritorious Service)'. These cumbersome titles were not destined to last and do not seem to have been used in any but the most formal documents, and both medals appear to have been colloquially styled 'The British Empire Medal' for a period after 1922.

The Medal of the Order for Gallantry 1922–40

Criteria for awarding the two medals, was established in June 1923. The medal for gallantry was to be awarded to those who performed individual acts of gallantry with the knowledge that their lives were thereby endangered. The standard would be high, but not so high as the standard required for the award of the Albert Medal (founded in 1866, awarded posthumously after 1949, and replaced by the George Cross in 1971); or for the Edward Medal (founded in 1907, awarded posthumously after 1949, and also replaced by the George Cross in 1971).

As with the Order, the medal was awarded for both Civil and Military service, the latter being distinguished by the central vertical red stripe. The ribbon remained purple and 1$\frac{1}{16}$ inches wide, the red stripe being about $\frac{1}{10}$ inch wide. On the obverse of the medal, the word 'FOR' appeared close to the base of Britannia's trident, and the word 'GALLANTRY' in the exergue; and the medal was suspended from the ribbon by a straight clasp ornamented with laurel leaves. With echoes of the 1916 debate, a number were inadvertently struck bearing the legend 'FOR GOD & EMPIRE', but before they were issued the mistake was realised and they were recalled and melted down. New dies were made and medals struck with the correct legend.

Ponsonby's complaint in 1922 about the lack of distinction between the two medals of the Order was in due course justified. By the early 1930s, the medal for gallantry had all but parted company with its companion for meritorious service. It was both sparingly given and highly regarded. Between January 1923 and March 1931 there were only thirty-six awards of the medal for gallantry, compared with more than 700 awards of the medal for meritorious service. With the rising prestige of the gallantry medal came calls, especially from the Admiralty, the War Office and the Air Ministry, for it to be more clearly distinguished from its companion.

In March 1931 the committee responsible for selecting and recommending recipients, acknowledged the concerns of the three ministries and agreed that the similar appearance of the two medals was confusing.

At a distance of about three or four feet . . . it is scarcely possible for an individual with normal eyesight to see whether the Medal is the Medal for Gallantry or the Medal for Meritorious Service.[23]

The committee recommended the addition of an emblem of silver laurel leaves attached to the ribbon of the medal, a smaller emblem for use with the ribbon alone, and also the use of the postnominal letters 'GM' (Gallantry Medal). 'This would probably enhance the value of the Gallantry Medal – and indirectly increase the prestige of the Order as a whole.'[24]

Sir John Anderson of the Home Office agreed with the proposal.

The two medals look very much alike except on close inspection and it is only by its position, before or after War Medals, Coronation Medals and Long Service Medals, that it can readily be told whether a medal is a gallantry one or not.[25]

He suggested the imposition of a silver buckle half-way down the ribbon 'exactly like the gold buckle which used to be worn on the ribbon of the CB before it was made a neck decoration'. On the use of the letters GM, he was not so happy. 'I am afraid that they would convey nothing to the ordinary person's mind but would merely set him wondering what they meant. Surely BEM would be better?'[26]

The recommendations of the Selection Committee were introduced in stages. During the course of its existence, the medal had become commonly known as the British Empire Gallantry Medal, or more usually the Empire Gallantry Medal, and by the revised Statutes, dated 3 November 1933, the title was confirmed and recipients were permitted to use the postnominal letters EGM. Anderson's silver buckle found no favour, and the silver laurel was adopted by an amending statute, dated 30 July 1937. The branch was fixed to the ribbon by two prongs pushed through the ribbon and then bent over. The reverse bore the Royal Cypher of George V, until 1937 when the cypher was changed to George VI and the words 'Instituted by King George V' added. At the same time, as with the Order, the ribbon of the Civil Medal was changed to rose pink, 1¼ inches wide, edged with pearl grey stripes. The Military ribbon was similarly changed but had an additional central vertical pearl grey stripe about 1/16 inch wide. Further acts of gallantry deemed worthy of an additional award were to be recognised by the addition of a bar to the ribbon. None was awarded in the few remaining years of the life of the Medal. In July 1940, almost on the eve of the abolition of the medal, after representations from the Air Ministry, King George VI authorised recipients of the EGM who had been awarded a bar, to wear a small silver rosette above the laurel leaf when the ribbon alone was worn.

It had become increasingly clear that the Empire Gallantry Medal had only a notional connection with the Order of the British Empire. Throughout the eighteen years of its existence, it had evolved into a highly prized decoration with a life of its own that really had nothing to do with the Order. Indeed, it could be argued that the medal was never really a part of the Order. When the two medals were instituted in 1922, it was decided that members of the Order should be eligible to receive the Medal for Gallantry, but ineligible to receive the Medal for Meritorious Service. This proviso effectively made the Medal for Gallantry into a gallantry decoration from the start, with the Order providing an historic background point and the colour of its ribbon.

The inevitable occurred in September 1940 when King George VI abolished the Empire Gallantry Medal and instituted the George Cross and the George Medal. The surviving holders of the Empire Gallantry Medal were authorised to return their medals to the Central Chancery and to exchange them for the George Cross. At the time of writing, there are eight living holders of the George Cross, who were first awarded the Empire Gallantry Medal.

A total of 130 Empire Gallantry Medals were awarded as follows: 64 Civil awards; 62 Military awards; and four awards to foreign nationals: a Belgian in December 1933; two Frenchmen in February 1936, and another Frenchman in January 1940. The first three involved gallantry during air disasters, and the fourth for gallantry on a blazing petrol tanker. In 1924 the Royal National Lifeboat Institution celebrated its centenary and a debatable decision was taken to give the EGM to each of the eight surviving holders of the Institution's Gold Medal (for gallantry). The recipients had received their medals at various dates between December 1895 and October 1922. Disregarding the foreign and RNLI awards, 118 awards were made in respect of 86 incidents between December 1922 and September 1940.

The Medal of the Order for Meritorious Service 1922–93

Under the criteria established in June 1923, this medal was to be awarded for a level of service higher than that required for the Imperial Service Medal. Normally long service was an essential factor, but awards could also be made in recognition of the performance of valuable work of an exceptional nature. 'At the same time the test is very considerably more severe than the Imperial Service Medal.'[27] Recipients of the Medal for Meritorious Service were those who were not considered eligible, at that time, for membership of the Order.

The medal could be awarded for both Civil and Military service, the latter being distinguished by the central vertical red stripe. The ribbon remained purple and $1\frac{1}{16}$ inches wide, the red stripe being about $\frac{1}{10}$ inch wide. The Medal was identical to the Empire Gallantry Medal, with the exception of the words MERITORIOUS SERVICE appearing in the exergue, and was also designed by J. Langford Jones. It was suspended from the ribbon by a straight clasp ornamented with oak leaves instead of the laurel leaves of the Empire Gallantry Medal. There are four types of reverse: George V, George VI (1st type, until 1948), George VI (2nd type, after 1948, without the 'I' for Imperator) and Elizabeth II. As with the Order and the Empire Gallantry Medal, the colour of the ribbon was changed on 30 July 1937 to rose pink, $1\frac{1}{4}$ inches wide, edged with pearl grey stripes. The medal for military service had a central pearl grey stripe about $\frac{1}{16}$ inch wide. At the same time, the words INSTITUTED BY KING GEORGE V were added to the reverse. Further awards of the Medal were to be recognised by the addition of a bar to the ribbon, authorised by the King on 14 March 1941. When the ribbon alone was worn the award of a bar was indicated by a small silver rosette on the ribbon, one rosette for each bar.

With the demise of the Empire Gallantry Medal in September 1940, the Medal of the Order for Meritorious Service became the sole medal of the Order of the British Empire. The Statute of 14 March 1941 authorised the medal, including those awarded between 1917 and 1922 to be known as 'The British Empire Medal', although the term was unofficially in use by 1922. The same Statute also authorised the wearing of the medal by ladies from a ribbon fashioned into a bow, and worn on the left shoulder. An additional Statute dated 10 June 1942 authorised the use of the post nominal letters BEM. These letters were permitted mainly because, with the abolition of the Empire Gallantry Medal in 1940, the majority of awards of the Medal for Meritorious Service during World War II, were made for gallantry. Until the institution of the Queen's Gallantry Medal in 1974, the medal continued to be used, as did the CBE, OBE and MBE, as a reward for gallantry.

From 1923 until 1939, 832 awards of the medal were gazetted. Up to March 1941, 801 awards to foreigners were made, though this figure includes awards of the 1917–22 medal. The number of awards after 1940, especially during World War II, was considerably greater. The following numbers were noted in the *London Gazette*.

1944	3,077
1954	782
1964	702
1974	828
1984	781

On 4 March 1993, the Prime Minister, John Major, announced to the House of Commons that no further recommendations for the award of the British Empire Medal would be made. The decision was taken in the belief that the distinction between service meriting the award of an MBE and that meriting a British Empire Medal had become increasingly tenuous.

It can no longer be sustained. I therefore intend in future to increase the number of recommendations of MBEs and to discontinue recommending awards of BEMs. I should make it clear that this change will not affect existing holders of the BEM, who will of course retain their medals. These are, rightly, highly treasured possessions. The change will apply to the lists recommended by my right honourable Friend the Foreign Secretary and my right honourable and learned Friend the Secretary of State for Defence. The Governments of those Commonwealth countries that recommend British Empire Medals in their own lists have been informed of these proposals.[28]

The decision to make no further recommendations was applauded by some, in the mistaken belief that the MBE and the BEM were awarded on the basis of the social class of the recipient. There may have been some truth in that belief in the earliest years of the Order's history, but as the Order stabilised, the choice of award came to be governed solely by the recipient's level of responsibility, and questions of class were not a consideration. Others criticised the abolition of the BEM for that reason, and voiced their concern that a very useful medal had been unwisely swept away. Whatever the rights and wrongs of the decision, one thing remains certain; the service rendered by the tens of thousands of recipients of the medals of the Order of the British Empire from 1917 to 1993, was not in any way downgraded or dismissed. In their quiet, local and unostentatious way, the holders of the British Empire Medal were the salt of the earth.

The demise of the Empire Gallantry Medal in 1940 did not affect the use of other grades of the Order to recognise acts of gallantry. From the foundation of the Order in 1917, many appointments to the CBE, OBE and MBE grades of the

The Emblem for Gallantry 1957–74

Order, and awards of the British Empire Medal after 1940, were made for gallantry. After 1940, the awards for gallantry or bravery were as follows:

The George Cross (*for gallantry of the highest order*)

The George Medal (*for gallantry of an extremely high order*)

The CBE, OBE, MBE and BEM (*for gallantry of a high order*)

The Queen's Commendation for brave conduct

The Queen's Commendation for valuable services in the air.

In 1942–3 proposals were made to introduce some distinguishing mark to separate awards in the Order for gallantry from all others. The debate arose mainly because of a campaign in the press on behalf of the Merchant Navy whose sailors, being in a civilian service, were not eligible for the military division of the Order. One national newspaper campaigned for the abolition of the military division on the ground that the Merchant Navy was only eligible for the 'lower' civil division.

One correspondent suggested that the continental custom of awarding an Order 'with swords' should be used. As this was the means by which foreign military awards were distinguished from civil awards, it was not adopted, the central stripe in the ribbon being considered a sufficient distinction. Further suggestions included adding the letter G (for gallantry) to the postnominal letters, giving CBEG, OBEG, MBEG and BEMG, and also of adding a sprig of laurel or oak leaves to the ribbon.[29] No decision was taken in 1943 because the government departments concerned were unable to reach agreement. So the issue was shelved, with the recommendation that the George Medal might be awarded more widely in the Merchant Navy.[30]

The matter was raised again in the summer of 1956, but because of the Suez crisis, detailed consideration was postponed until the following year. Among the proposals was one from the Admiralty for a new gallantry medal to be styled the British Empire Star for Gallantry. This proposal was vetoed because it was thought to bear too much of a resemblance to the abolished Empire Gallantry Medal. After an experiment with oak leaves woven in green on to the existing ribbon, Sir Robert Knox proposed that two crossed oak leaves in silver be added to the ribbon of the OBE, MBE or BEM as appropriate. Although the higher classes could be granted for acts of gallantry, the circumstances would be clear and no special marking would be necessary.

The silver oak leaves were manufactured by the Royal Mint, although their first two efforts were described by Knox as 'terrible and very disappointing'.[31] The final design was the work of James Woodford, OBE, RA, who, at Knox's request, was called in by the Mint to produce a suitable design. The emblem was authorised by an additional Statute dated 6 December 1957, and gazetted on 14 January 1958; it was not to be awarded retrospectively. At the same time it was decided that the description of the appointment published in the *London Gazette* should contain the words 'for gallantry'. Instead of 'to be an additional Member of the Civil Division of the Most Excellent Order of the British Empire', the announcement would henceforward read 'to be an additional the Civil Division of the Most Excellent Member of the Civil Division Order of the British Empire for Gallantry'. During the period 1958–74, a total of 972 awards of the Order were made for gallantry, entitling the recipient to use the emblem for gallantry.

They were made up as follows:

CBE	1
OBE	10
MBE	136
BEM	825

The only known appointment for gallantry to the grade of CBE was that of Brigadier Jacques Alfred Dextrase on 16 October 1964. Dextrase, an officer in the Canadian army, and already an OBE, was appointed for leading a daring operation to rescue a group of missionaries in the Congo.

Although the use of the Order to recognise acts of gallantry did, in a sense, link the Order with its origins in World War I, the level at which it was awarded was anomalous. The choice of level in the Order depended not on the level of gallantry, but on the rank and level of responsibility of the individual concerned. There was a quite understandable tendency to assume that the award of the OBE represented a higher degree of gallantry than the MBE or the BEM, but this was not the case. At whatever level the Order was used, it denoted only the same degree of gallantry, namely that which fell after the George Cross and the George Medal, but before the Queen's Commendation for brave conduct.

Rank and level of responsibility were not relevant to an award for gallantry, and it was invidious, illogical and confusing that they should enter into decisions about such awards. There was, in any case, an inconsistency about a low level of gallantry being recognised by admission to an Order, while a higher level was recognised by the award of a medal. It was moreover, somewhat confusing to use as a gallantry award an Order primarily designed to recognise meritorious service over many years.[32]

The debate on the use of the Order as a gallantry award began in 1964 and continued, intermittently, for ten years. With echoes of the discussions of 1943, some consideration was given to a new set of postnominal letters for those admitted to the Order for gallantry. Instead of MBE, the recipient would use MBEV (for valour) or MBEC (for courage). Another proposal called effectively for a revival of the Empire Gallantry Medal, by using only the BEM as a gallantry award within the Order. The debate concluded with the institution of the Queen's Gallantry Medal on 20 June 1974. Awards of the Order of the British Empire for gallantry were not made after that date, and the oak leaf emblem ceased to be issued.

TWELVE

The Quest for a Chapel: 1

ST MARGARET'S CHURCH, WESTMINSTER AND OTHERS

While Registrar and Secretary of the Central Chancery, I worked hard to try and associate all Orders of Knighthood with some Cathedral or Chapel. . . I have never lost sight of the desirability of similar association for the . . . British Empire Order. As regards the latter, I have an idea which I would put to you one day confidentially, if you cared to listen to it.

Sir Douglas Dawson to the Earl of Cromer, November or December 1923

Although the Order of the British Empire was founded in 1917, forty years were to pass before the final decision in 1957 to establish a chapel for the Order in the crypt of St Paul's Cathedral in London. During those forty years, a number of different locations were proposed, and some were given more serious consideration than others. This chapter and the following two chapters tell the story of that architectural and spiritual odyssey.

St Paul's Cathedral 1917–18

The 1957 decision to choose St Paul's Cathedral brought the search full circle, since the cathedral had been proposed and briefly considered in 1917–18. The earliest reference is a memorandum prepared by Sir Lawrence Weaver in 1917. Weaver an architect, and Editor of *Country Life*, suggested that St Faith's Chapel in the crypt of St Paul's would be ideal.

In the Crypt . . . and beneath the Cross which surmounts the dome, lies the body of Nelson, who died fighting in the great struggle of a century ago for European liberty. Hard by the great Admiral's tomb rests Wellington, who crowned the work of Trafalgar at Waterloo. Near them are the tombs and memorials of many another great builder and defender of the Empire. . . Further east and immediately beneath the cathedral choir is the Chapel of St Faith, but rarely used for services and almost wholly unoccupied by memorials. It is suggested that this shall be devoted for use as the Chapel of the Order.[1]

Lord Lee of Fareham, GBE, Director-General of Food Supplies, enthusiastically supported the choice of the chapel. Charles Peake, his private secretary at the time, recalled, in 1950, 'sitting in and taking notes of several conversations which he had with Lutyens who eventually produced designs'.[2] Sir Edwin Lutyens submitted designs in 1918, proposing a new altar and reredos, forty stalls for the senior Knights and Dames Grand Cross, with plates of arms affixed to the backs of the stalls. Forty decorative shields would bear the arms of the Dominions and Dependencies of the Empire. The floor would be paved with iron plates 'as typical of war conditions',[3] which could be inset with brass armorial plates commemorative of deceased Knights and Dames. The total cost was put at about £35,000. Lee raised the possibility with Lord Stamfordham, the King's Private Secretary, who in turn brought it to the King's attention. King George V wisely declined to offer any opinion until the Cathedral Chapter had been consulted. The Chapter was not enthusiastic, and the proposal was dropped.

In November 1918 the Dean of York proposed that York Minster be used for the purpose. Transportation being a good deal more primitive in 1918 than it was later to become, the distance from London to York prevented any serious consideration of the Minster.[4] In 1924, at the suggestion of Sir Frederick Radcliffe, the Earl of Derby proposed that the chapel of the Order should be located in the unfinished Liverpool Cathedral. The thought of linking a new Order with a new Cathedral was imaginative but, again, distance from London was the main objection.

In May 1924 Colonel Sir Edward Ward, GBE, suggested that a service of the Order should be held, although he offered no suggestion on location, and he received a holding reply from Sir George Crichton, the Secretary of the Central Chancery.

This point has not been lost sight of, but the question opens up a great many difficulties, e.g. there are at present no Collars and no Mantles for the Knights Grand Cross of the Order, and there is also the problem of finding a suitable Chapel or Church. You may rest assured that we shall endeavour, as soon as possible, to arrange matters so that the Order may be placed on a par with the older Orders and its value enhanced in the public estimation.[5]

In June 1925 Crichton fielded another correspondent with much the same comment. 'This question has received attention and that it is hoped in due course to place this Order on the same basis as the other Orders.'[6]

In 1928, Lieutenant Commander Pirie Gordon of *The Times* brought the debate back to St Paul's Cathedral by suggesting the Chapel of St Dunstan, in the north-west corner of the cathedral, opposite the Chapel of St Michael and St George.

In 1931, Mr E. Gibson suggested that, given the title of the Order, an annual service of the Order should be held on Empire Day (24 May) in St Paul's Cathedral. The suggestion was taken up by the Prelate of the Order, Bishop Arthur Winnington-Ingram of London, who in turn consulted Sir Frederic Kenyon, Gentleman Usher of the Purple Rod. As there was no space large enough to accommodate a separate chapel for the Order, the best solution was to hold a service in the whole cathedral rather than a special function in a chapel where there would only be room for the Knights and Dames Grand Cross and possibly the Knights and Dames Commander. 'I think there is something to be said for it', wrote Kenyon to Sir Warren Fisher, Secretary of the Order, 'though I am not particularly enthusiastic.'[7] Fisher accepted that the Order should have a chapel in which services of the Order would be held periodically, but where it should be was quite another matter.

One of the great proponents of the provision of a chapel was Sir Douglas Dawson who, with Ponsonby, had done so much of the groundwork of creating the Order in 1916–17. As the question of mantles and collars was beginning to surface in 1923, Dawson wrote to Lord Cromer towards the end of the year asking for a confidential conversation in which he would outline his proposal for a chapel. Whether or not the conversation took place is unknown but in 1932, Cromer himself proposed Southwark Cathedral.

Before anything definite is done in Ecclesiastical quarters the first thing would be for the Officers of the Order themselves to arrive at some definite project, which could afterwards be elaborated in further detail.[8]

The idea of providing a chapel was brought before the Committee on the Distribution of the Permanent Establishment of the Order in 1933 by Fisher, but the members were not asked to give any serious consideration to the matter. Fisher merely felt that they should be acquainted with some of the proposals that had surfaced since 1917. 'Nothing definite has been settled and it is possible that Members of the Committee have views on the subject which they may wish to record.'[9] The committee debated the question but decided that 'as they could come to no satisfactory conclusion, to make no recommendation'.[10]

In the summer of 1936, William Murdoch, a member of the Grand Council of the Primrose League, wrote to Stanley Baldwin, the Prime Minister, urging that Southwark Cathedral be chosen. His letter was filed without action, but in March 1937, Sir Edward Barton, the junior Knight Grand Cross of the Order, wrote to Bishop Winnington-Ingram.

Assuming that members of the Order are to be found in most parts of the Empire, would the occasion of the Coronation be a suitable one for the inauguration of a movement to provide a Chapel of the Order in London. . . No doubt the idea bristles with difficulties and I myself have been too long resident in the Back Blocks to be able to estimate what room exists today for the pious traditions of chivalry.[11]

The bishop then took the matter to Sir Alexander Hardinge, the King's Private Secretary.

His Majesty certainly thinks that in principle the idea is a good one. But before giving a definite answer the King would like the proposal to be put before Sir Warren Fisher, and then submitted to Queen Mary as Grand Master.[12]

Another alternative was submitted in the summer of 1937 by Lord Plender, GBE, who offered the suggestion of the Church of St Bartholomew-the-Great in the City of London. As the church was only half its original size, he proposed rebuilding the 13th-century nave.

The continuing flow of suggestions and the approval in principle now given by King George VI caused the matter to be given serious consideration after the Coronation in May 1937. Having been unable to come to any satisfactory conclusion in 1933, the committee gave the matter priority in 1937. Fisher circulated a memorandum to the members that outlined the required criteria for choosing a chapel and discussed the proposed locations.

1. It was essential that there should be space to hang at least some of the banners of the approximately 114 Knights and Dames Grand Cross.

2. It was desirable to provide stalls under the banners.

3. The service should be held within a short walking distance of the place where the banners were hung.

4. The building should be large enough to accommodate adequate representation of the various classes.

5. It was desirable to avoid using a crypt 'and thus adding unnecessarily an air of melancholy to the proceedings'.

6. It was desirable that the Chapel should be located in a building not used by any other Order.

7. The Chapel should be located in London, and should be 'conveniently and centrally placed, and the surroundings pleasing'.

8. The building should be well-known, and, if possible, 'mean something to Overseas members who may never have the opportunity in the future of visiting it'.[13]

Working on these principles, Fisher ruled out Canterbury, York and Liverpool Cathedrals. 'There is no doubt . . . that the inconvenience of travel from London, even to Canterbury and back, would prevent many who would otherwise attend the Services, from visiting the Chapel at all'.[14] Accepting the principle of locating the Chapel in London, Westminster Abbey and St Paul's Cathedral were obvious choices, but both provided homes for other Orders; the Order of the Bath at the Abbey, and the Order of St Michael and St George at the Cathedral. To choose one or the other would reduce the sense of exclusiveness for members of the Order of the British Empire, but as St Paul's had often been mentioned, Fisher gave it brief consideration. He reiterated his belief that the choice of a crypt would be an 'unnecessarily mournful proceeding' but the Chapel of St Dunstan in the North Aisle near the West Door might be considered. As the Chapel of St Michael and St George occupied the opposite location in the South Aisle, 'there would be an interesting effort at mimicry . . . a kind of mirror reflection', but it might lay the Order open to the charge of aping the Order of St Michael and St George.[15]

Southwark Cathedral was a more interesting possibility, although its surroundings were a little less than pleasant. 'There is a railway viaduct level with the clerestory. A fruit market is close by. Pungent scents not always pleasant, and the odour of a brewery, filter into the Cathedral from time to time.' Although the interior architecture was 'pleasing and Gothic', 'the Cathedral authorities state that it is gradually falling to pieces, owing to the passing trains and the lack of repair'. The principle objections were its drabness and its distance from the centre of London. 'It is not well known and an announcement that it had been adopted for the Chapel of the Order of the British Empire would probably arouse little interest among the members of the Order here or overseas.'[16]

St Bartholomew-the-Great was not a serious contender in Fisher's opinion. The church was surrounded by tall buildings and wedged between St Bartholomew's Hospital and Cloth Fair. Although with extra chairs it might accommodate 1,000 people, this was far fewer than could be accommodated at Southwark. With regard to the possibility of building a new nave on the site of the garden between the church and the gatehouse, Fisher's opinion was quite clear: 'It is to be hoped that the money will not be forthcoming'.[17]

The convenience of St Martin-in-the-Fields in Trafalgar Square was matched by its capacity to seat 2,000 people 'if carefully packed', but the chief objection was the 18th-century design which allowed only a very shallow chancel. There would be no possibility of erecting stalls and hanging banners above them.

Having disposed of all other competing claimants, Fisher then moved to propose the building that was clearly his personal choice, St Margaret's Church, standing next to and in the shadow of Westminster Abbey. The location was central, the surroundings were pleasing and it was well known. 'It has not perhaps the wide democratic appeal of St Martin's, but it is not so drab as Southwark.'[18] The church could hold about 1,000 people and a clear view could be obtained from almost anywhere inside. Although there was no space to marshal a procession,

St Margaret's, Westminster 1937–9

this could be done across the road in Westminster Hall. 'Those who fail by ballot among the second to fifth Classes for places in St Margaret's could attend the
marshalling of the procession in Westminster Hall.' The church was not really
large enough, but nothing would be except the Abbey or St Paul's Cathedral, and
these had already been adopted by other Orders. 'St Margaret's does pass
perhaps a greater number of the tests mentioned at the beginning of this note than
some of the other places recommended.'[19] The committee duly accepted Fisher's
suggestion and, on 21 July 1937, recommended that St Margaret's Church,
Westminster, be adopted as the chapel of the Order.

A copy of the report was passed to Queen Mary, the new Grand Master of the
Order, who read it 'with much interest',[20] and to the Prelate, for his comments.
Bishop Winnington-Ingram made a final attempt to secure St Paul's Cathedral,
'as I was very anxious that the Order of the British Empire should be connected
with the Central Church of the Empire',[21] and raised the matter with the Dean of
St Paul's. Dean Walter Matthews suggested in reply that the cathedral should be
used for services but the banners should be hung in the Church of St Martin
Ludgate, a short walk down Ludgate Hill from the cathedral. The Prelate repeated
the proposition to Fisher, who carefully considered it for three weeks and then
vetoed it.

It would, I fear, be quite impracticable to hang there the Banners of the Knights and
Dames Grand Cross of the Order, for although it certainly possesses many pleasing features, it would, I feel sure, be too great a distance from St Paul's for the Processions, and
moreover the thoroughfare is always very congested.[22]

With the dismissal of St Paul's Cathedral, serious and detailed exploration of
the possibility of using St Margaret's Church began at the end of November 1937.
A preliminary letter of enquiry from Fisher to Vernon Storr, Archdeacon of
Westminster and Rector of St Margaret's, produced agreement in principle. St
Margaret's being the church of the House of Commons, Storr had also consulted
Edward Fitzroy, Speaker of the House, who was 'cordially in favour',[23] but there
remained the question of consultation with the twenty-five member Parochial
Church Council. With this tentative approval, there began two years of detailed
planning that was to end in failure.

Fisher convened a meeting of the Officials of the Order on Tuesday 25 January
1938 to obtain their approval. Abandoning the thought of using Westminster
Hall, he proposed that the first part of any service of the Order should be held in
Westminster Abbey, followed by a procession to St Margaret's where the Banners
would hang. The total strength of the Order was about 30,000, of whom approx-
imately 30% lived overseas. With the use of the Abbey as well as the church, there
would be sufficient accommodation in St Margaret's for all the GBEs, KBEs and
DBEs together with their friends, and a large representative number of CBEs,
OBEs and MBEs could be housed in the Abbey. After further consultation with
Canon Storr and Paul de Labilliere, the new Dean of Westminster Abbey, the
Officials agreed to submit a formal recommendation to the Grand Master and to
the Sovereign. They were unanimous in recommending that the Banners of all
the 126 Knights and Dames Grand Cross should hang in St Margaret's. To make
provision for a smaller number would extend the waiting period for a banner
vacancy to many years because of the enormous size of the Order. It was also
agreed that a permanent stall plate for each GBE should also be affixed, and both
banners and stall plates would be paid for by the Knight or Dame concerned.

Services would be held every three years, but because of lack of funds, and the work that would need to be done to the church, it would be impracticable to hold a service before 1942. It was agreed that an Order fund should be created with each member being invited, by letter, to contribute a sum, ranging from £3 from a GBE to 2/6d from an MBE.

Something of a rude awakening came on 3 March 1938 when Canon Storr and Sir Robert Knox, the Treasury Ceremonial Officer, met Sir Charles Peers, Surveyor of the Fabric of Westminster Abbey, at St Margaret's. Peers proposed enclosing the whole of the nave with stalls, and turning the side aisles into passages. Knox was worried.

Sir Charles Peers – first architect

Peers put the cost of the scheme up from £10,000 to £15,000, and then to £25,000 in a few moments. Stockley and I feel that a figure of the order of £25,000 will put the whole scheme out of court. It will be very difficult to raise £10,000. A figure in the region of £3,000 to £5,000 would bring the idea more within the bounds of possibility.[24]

Storr agreed and replied that 'all architects have a way of disregarding money'.[25] Knox was firm in his belief that the Order must pay its way and could not be allowed to run into debt. He put pen to paper and broke the news to Peers, who issued a withering and slightly petulant reply.

If you really think that so large an Order as the British Empire can't produce a reasonable sum for making its chapel as good as it can be, it will have to have something not so good. . . If you think that no more than a sum of £5,000 can be raised you had better get hold of some poor architect and tell him that this is all there is and he had better do his best. . . I am sure you will be able to approach other architects who can give you an economical design.[26]

Storr convened a meeting of the Parochial Church Council on 16 March, and reported that the members had given their unanimous approval to linking the Order with St Margaret's, although they were not prepared to allow the extension of the stalls from the chancel into the nave without first seeing the stalls in the chancel. The Council was to prove a troublesome body. St Margaret's was a parish church, and any parishioner had the right to stand for election to the Parochial Church Council, but Canon Storr's predecessor as rector had refused to have anybody except Members of Parliament on the Council. The body became known, unofficially and without any authority, as the Parliamentary Church Council, and to all intents and purposes, a committee of the House of Commons.

With the departure of Sir Charles Peers, Knox turned to Sir Charles Nicholson, consulting architect to Lincoln, Wells, Lichfield and Norwich Cathedrals. Nicholson visited St Margaret's on Monday 4 April and estimated that a set of canopied Gothic-style stalls in oak could be erected on either side of the chancel at a cost of £4,000, a figure that was generally acceptable. What was beginning to cause misgivings in certain quarters was the prospect of extending the stalls out of the chancel and into the first bay of the nave, because of the large numbers of Knights and Dames Grand Cross. Some members of the Parochial Church Council were in favour, others 'and these form quite a considerable party'[27] were not prepared to sanction this without further consideration and without meeting the architect on the spot. 'I believe that most of the PCC will come into line',

Sir Charles Nicholson – second architect

wrote Storr to Knox, 'but they cannot be rushed.'[28] Restricting the stalls to the chancel would allow spaces for only 24 GBEs, far fewer than had originally been hoped and Nicholson himself regretted this development.

If you merely have a single bay of stalls the result will be a rather fine but definitely commonplace parish church of the later Victorian sort, with a rather overpowering set of Choir Seats and that in that case would be disappointing in emphasising the fact that the building was especially appropriated to the Order.[29]

Nothing very much happened during the spring and summer of 1938. Canon Storr was away on holiday in South Africa from 21 April until 8 August, and Sir Charles Nicholson, occupied with many other commissions, did not produce a sketch drawing of the proposed stalls until the end of September. Responding to the concern at the small number of stalls, he produced a design which planned not for 24 but for 38 stalls, in four rows, each stall being 30 inches wide. Knox asked whether the width could be reduced to provide an extra ten stalls, but was warned that the stalls would have to be only 24 inches wide, 'a little small for comfort and dignity'.[30] He then asked for a model of the proposed stalls to be produced, but was again cautioned.

The model would be rather a large affair and unless it is insisted upon I should advise discouraging it because directly anyone puts up a model the certain result is a tremendous outcry and the scheme is very likely to fall through.[31]

It would give a very incorrect idea of the finished work and would lead to virulent letters to the 'Times'.[32]

Throughout October 1938 letters went back and forth between Knox and Nicholson, all concerned with trying to squeeze more and more stalls into the chancel, and, by the middle of the month, the number had risen to 46.

At the beginning of November, Storr reported developments at the Chapel to Knox. He had drafted a letter to members of the Parochial Church Council which he proposed to distribute, accompanied by a copy of Nicholson's sketch. 'I have pointed out the uselessness of having a model put up. . . I hope this will squash the idea.'[33] But Storr had yet again consulted the Speaker who, while personally in favour, declared that he had to consider the views of the House of Commons.

He said that it would in his judgement be wise to put the sketch, together with a few explanatory notes, in the Tea Room of the House of Commons, because there was always some danger that an MP might raise an outcry, which might get into the press, about vandalism, spoiling the House of Commons Church etc. Whereas if all had had a chance of seeing the plan they could not complain. I do trust this suggestion of the Speaker, on which I feel one must act, won't cause any trouble. If there were opposition, it would probably come from some MP who ordinarily took not the slightest interest in the Church![34]

From this point onwards, the scheme started to run into trouble. It seems that the Speaker, although motivated by good intentions, was beginning to realise that he himself could be in trouble with the House of Commons, if he were to act on his own authority and allow the implementation of such a major and possibly contentious scheme. Knox immediately realised that he was now in a difficult position. Were he to agree to the Speaker's suggestion and put up a public notice in the House of Commons Tea Room, he would effectively be submitting provisional plans for approval by the House of Commons, albeit in a quite casual and informal way, before they had been approved by the Officials of the Order, let alone the Grand Master and Sovereign, but in view of what the Speaker had said, he had no choice.

By the end of November 1938, the plans were now becoming common knowledge among members of the House of Commons, and not only those who were members of the Parochial Church Council. Storr reported to Knox that the Speaker had been taking a personal interest in developments, and that the Amenities Committee of the House had also now taken an interest and called in Alfred Charles Bossom (later Lord Bossom), MP for Maidstone and also a qualified architect, to visit the church and produce a report on Nicholson's plan. Bossom visited St Margaret's on 21 November and firmly pronounced that any extension of the stalls into the first bay of the nave would ruin the church. If such an extension was needed, it should go eastwards into the sacrarium or sanctuary.

With a hint of reluctance, Storr gave his support to Bossom's opinion, but the scheme was now beginning to run into deep trouble.

Most of my Church Council have written approving of the other scheme; but some are in opposition. The point, however, is that the Speaker and the Amenities Committee are not in favour of the scheme as we have it now. . . I write in advance of the meeting of the Church Council tomorrow; but there is no doubt that they will vote for delay until the scheme for an eastward extension has been considered.[35]

Storr's fear proved justified. The Council asked Nicholson to redesign his scheme and extend the stalls eastwards into the sacrarium and, as a parting shot, asked if the Order would be willing to make a contribution to the £4,000 needed to restore the church organ. 'The ground of this request was that the OBE was being offered a very beautiful and important church as their home.'[36]

Nicholson was displeased to hear the news of Bossom's involvement. With more than a suggestion of professional resentment, he stated that he was quite sure that he and Bossom would never be able to agree upon any matter concerning church architecture and, in a cross letter to Knox, he abruptly resigned.

If he (Bossom) is delegated by the House of Commons to act as their spokesman in this matter, there would be no good purpose served by my retaining any connection with the proposals. . . I am aware that he was at one time a practising architect, but I do not think his particular line of experience . . . is such as to give weight to his views upon the matter under consideration, and this opinion of mine is confirmed by the fact that he has suggested encroaching upon the sanctuary . . . which would in my opinion destroy all sense of space and openness in the place where it is most needed. Of course I may be quite wrong and he may be quite right, but the fact remains that I do not feel justified in undertaking works unless I have discretion on certain essentials. And I am getting too old to embark on matters that involve a good deal of controversy.[37]

Despite swift and soothing letters from Knox and Storr, Nicholson refused to reconsider, beyond making a half-hearted suggestion to use the south aisle instead, and the scheme reached a full stop. As Storr wrote to Knox, 'What a muddle it all is! There are only two alternatives (a) to employ a new architect, (b) to drop the idea of using St Margaret's. And that decision rests, of course with you at your end.'[38] Knox was willing to persevere with the choice of St Margaret's, but the scheme had effectively moved beyond his control and into the jurisdiction of the House of Commons, and there was still more grief to come.

On 1 December 1938, Knox set the debate moving again in a letter to Storr, in which he recognized that any scheme would have to carry the approval of the House of Commons.

It is obviously desirable, however, to obtain if we can from the Parochial Church Council as detailed a statement as possible of what they *do* consider to be suitable so that the third Architect, if he starts work, may not decamp too early in the negotiations. If the Councillors have views about the selection of an Architect it might of course be helpful to learn what these are. Trouble later on in that direction might thus be avoided.[39]

Storr suggested the name of Sir Giles Gilbert Scott, the architect of Liverpool Cathedral, but Knox, on the strong recommendation of the Lord Chamberlain, and with the support of the Office of Works, invited Roger Pinckney, a young and comparatively unknown architect, to accept the task of rescuing the scheme from the bog into which it had sunk.

Roger Pinckney –
third architect
Pinckney had seen the church before Christmas 1938, and submitted his plans in the middle of January 1939. Although he preferred Nicholson's design, he realised that it was a lost cause. Pinckney's design provided for 42 stalls extending into the sacrarium, but he moved them further back to create a chancel aisle 5ft wider than that allowed by Nicholson. The total cost was estimated at £6,000; the cost of the stalls would be £5,000 and the cost of tiling the chancel floor would be £250, with architect's fees accounting for the rest. The scheme was approved by the Officials in March 1939 and, with minor alterations to the canopies of the stalls suggested by Queen Mary, the final design was approved at the beginning of June. On 15 June approval was given by the Royal Fine Art Commission, and on 22 June the Parochial Church Council gave its unanimous approval. Everything now seemed to be set and everyone now seemed to be satisfied. Either thinking or hoping, or both, that it would be little more than a formality with such general support, the plans were forwarded by Canon Storr to the Diocesan Advisory Committee of the Diocese of London.

In respect of the interior of its church buildings, the Church of England is exempt from all state planning controls, but this is allowed on the understanding that the Church regulates itself in this respect. This is achieved by the means of an Advisory Committee in each diocese. All alterations to the interior of a church must be submitted to the committee to make a recommendation to the Diocesan Chancellor for the grant of a faculty to enable the work to go ahead. Albeit with its peculiar parliamentary connections, St Margaret's was a parish church of the Church of England, and therefore any alteration to the interior fell within the faculty jurisdiction of the Church.

Knox's hope that the way ahead was now clear, proved to be premature. The London Diocesan Advisory Committee, although expressing its general support for the scheme, and also being willing to support the faculty application, voiced disquiet at the extension of the stalls into the sanctuary, and referred the issue to its own architect, Dr F. Eeles. Eeles disapproved of the eastward extension and recommended the petitioners to re-consider the Nicholson plan and use the first bay of the nave.

I should not be afraid of the effect of this in the very least . . . Not only is there no chancel arch, but there is no architectural division of any sort or kind . . . The only question is proportion. At present you have six bays in the nave, two in the chancel. Such a proportion as five in the nave and three in the chancel has abundant precedent and I doubt if any people would know there had been any change in this respect once the work were done. Your only real trouble, as I see it, would arise from taking away seats. But you are really turning a parish church into a collegiate church and it cannot be done without some sacrifice. . . I should counsel delay so as to give time for a good deal more consideration.[40]

Further consideration was given, and a new scheme, effectively a slightly revised form of the Nicholson plan, was approved by the Royal Fine Art Commission and presented to the Parochial Church Council at a meeting on Tuesday 18 July that, unusually, was chaired by the Speaker. Unfortunately, debate at the meeting was both pre-empted and influenced by a question in the House of Commons on the very same day. Rupert De la Bère, Member of Parliament for Evesham, who was not a member of the Parochial Church Council, asked Captain Crookshank, Financial Secretary to the Treasury:

whether some additional provision for honourable Members of this House will be made at St Margaret's Church, Westminster, in view of the provision which is being made for members of the Order of the British Empire.[41]

On being reassured that the provision for Members would not be rendered inadequate, he asked a supplementary question. 'Will the right honourable and gallant Gentleman bear in mind the fact that the feelings of the House have been somewhat hurt by the unhappy way in which this matter was handled?' Crookshank correctly replied that the plan for St Margaret's had nothing to do with him or with any other member of the government. It seems likely that De la Bère was among those who had originally objected to the extension of the stalls into the first bay of the nave and, realising that his cause was lost, used his position as a member of the House of Commons to make one last public objection.

No decision was taken by the meeting of the Parochial Church Council on 18 July and the debate was adjourned for further informal consultation. Knox later reported that full agreement on all points had not been reached by the beginning of August but that he hoped to be in a position to launch an appeal within six months. In a memorandum to Sir Edward Bridges, he was more forthright.

It was only at the end, about July 1939, after I had brought it on several occasions before the Parliamentary Church Council of St Margaret's and the Speaker, and twice before the Royal Fine Art Commission, and after it had been examined by the London Diocesan Advisory Committee and the Central Council for the Care of Churches, that an opposition party appeared on the Church Council. Prior to that, they and the Speaker were most anxious for us to go ahead. (We were kind people who were going to improve the House of Commons Church free of charge) . . . I believe that in August 1939 the Speaker took alarm and sped off to His Majesty. This was an unnecessary move on his part as it was quite clear by then that we had lost. This was very disappointing after many month's work.[42]

With the outbreak of the Second World War in September 1939, all the plans were shelved, and Knox could do no more than commiserate with Storr on the fact that all their plans had come to nothing.

We cannot proceed with the scheme at present; we could not possibly set it going in present circumstances. I greatly regret this for many reasons, not least, because I always so much enjoy meeting you at St Margaret's. Let us hope that we shall be able to start again in a year or two's time.[43]

The outbreak of war coincided with the retirement of Bishop Winnington-Ingram, the first Prelate of the Order, in September 1939. Eighty-one years old, Bishop of London for thirty-eight years and Prelate of the Order of the British

Empire for twenty-one years, he expressed his sorrow in having no part 'in what I have long desired, to see a Chapel for the Order and a Service'.[44]

The outbreak of war in fact ended any thought of creating a chapel for the Order in St Margaret's Church. There is also evidence that the difficulties encountered in trying to deal with a 'Parliamentary' Church Council and, behind it, the House of Commons, had been, for those who had initiated it, an experience unpleasant enough to make them wary of reviving the scheme. In 1942–3, Canon Alan Don, who had replaced Canon Storr as Vicar of St Margaret's suggested placing the matter again on the agenda of the Parochial Church Council before the end of the war. Knox's cautious reply indicated that there was no enthusiasm for reviving the protracted and difficult negotiations of 1938–9.

I have put it to him that our attitude now . . . is that we should prefer not to make any further approach to the Rector and Churchwardens . . . but would wish rather that this should come from them.[45]

That, it seems, was the end of any thought of using St Margaret's Church, Westminster.

THIRTEEN

The Quest for a Chapel: 2

SOUTHWARK CATHEDRAL AND OTHERS

It is evident that the institution of a Chapel of the Order of the British Empire south of the River would be an honour for that area. From the point of view of those belonging to the Order, however, there is no doubt that the Cathedral would be very difficult of access for Services. On all weekday mornings the vegetable market is in full swing outside the churchyard wall, and there is, moreover, in the Cathedral almost a continuous noise from the railway.
Report of a meeting of the Officials of the Order, 30 April 1947

As the Second World War drew to a close, attention turned again to the question of a chapel for the Order, and new suggestions began to appear. Admiral Sir Reginald Tupper, GBE suggested to Sir Richard Hopkins in 1944, that since an Empire Day Service was to be held in St Paul's Cathedral on 24 May, might there not be some thought of reserving a block of seats for members of the Order? The suggestion was supported by the Empire Day Movement, but treated with caution by Robert Knox. Without wishing to be discourteous to the Movement, he was concerned that such a 'joint' Service might be taken as an indication that the Order and the Movement shared the same aims and objectives.[1] Knox's caution proved to be prescient. The Empire Day Service at St Paul's Cathedral petered out in the years immediately after the War, partly due to bad management, and partly due to constitutional changes in the Commonwealth.

In 1945, the Bishop of Kensington offered the bombed church of St John's, Smith Square to the Order. On this occasion it was Sir Harry Stockley who was cautious.

Perhaps, a little later on, we might look at this Church, but I think we ought to ascertain what the arrangement is going to be in the future for the rebuilding of other City Churches. I believe St John's is very badly damaged. Perhaps this offer is made in the hope that the Order might pay for the restoration![2]

The idea was raised again in February 1947 by the Dean of Westminster who, with motives that were less than altruistic, was taken with the idea of moving, from the Abbey to St John's Church, some of the monuments of those who had taken a conspicuous part in building the Empire. The Dean's motive was largely to provide space in the Abbey for more monuments. The thought of using St John's Church lingered a little longer, but was never given serious consideration.

In 1946 the Dean of Canterbury Cathedral offered the use of one of the cathedral chapels for the use of the Order, but the offer was refused, again on the grounds of distance, and also because of the now established policy to locate the Chapel in London.

The Dean's offer was brought to the attention of King George VI who was of the opinion that Canterbury was too far. But the suggestion of Canterbury was sufficient to stimulate renewed interest and, in December 1946, the King and Queen Mary directed that consideration should be given to another previously rejected candidate, Southwark Cathedral. Rejected in 1937 because, in the opinion of one correspondent, its surroundings were 'sordid and forbidding', it re-entered the field ten years later with the support of the Sovereign and the Grand Master.

The first church on the site of Southwark Cathedral was said to have been built in the 7th century by a ferryman, whose trade had made him wealthy at a time when there was no bridge across the Thames, and the church was historically known as St Mary Overie (i.e. 'over the river'): the present title is 'The Cathedral and Collegiate Church of St Saviour and St Mary Overie'. Of the present building, only the 13th-century choir remains from the medieval church. The tower is 17th century and the rest of the cathedral is the result of an extensive 19th-century restoration. The increasing population of south London made a nonsense of its location in the Diocese of Rochester and, in 1897, it became the pro-cathedral for south London, and in 1905 Edward Stuart Talbot was enthroned as the first bishop of the new Diocese of Southwark.

As the building was the cathedral church of another diocese, the Bishop of London, as Prelate of the Order, informally consulted the Bishop of Southwark about the possibility of using his cathedral. The two bishops had met by 26 April 1947 and the Bishop of London reported that his colleague was 'very interested in the suggestion and affirms that the Provost will be even more so'.[3]

On 29 April 1947, the Officials of the Order, accompanied by the Private Secretaries to Queen Mary and to the Prime Minister, drove across the river to look at the cathedral. The group was met by the Bishop of Southwark, and by representatives of the Traffic Branch of the Metropolitan Police. The group submitted a less than enthusiastic report. For the location of stalls, stall plates and banners, the options were to use the 13th-century Lady Chapel, the Harvard Chapel, the Choir, or the Nave. For various reasons, the first three were ruled out, leaving the Nave, and the North and South Aisles, as the best location for banners and stall plates 'although it might be necessary to dispense with personal stalls'.[4] The decision to give the erection of stalls a low priority was perhaps as much to do with the experience of St Margaret's as with the geography of Southwark. The cathedral could seat 1,700 people and, although the membership of the Order was 55,000 strong, the capacity was felt to be as adequate as any other church or cathedral.

The insurmountable difficulty at Southwark was the inadequacy of parking facilities, and the police advised that parking of cars for large congregations would give rise to the greatest difficulties.

It is evident that the institution of a Chapel of the Order of the British Empire south of the River would be an honour for that area. From the point of view of those belonging to the Order, however, there is no doubt that the Cathedral would be very difficult of access for Services. On all weekday mornings the vegetable market is in full swing outside the churchyard wall, and there is, moreover, in the Cathedral almost a continuous noise from the railway.[5]

Because of these disadvantages, the group felt it wise to submit to the King and to Queen Mary other possible options.

After leaving Southwark Cathedral, the group drove back across the river, once *St Paul's Cathedral*
again to consider St Paul's Cathedral. On this occasion, the use of the cathedral *again*
by the Order of St Michael and St George was not thought to be a problem,
although the use of the previously considered Chapel of St Dunstan was firmly
discounted, and attention turned to the crypt.

It has previously been considered to be too funereal, but the Altar and the tombs are now
perhaps better lit than they were some years ago. The windows are barred on the outside,
which emphasises the position below ground. It might be possible to conceal this by the
use of coloured glass. There is a simplicity in the architecture of the crypt which those in
authority will obviously wish not to disturb. Whether very simple Stalls for the Knights
Grand Cross might be placed between the pillars near the Altar is a matter for careful consideration. If they should be thought unsuitable, it might be necessary to be content with
Stall Plates on the walls. Banners also would present a difficulty, and it might be necessary to dispense with these. . . The advantage of using St Paul's would be that a great
many people could be accommodated for a Service in the Cathedral itself, while the Crypt
could be used for the special purposes of the Order.[6]

The group also considered the option of St John's, Smith Square. Obviously
the church would require rebuilding for 'a considerable sum', and with galleries
could seat possibly 1,000. The surroundings were pleasing and the Chapel would
not be underground. 'The authorities of Westminster Abbey would favour the
use of this church but the small number which could be accommodated is, in our
view, a serious disadvantage.'[7]

Of those present on the tour of the two cathedrals, all the Officials of the Order *Divided views*
favoured the use of St Paul's Cathedral, while Major Wickham, Queen Mary's
Private Secretary, favoured Southwark Cathedral. Nobody considered St John's,
Smith Square to be a serious contender. Wickham was almost certainly
influenced by Queen Mary's intense interest in Southwark. He felt that, for banners, stalls and stall plates, Southwark was better than the crypt of St Paul's,
although for an annual service, the nave of St Paul's was a much better location.

If the Chapter of Southwark smile more cordially upon the scheme than the Chapter of
St Paul's, then I should come down in favour of the former. . . I do not think that traffic
considerations need weigh too heavily for only one occasion in the year;[8]

and as a parting shot he added, 'Queen Mary asked me all about yesterday's expe-
dition, and I think it is very probable that Her Majesty will herself pay a visit to
Southwark Cathedral one day soon'.[9] Early in May the Bishop of London tele-
phoned Bridges and reported that he had met Queen Mary and gathered 'that she
had firmly made up her mind in favour of Southwark and she thought the King
was of the same view'.[10]

Knox himself was inclined against the use of St Paul's crypt.

It has, in my view, the general view of a distempered vault. . . Personally, I do not even
much like the idea of inviting GBEs to put their stall plates in a Crypt. Most of them are
getting on in years and it seems . . . to resemble an invitation to them to make some prepa-
rations for removal elsewhere. . . Nevertheless, the Cathedral itself has so many advantages for our purpose that no doubt something could be done to improve the Crypt. All I
am anxious about at the moment is that we should not have a report on record which suggests that it is suitable in every possible way.[11]

The formal report of the group was submitted on 27 May 1947. The report
surveyed all the options, laying out in detail the advantages and disadvantages of

St Paul's and Southwark Cathedral. St John's, Smith Square was all but dismissed on the grounds of its small size and the expenditure required to restore it. The report formally advised against Canterbury and York because of the problem of accessibility, and St Margaret's, Westminster was firmly and finally rejected, because of parliamentary problems.

Southwark confirmed

Queen Mary visited Southwark Cathedral on 23 September 1947, and was escorted around the building by the Bishop and the Provost. The Queen was 'greatly impressed'[12] by the building and asked the Provost privately to consult the members of the Chapter. He did so, and reported them to be 'unanimously and enthusiastically in favour'.[13] By 6 December, Sir Alan Lascelles, Private Secretary to the King, informed Bridges that the King and Queen Mary had definitely decided that they wanted the Chapel established at Southwark. Knox visited the cathedral for the morning service on Christmas Day and made careful notes of a variety of details, ranging from the way the cathedral was lit, to the badges worn by the sidesmen, and the robes and badges of the choir, and the possible locations of banners and stall plates.

A delay of four months occurred because of the impending change of Provost. Provost Cuthbert Bardsley was consecrated Bishop of Croydon on 1 November 1947, but remained Provost of the cathedral until the arrival of his successor, Edward Ashdown, in April 1948.

After a first meeting of Bridges, Knox, Ashdown and Wickham on 14 June 1948, the new Provost wrote to Knox on 1 July with an alternative suggestion. Rather than use existing space within the cathedral, why not consider a longer term plan to extend the cathedral by building an entirely new chapel for the Order attached to the west end of the south transept. The suggestion was greeted unfavourably by both Knox and Wickham, the latter remarking that 'however desirable a long term scheme for building a permanent Chapel at Southwark may be, this is not the time to contemplate putting money into bricks and mortar'.[14] Ashdown himself had a meeting with Queen Mary on 10 July to discuss the general plan of giving the Order a home at Southwark and was impressed by her interest and her grasp of the details. 'She showed quite amazing understanding and sympathetic interest. It is clear that she hopes that our plans will take definite shape before very long.'[15]

The first difficulties

With the rejection of his suggestion for a purpose-built chapel, Ashdown duly reported his alternative plans to a meeting of the Officials at the cathedral on 25 October 1948. He recommended that the banners should hang not in the nave but in the north and south aisles, two banners to each bay, with a small name plate near each banner to facilitate identification. Each banner would be no larger than 2ft 3in square and suspended from a bronze bracket. The armorial plates would be affixed to oak panelling erected in the arcade at the west end of the nave, one panel in each bay of the arcade. No stalls would be provided for the Knights and Dames Grand Cross, although the Provost later suggested that temporary stalls might be erected beneath the central tower for services of the Order. He added that it was quite impossible to find a chapel within the cathedral that could be devoted solely to the use of the Order. Legal difficulties might arise with the Retro-Choir as it was a parish church, and the use of the Harvard Chapel was out of the question as Americans subscribed to its upkeep.

The meeting approved the enlargement of the banners to 2ft 9in square, and the size of the armorial plates as 6in by 5in, and further agreed that, because of the difficulties of finding space for a chapel within the cathedral, it would be best to treat the whole cathedral as the Order chapel. The plan was referred back to the cathedral chapter who, although in favour of the general scheme, vetoed the positioning of armorial plates below the relevant banner because of a fear that it might produce 'a spot-like effect' on the walls of the cathedral.[16]

As the St Margaret's scheme had run into trouble ten years earlier, so now the Southwark scheme was beginning to run into trouble. Queen Mary herself was an enthusiastic supporter of taking the Order to Southwark, but she would have liked to see a chapel within the cathedral reserved specifically for members of the Order, and she was reported to be 'sorry' on hearing that this would prove impossible, and 'disappointed' that the banners would not be hung in the nave. [17]

Ashdown took note of Queen Mary's wishes, and consulted Godfrey Allen, the cathedral architect in December 1948. Allen gave the matter careful thought, and produced another plan which would accord with Queen Mary's wishes, and was presented by Ashdown to the Officials at a meeting on 3 February 1949. He proposed establishing a small oratory for the Order by enclosing the north-west corner of the nave with railings. There would be no space for banners, and seating for no more than three or four people, but it would provide a home for the 'roll' of the Order, and it would be a place that the Order could call its own. It was in fact little more than a cupboard.

Twenty banners would still be hung in the north and south aisles, and the banners of the Sovereign and the Grand Master, with perhaps two additional GBE banners, could be hung prominently from the west wall of the nave. The name of each Knight or Dame Grand Cross would be painted on a small shield at the base of the staff of the Banner. Armorial plates would be attached to a narrow panel of wood attached to the walls, about 7ft from the ground, below a stone string course, and between the plates would be carvings symbolising different parts of the Empire. Ashdown warned the committee that the Chapter had not yet approved this proposal, and their attitude 'was as yet doubtful'.[18]

Another architect

The 'oratory' plan was less than satisfactory and nobody was at all enthusiastic about implementing it. At Queen Mary's suggestion, the distinguished church architect, Ninian Comper, was consulted about the scheme. Comper produced a different and very grand scheme. He proposed to retain the concept of the whole cathedral being the chapel of the Order but, in placing the banners, he suggested following the plan of the Order of the Garter in St George's Chapel, Windsor Castle, and the Order of St Patrick in St Patrick's Cathedral, Dublin, and placing the banners, not in the side aisles but over the choir stalls. He proposed erecting an altar at the crossing, covered by a ciborium, and that both altar and ciborium would carry appropriate decorations emphasising the connection with the Order. This altar would be the one in general use, while the high altar behind would be used for special occasions, and the choir would become a focus for the Order.

Bridges was impressed by the plan.

Assuming the cost could be found, there would be a touch of grandeur in a scheme of this kind. If adopted in its entirety, it would be much more attractive than anything offered up to now by Southwark and might go some way to make up for the awkward journey and the dull surroundings.[19]

Wickham was not so impressed:

in addition to reducing the seating accommodation, it would partly obscure a view of the high altar. I feel sure, too, that the Provost and Chapter would not fall in with Comper's suggestion that the nave altar should be the one in general use and the high altar reserved for special occasions.[20]

Continuing unease

The 'dull surroundings' were a constant worry for Sir Robert Knox. In January 1949 he placed a note of his thoughts in the file relating to Southwark Cathedral.

There is some feeling, I cannot say how strong it is, that it might possibly be wise to consider the practicability of recommending an alternative scheme. There probably is no alternative which could be made very attractive, but there may be some scheme with fewer disadvantages than Southwark. It is very much out of the way for the average person and the surroundings are so dismal, and there may be little response from GBEs or others in the Order. A factor in the selection of Southwark is that the arrival of the Order . . . south of the river would help on the scheme for improving the South Bank. Having regard to the general condition of the country, it must surely be many decades before the surroundings of Southwark can be substantially improved. . . It has taken some 20 years to bring the Order of the British Empire up to its present place in public regard. A certain number of persons refuse appointments still and it remains the junior of the great Orders. It may therefore probably be said with truth that in going south of the river, and as far off as Southwark, the Order is conferring some benefit on that area. The Order, in the view of many, will not be so well established or have such a long history that it can afford to do this. The scheme for a Chapel should improve the standing of the Order. It seems likely that the placing of a Chapel under the Southwark scheme might well have the opposite effect on the Order.[21]

This note is dated 15 January 1949, and there is no evidence that it was seen by anyone else, but even as Comper's plans were being discussed, Knox was asking Wickham to consider other possibilities. Towards the end of January, the two men visited St Bartholomew-the-Great and St Peter's, Eaton Square. Wickham ruled out the latter on the ground that Queen Mary would prefer an 'old' church. Knox also mentioned St Michael's, Chester Square; St Dunstan's, Fleet Street; St Peter's, Cornhill; and St Mary-le-Strand; but Wickham ruled out all of them.[22]

The feelings of the Officials of the Order were similar to those of Knox. On 29 January, the Registrar, Sir Ivan De la Bere, delivered his shot:

I still think Southwark Cathedral is NOT a suitable place for the Chapel of the Order. I consider it to be too far out and in too noisy and sordid a locality, and though it is a Cathedral, I feel that its name means nothing to the majority of those Members of the Order who are domiciled out of London and particularly to those resident overseas. I do not believe that, if the Chapel is located at Southwark, there will be much enthusiasm for attending services of the Order there, which perhaps would be lucky in view of the transport difficulties, nor can I visualise many Members using the Chapel for Wedding or Christening services, which I suppose should be the object of having such a Chapel. Nor do I think many Members will contribute financially towards the beautification of a place about which they know little and which they do not intend to visit.[23]

The King of Arms, Air Marshal Sir Roderick Carr, thought the use of Southwark would be 'a pity'.[24] The Gentleman Usher of the Purple Rod, Sir Frederic Kenyon delivered a critique on the grounds of equality.

I am not, myself, in favour of a Chapel of the Order, decorated with the insignia of the GBEs at all. I think that (especially in these days of reduced incomes) many of them would be unwilling to incur the expense (I should myself for one); and I don't like the idea of a monument for the special glorification of the GBEs.[25]

He proposed simply an annual service to which all members of the Order would be invited. 'Such a service almost necessarily implies the use of St Paul's which (as I think everyone recognises) would be a much more attractive home of the Order.' The Prelate was, not unnaturally, in favour of his own cathedral church. 'I think we have all agreed that it is particularly appropriate to an Empire institution.'[26] All these comments, were incorporated in a final report, dated 22 February 1949, which was submitted to Queen Mary on 26 February. The report outlined the plans of the Provost, listed the drawbacks to the use of Southwark, and then finally recommended that St Paul's should be considered once more.

We are convinced that if a satisfactory scheme could be prepared for using St Paul's for the Services of the Order, such a scheme would be far more likely to win the approval and support which we fear may not be given to the Southwark scheme. . . We wish humbly to ask that we may be given further directions by the Sovereign and the Grand Master of the Order.[27]

The report was forwarded to Queen Mary by Sir Edward Bridges, with an accompanying note to Wickham stating that if the Southwark scheme should be preferred, 'we shall, of course, all put our backs into it and be determined to make the scheme a success'.[28] Wickham discussed the scheme with Sir Alan Lascelles, Private Secretary to the King, who suggested that the whole idea of a chapel should be dropped for the time being. Lascelles took the position that there was no money available, that Southwark was unsatisfactory, that he had learned that the Dean and Chapter of St Paul's were 'strongly opposed' to the use of the Crypt of their cathedral, that members of the first class were unlikely to wish to pay for banners and armorial plates, and that he had not heard of any strong demand for either a chapel or services.[29] Given all these factors, Lascelles suggested that the wisest course would be for any question of a chapel to be abandoned. Writing to Lascelles on 5 April 1949, Bridges confessed his disappointment that the efforts of the committee should have failed to find a satisfactory scheme, but he agreed that dropping the whole scheme was 'much the wisest course'.[30] On 19 April, Lascelles confirmed that the King and Queen Mary agreed that the attempt to find a permanent Chapel for the Order should, for the time being be abandoned,[31] and the news was conveyed to the Provost of Southwark on 26 April.

The demise of the Southwark scheme did not rule out the possibility of holding annual services for members of the Order, and King George VI made the suggestion that Services for the Order 'shall be held at such times and in such places as may be found most expedient'.[32] His wish was echoed by Queen Mary who 'cordially approves'[33] the idea of holding Annual Services in different Cathedrals around the country. Wickham reported to Bridges on 3 May that Queen Mary entirely understood and appreciated all the efforts of the committee.

Queen Mary shares the appreciation expressed by the King of the work of the . . . Officers of the Order and is not a whit the less grateful to them because their endeavours proved unavailing. Her Majesty particularly wished me to say this.[34]

This generous response on the part of Queen Mary, who had clearly set her heart on Southwark Cathedral, was all the more poignant, because she was eighty-two

The scheme abandoned

years old, and it was now unlikely that she would live to see the establishment of
a permanent chapel for the Order.

So it proved to be. Her Majesty Queen Mary, second Grand Master of the
Order of the British Empire, died on 24 March 1953.

FOURTEEN

The Quest for a Chapel: 3

ST PAUL'S CATHEDRAL

The essential would seem to be that some Church or Cathedral should be formally adopted as the Church of the Order of the British Empire, and periodical services of the Order held there. I submit that it will be felt by many that St Paul's Cathedral is pre-eminently suitable to be formally adopted . . . both by virtue of its being the Cathedral of the capital city and because it lends itself to services attended by a large congregation.
Sir Edward Bridges to The Grand Master, 30 June 1954

The thought of holding a service for the Order, lingered for a while after the demise of the Southwark scheme in April 1949. King George VI gave his provisional approval for a service to be held on 24 May 1951 in St Paul's Cathedral, and a planning meeting was held on 22 February 1950. Those present included Sir Edward Bridges, Secretary of the Order, Brigadier Ivan De la Bere, Registrar of the Order, and the Private Secretaries to the King and to Queen Mary. The plan was eventually abandoned because of a decision to hold a service of the Order of the Bath on that day in Westminster Abbey for the purpose of installing the Duke of Gloucester as the new Great Master.

The possibility of locating a chapel for the Order in St Paul's Cathedral resurfaced early in 1953. On 17 February, Dean Walter Matthews wrote to Sir Edward Bridges with a suggestion that, once again, St Paul's Cathedral might be considered. 'We wasted a lot of time before in discussions, and I do not want to start a hare which is unlikely to be caught, but the situation has now changed in one respect. We are restoring the north transept, and I think it is possible that something might be done there, at least to put up some banners, and perhaps to make an open chapel.'[1] Bridges courteously explained to the Dean that although the matter could be re-opened, Queen Mary had been much in favour of Southwark Cathedral and, in view of her great age, it would be kinder not to raise the matter again until after the appointment of a new Grand Master.

The death of Queen Mary in March 1953, and the Coronation of Queen Elizabeth II in the summer of that year, excluded any serious consideration of the Dean's proposal during that period, but Matthews wrote again, this time to Bishop William Wand of London, in March 1954.

It now becomes rather urgent that some decision in principle should be made, because the scheme which was generally regarded as most acceptable . . . was that the North Transept should be used for the purpose . . . and, as you know, the restoration of this part of the Cathedral is now at a fairly advanced stage. . . We should welcome the Order and are prepared, under certain conditions, to make use of the North Transept.[2]

During subsequent investigation, it became clear that, although an altar and a few banners could be positioned in the north transept, the construction of stalls would alter not only the character of the transept, but also the symmetry of the cathedral. One of the most forceful criticisms came from a member of the cathedral chapter, Canon George Prestige.

I am confident that the Surveyor would be still more hostile; he would regard it as treating a classical Renaissance building as if it were a Gothic building, and the whole business as a purely Gothic act of barbarism. . . The transept must remain in every sense an integral part of the Cathedral structure: but granted that, we should be happy enough . . . with a special focus at one point which is permanently in and of the total Cathedral – a wayside shrine but not so as to check the flow of general traffic.[3]

The canon's view was indeed supported by the Surveyor of the Fabric who was none other than the same Godfrey Allen, Surveyor of the Fabric to Southwark Cathedral, whose plans for an Order chapel in that building had been rejected five years earlier. Allen vetoed the use of the transept, and by June 1954 attention had turned yet again to the cathedral crypt.

Before serious consideration began, it was observed that the Order probably included a sizeable number of non-Christians, and was it therefore appropriate for its spiritual home to be located in a Christian church? An investigation concluded that from a total of 85,000 substantive members, possibly 5,000 at most were non-Christian. Although the point was well made, it was felt that the experience of the Coronation and the many Coronation Thanksgiving services, held throughout the country, provided evidence that non-Christians, and Christians who were not members of the Church of England, felt no scruple about attending special services of a commemorative character held in an Anglican church. The experience of non-Christian appointments to the Order of St Michael and St George had caused no difficulty and, furthermore, no recommendations for appointments to the Order of the British Empire were now being made from the largely non-Christian countries of India and Pakistan.

Consultation

At a meeting on 30 July 1954, the Officials of the Order declared themselves to be 'enthusiastically in favour'[4] of St Paul's Cathedral, but the establishment of a chapel for the Order within the Cathedral was deferred for wider consultation with the membership of the Order. A representative selection of twenty-one Knights and Dames Grand Cross were asked three questions:

(1) Did they approve of the suggestion of St Paul's?

(2) Would an appeal for funds have their support, and did they think that such an appeal would be successful?

(3) Could they offer any suggestion as to how the appeal should be made, and how much should be asked of each grade of the Order?

Of the 20 replies, 18 indicated their broad approval, although two of them were concerned that non-Christians might feel excluded, and one (the Countess of Limerick) suggested that Westminster Hall might be a better location in this respect. Of the two 'noes', one felt that the proposal was an artificial attempt to inject corporate reality into a large Order where none existed and none was possible. The other objector, probably unaware of the repeated suggestions and attempts to find a chapel for the Order since 1917, felt that that the proposal had come too late in the Order's history.

When the Officials met again on 6 October 1954, they agreed to submit to the Grand Master a request that a representative group of five Knights and Dames Grand Cross should be added to the committee, to widen the consultatory process. The five chosen were the Earl of Crawford and Balcarres, Sir Malcolm Trustram Eve, Lady Freyberg, the Countess of Limerick and Field Marshal Lord Wilson. Lord Wilson declined because of ill-health, and Lady Limerick offered her excuses on the grounds that she would often be travelling abroad in connection with her work with the British Red Cross Society. They were subsequently replaced by General Sir Brian Robertson and Admiral Sir Cecil Harcourt.

At the same meeting Dean Matthews, bearing in mind the strong opinions of Canon Prestige and the Surveyor, formally advised the committee that the Chapter would probably favour the use of the Crypt rather than the North Transept. An informal meeting was held in the Crypt on 21 October at which Godfrey Allen outlined his proposals to create an Order Chapel at the east end of the Crypt, and undertook to produce detailed plans for the committee. Allen subsequently had a meeting with the Dean, whom he, somewhat surprisingly, reported to be 'rather non-committal' about the whole project, and then with Canon Prestige, whom he found to be 'vehemently hostile'.[5] Cathedral Chapters are never the easiest of groups to deal with and, as the employee of a divided Chapter, Allen was clearly in a difficult position. The prospect of establishing a chapel in the near future looked unlikely in the face of such trenchant opposition.

The situation changed on 19 January 1955 with the sudden death of Canon Prestige. Dean Matthews then suggested that the Officials submit a formal application as soon as possible, before any new appointment was made of some person whose views might also be hostile![6] Without delay, Allen submitted a scheme at the end of February. His plan was not unlike the Lutyens design of 1917, providing 36 stalls for the GBEs and a further six stalls for the Officials. He provisionally estimated the cost to be in the order of £35,000–40,000, but by the summer of 1955, he had refined the figure to £32,000.

Acting entirely on his own initiative, Oswin Gibbs-Smith, Archdeacon of London and a Canon Residentiary of the Cathedral, showed the proposed design to the distinguished architect, Professor Albert Richardson, a member of the Royal Fine Art Commission, the Royal Commission on Historical Monuments, and the Central Council for the Care of Churches. Richardson broadly agreed with Allen's design, but suggested the introduction of return stalls to give a slightly enclosed effect to the crypt chancel, which would form the Chapel of the Order. The committee vetoed this suggestion but asked for further proposals on how to separate the chapel from the rest of the crypt. Allen proposed an ironwork grille but this was rejected in January 1956, and he was asked to substitute an oak screen. Allen, who preferred the use of iron, produced another design in June, this time for a low iron screen. The committee supported the new design, and resolved to submit the scheme to the Grand Master for his approval.

The cost of the work had now risen to approximately £60,000, and caused the the valid observation that an appeal for such a sum might raise criticism. In the interests of simplicity and economy, there came the suggestion, in August 1956, that although St Paul's Cathedral should be used for major services of the Order, the Queen's Chapel, Marlborough House might be used as the Chapel of the Order for smaller events. This could continue until a reasonably accurate assessment could be made of the need and support for a purpose-designed Chapel.

The Queen's Chapel, Marlborough House

The proposed use of the 17th-century chapel, designed by Inigo Jones, itself raised problems. The Archdeacon of London strongly opposed the suggestion, on the strange ground of the distance between the Chapel and the Cathedral. Nevertheless, in August and September 1956, consideration was given to the possibility of using the Queen's Chapel. The suggestion was supported by the Lord Chamberlain, the Earl of Scarborough, although with some reservations.

> With regard to the hanging of banners, etc., I mention this because this chapel, as it is now restored, is a unique and beautiful example of the work of Inigo Jones, and it would be a pity to mar the homogeneity of the chapel by too many banners and insignia.[7]

The idea of using the Queen's Chapel did not command widespread support, but the suggestion was rooted in a genuine concern at the high cost of Allen's design.

Lord Mottistone   Time had now run out for Godfrey Allen. He was due to retire as Surveyor of the Fabric of the Cathedral at the end of 1956, and the Archdeacon proposed that Allen's designated successor, Lord Mottistone, should be invited to produce a completely new and less expensive design on taking office at the beginning of 1957. The members of the committee were in agreement, and Sir Edward Bridges was faced with the task of writing a sensitive and tactful letter to Allen.

Mottistone was asked to produce a design at fairly short notice. The Duke of Edinburgh was due to leave the country on 14 October for an extended tour of Australasia, returning at the end of January 1957, and a provisional scheme would need to be submitted to him before his departure. Lord Mottistone was notified of the commission on 18 September 1956 and, astonishingly, produced a provisional and very imaginative design only six days later. He abandoned any thought of stalls and panelled woodwork, producing a design including wrought iron-work, glass panels painted in grisaille, and benches and faldstools upholstered in the colours of the Order.

The design was discussed by the committee at its meeting on 28 September and favourably received.

> The general feeling . . . was that, while the previous scheme had great dignity, it had involved the erection in the comparatively low Crypt of a great structure of wood in the style used by Wren for such furnishings in lofty parts of the Cathedral. The scheme proposed by Lord Mottistone followed different principles. It made the most of the Wren architecture of the Crypt, and in principle, it was on the right lines. It might nevertheless be expected to give rise to criticisms in some architectural circles. The architect had shown great courage in proposing the use of iron columns with inset grisaille work on glass, not seen elsewhere in the Cathedral. These black iron pillars would contrast with the colours of the Order seen on the Altar and in the carpet and other furnishings.[8]

The Grand Master gave his formal approval to the new design on 10 October, suggesting that emblems representing (a) the different countries of the Commonwealth, and (b) the different types of activity in respect of which the Order is awarded, might be worked into the design for the glass panels.

The Cathedral Chapter had formally approved the location of the Order Chapel in the crypt in January 1956, and with the design now agreed in principle, a Deed of Agreement was exchanged on 20 March 1957.[9]

The establishment of the Chapel of the Order in the cathedral also led to the creation of three new Officials: Dean, Sub-Dean and Prelate Emeritus. The Archdeacon of London, also a Canon Residentiary of the cathedral, proposed that the Dean of the Cathedral should become Sub-Prelate of the Order. The suggestion was taken up by Sir Robert Knox, who additionally suggested that the Archdeacon should receive the title of Assistant Prelate, and he proposed the titles to the new Bishop of London in May 1956 only to receive a cool response. 'The Prelate thinks that any description including the word "Prelate" is not perhaps entirely satisfactory for a clergyman who is not a Bishop.'[10] The suggestions were dropped and it was agreed that the Dean should be ex-officio Dean of the Order, and act as an assistant to the Prelate. Provision was made for the appointment of a Sub-Dean, to be held in the first instance by the Archdeacon of London, but not to be held ex officio. The title of Prelate Emeritus was given to William Wand, recently retired as Bishop of London, and now a Canon Residentiary of the Cathedral.

The establishment of a Chapel for the Order of the British Empire was announced in the *London Gazette* on the Queen's Birthday, 13 June 1957, along with the new clerical appointments, the Dean, the Sub-Dean and the Prelate Emeritus. The day was also chosen to launch the appeal to fund the establishment of the Chapel. Notices of the appeal were sent to all GBEs, KBEs, DBEs, and CBEs, and to all OBEs and MBEs who had received their appointments from June 1956. Limiting notice of the appeal to the most recent additions to the fourth and fifth classes was the result of the difficulty in maintaining an accurate register of the names and addresses of the members. However, a good number of the earlier appointments complained that they had not been invited to subscribe to the fund, and a subsequent notice was sent to all members still recorded as being alive, no matter how ancient the registered address. Inevitably many letters were returned marked 'Not known' or even 'Dead', but a considerable number did eventually reach the intended recipients. Brigadier Ivan De la Bere reported in May 1958, that this extension of the appeal was bringing in donations of £100–150 per week:

but with many thousands of address cards to cope with, it is a longish business and for reasons of economy has to be fitted in with the other work of this office: at present we have only got as far as the letter 'E' and it will not be practicable to complete the issue of the 'appeal' until about the middle of next year.[11]

Ivan De la Bere was not greatly enamoured with the cathedral crypt, and thought a great deal of work would need to be done.

Though like most places underground it is a bit depressing . . . provided we do not stint our Architect and Artist unduly, I feel sure that our Chapel will eventually be bright and beautiful. But each time I enter the Crypt and go through St Faith's Chapel towards the place selected for the British Empire Chapel I get more depressed by the general appearance of St Faith's Chapel. With its piano on a platform and its generally gloomy lay-out it reminds me of a rather scruffy mission-room.[12]

Fears of a poor response to the appeal proved to be unfounded. More than 20,000 people responded, including not only living members of the Order, but also relations of deceased members. The required sum of £10,000 was raised within two weeks, and by 20 September, the fund stood at £30,000. By May 1959 it had risen to £58,000, and by the date of the first service on 20 May 1960, to £100,000. The total cost of the refurbishment of the crypt for the Order was £41,000, including £5,565 for an organ by Henry Willis.

The best introduction to the Chapel of the Order is to read the words of Lord Mottistone, its designer.

The design of the Chapel

The underlying idea in the design of the Chapel is that, although there should be a sense of enclosure to the sanctuary, the simple beauty of Wren's masonry should not be obscured. I therefore omitted from the design any solid woodwork of stalls and canopies, and instead formed the enclosure by wrought-iron screens after the manner and in the tradition of the master craftsman, Jean Tijou, whose exquisite work is one of the glories of St Paul's. They carry representations of the star and badge of the Order surmounted by the Royal Crown, and contain sixteen glass panels designed and painted in grisaille by Mr Brian Thomas. All the ironwork was hand-forged to my designs and from my drawings by Mr William Norris at his forge at Brentford.

As it was desired to portray likenesses of the Royal Founders and Sovereigns of the Order and also to illustrate – by way of symbols and emblems – various of the types of service which at home and overseas have earned recognition in its several grades, these subjects were painted in reticent tones on the glass panels which were set in the wrought-iron screens. Treated in this way, the black iron and neutral tints of the panels form an admirable foil to the colours of the Order – pearl grey and rose pink – which occur in the soft furnishings, and to the still richer colouring of the Royal banners and the stained glass windows in the ambulatory.

The lighting of the shrine is derived from fittings which, surmounting the screens, contain electric candles for direct effect and lamps within their sconces to illuminate the vaulted ceiling.[13]

The glass panels   The chapel has a number of distinctive features, of which the most unusual are the grisaille glass panels. Two panels flank the entrance to the chapel: the panel on the north side shows King George V and Queen Mary (the Queen being habited in the mantle and collar of the Order); the panel on the south side shows Queen Elizabeth II and the Duke of Edinburgh (the Duke also being habited in the mantle and collar of the Order).

The panels on the north side of the Chapel illustrate the continents and hemispheres, and contain emblems of the countries of the Commonwealth. The panels on the south side represent the various forms of service given to the community for which awards are given by the Sovereign. Beginning on the north side of the chapel, and moving clockwise around the apse to the south side, the panels display the following representations.

The first panel represents Australasia and incorporates a gold prospector's equipment, a kangaroo, a Maori, a kiwi, sheep, apples, wattles and a tree fern. The second represents the Americas and shows a moose, a Mountie, a totem pole, a grain elevator, timber, sugar-cane and pineapples. The third represents Europe and the Mediterranean and shows a classical temple, a Gothic cathedral with two doves of peace, an English country cottage, an owl of wisdom sitting on a book, and emblems suggesting agriculture, science, music, industry, justice, exploration and sport. The fourth represents the northern and southern hemispheres and shows the constellations of the Great Bear and the Southern Cross, a polar bear, a whale, a seagull, an octopus, a sea-urchin, a sea-horse, a conch shell, a star fish, a crab, a sea-anenome, penguins and various other sea creatures. A central medallion shows the globe set between the points of the compass. The fifth represents Asia and shows an Asoka lion, an elephant, a pagoda, a peacock, a hooded cobra, a tiger, and cotton, tea, coffee and rice plants. The sixth represents Africa and shows a voortrekker's wagon, a prospector's tools, native weapons, a lion, an antelope, a wildebeest, a fruit tree, flame lilies, cocoa, and ostrich feathers. The seventh and eighth depict Queen Elizabeth The Queen Mother, consort of King George VI, above Glamis Castle, her ancestral home and King George VI himself. The ninth represents the Church (the cross, the bible, a chalice, a crozier, a font and a church) and agriculture (various fruits, crops, fish and a milk churn). The tenth represents commerce (a hive, a ledger, bags of money, a factory, etc.) and transport (an aeroplane, a man carrying a burden, and a ship). The eleventh represents fine arts and education (an artist's palette, the tools of an architect and a sculptor, a muse with a lyre, a violin, an open book and actors' masks) and the skilled crafts (blacksmith at his anvil, a saw, a spade, a pickaxe and building tools). The twelfth represents science and medicine (a globe measured by a hand holding a compass, the staff of Aesculapius, and a DNA model) and communications (a telephone, a radio, a camera, a typewriter, and a mountain of paper). The thirteenth represents justice (the judgement of Solomon, scales, and crossed swords) and administration (a town hall, an office, a mayor's insignia, maces, a filing cabinet, a briefcase, a topee, and an umbrella). The fourteenth represents the armed forces (a shield, wings, two swords, a trident, and a castle) and sport (three athletes, a football, a hockey stick, a rugby ball, golf clubs, boxing gloves, a tennis racket, a cricket bat, and a trophy).

The altar is constructed of Portland stone with carved and gilded enrichments. In the centre is a carved and gilded wreath enclosing a chi-rho. The altar is covered with a Laudian frontal of rose-red velvet lined with gold and embroidered by the Royal School of Needlework in silver and gold thread, with a representation of the Star of a Knight Grand Cross. The dossal curtain behind the altar was specially woven with gold and silver permanent Lurex threads, and the other dossal curtains, of cloth of gold, were also specially made and woven. The cross and candlesticks are of iron and bronze and were made by Adrian Stokes, who also made the screens. The altar plate, usually to be seen in the cathedral treasury, was executed by Meadowcroft & Sarll.

The altar and other furnishings

The chairs and faldstools are of silvered wood and upholstered in rose and grey brocade. The font is also of silvered wood, with a spun and polished aluminium bowl underneath the cover.

The lectern is made of oak and contains, in the vertical column, a wrought-iron panel carrying the cross of the Order in colour. It was designed by Paul Paget.

The floor of the chapel is laid with specially made dove-grey and white polyvinyl tiles. The original intention to relay the floor in marble was abandoned. The carpet was designed by Lady Maufe and woven by the Wessex Weavers.

The organ was presented to the cathedral by the Order and made by Henry Willis and the enclosing case was designed by Lord Mottistone. The organ is badly affected by damp and is no longer in working condition.

The four hundred hassocks were completed by a band of three hundred and eighteen embroiderers under the supervision of Lady Freyberg, GBE, in 1972. Two hundred and three hassocks are embroidered with the star of a GBE, and one hundred and ninety-seven show the badge. Each one bears the name of a Commonwealth country and, in certain cases, the names or initials of a member of the Order to whom the embroiderer had dedicated it. The designs were prepared by the Royal School of Needlework and all the hassocks were made up by Wippell & Mowbray. They were dedicated on 22 November 1972.

The registry, panelled throughout in oak, is built between two piers on the north side of the Chapel and was dedicated in 1971. It contains a built-in cupboard in each corner and a desk on the west side. Designed by R. F. Rushton, Deputy

The registry

Surveyor of the Fabric, the joinery was executed by Martyn of Cheltenham. The stool, presented in memory of Herbert Sammons, was designed by Rushton and followed the general pattern of the Mottistone furniture in the Chapel. A crystal inkwell, with silver lid in a silver tray complete with silver penholder, was presented by the Order.

The windows   The nine stained glass windows in the chapel were designed by Brian Thomas and made at the Whitefriars Studio. They were installed at various dates between 1959 and 1964. It was at first thought that the windows should contain the arms of Canada, Australia, New Zealand, South Africa, India, Pakistan, Ceylon and Ghana – the first eight countries of the Empire to become independent. The idea was abandoned when it was pointed out that such an arrangement might offend sentiment in other Commonwealth countries. The Commonwealth Relations Office warned that:

it would look very odd at this date to put up the coats of arms of countries no longer interested in recommending for honours... We should ... in any case have to consult the other Commonwealth Governments concerned before putting their coats of arms into the windows of the chapel: [14]

and, quite apart from the then problem of South Africa, the proposal might not get a warm reception. A compromise proposal incorporated floral emblems of certain countries instead of the armorial bearings.

The Bishop of London was worried about the stained glass darkening the chapel. Thomas replied.

I have left as much plain glass as I can without allowing the grille behind the glass to show through as prison bars. I hope that any obscuration will be compensated for by the warming of the light by the gold pattern of the design. [15]

Beginning from the bay adjacent and to the east of the organ bay, on the north wall, and moving clockwise, the windows are as follows.

The first window represents the theme of 'Service' as exemplified by Christ washing the disciples' feet at the Last Supper on the night before his crucifixion (John 13:5). The illustration is flanked by the Civil and Military ribbons and the badges of the Knights Grand Cross (above) and Dames Grand Cross (below). The ribbon of the Military Dame Grand Cross is that in use from 1937–70 (i.e. without the central vertical pearl grey stripe). The ribbons and badges replaced the original proposal for the armorial bearings of Canada, Australia, New Zealand and South Africa.

The second window, in a chapel on the north side of the British Empire Chapel, shows Christ healing the sick (Matthew 4:23), flanked by the armorial bearings of the second and third Grand Masters, Queen Mary and the Duke of Edinburgh, with inscriptions recording their dates of office.

The third window, the first of three in the apse, has been called the 'Royal Window'. In the centre are the Royal Arms, and above, the crown of the Queen, Sovereign of the Order. Below the arms is a princely coronet with black and white ostrich feathers, which is the crest of the Grand Master, the Duke of Edinburgh. The arms are imposed on two lances with fluttering standards bearing the cyphers of King George V and Queen Elizabeth II. On either side are terrestrial globes showing the two hemispheres, representing the world-wide fellowship of the Commonwealth, and symbols suggesting the blessings of Security (a shield and sword for the army, a trident for the navy, and wings for the air force), Prosperity (a cornucopia), Justice (scales) and Religion (the cross and the bible). Below the emblem for religion can be seen the date 1960 in Roman numerals. The four swags are composed of the emblematic flowers of the Commonwealth countries in 1960: the maple leaf of Canada, the wattle leaf of Australia, the tree fern of New Zealand, the lotus of India, the protea of South Africa, and the flame lily of Zimbabwe (formerly Rhodesia).

The fourth window, called the 'Members' Window', can be seen in the centre of the apse, above the altar, and illustrates the stars, badges and medal of the Order. In the centre is the star of the GBE surrounded by a collar. At the top left is the star of the KBE and DBE. At the top right is the badge of the CBE. At the lower left is the badge of the OBE, and the MBE badge can be seen at the lower right. The heraldic sea-lions, bearing tridents, are a feature deriving from the collar of the Order, and between them can be seen the medal of the Order.

The fifth window, called the 'Officials' Window' is the third in the apse, and shows the insignia or emblems of the Officials of the Order: the crown and rod of the King of Arms; the purple rod of the Gentleman Usher; the book of the Registrar; the crossed quill pens of the Secretary; the badge of the Prelate; the badge of the Prelate Emeritus; the badge of the Dean; and the badge of the Sub-Dean. The window is embellished with various sea-lions, tridents, anchors, and the Motto of the Order.

The sixth window, is located in a disused chapel on the south side of the British Empire Chapel, now partitioned from the aisle leading to it. Consequently the window can only be seen above the partition by standing some distance away. The window illustrates the parable of the Lost Sheep (Luke 15:4–7) above crossed shepherds' crooks. It is flanked by medallions showing Britannia, the cypher of King George V, the conjoint crowned effigies of King George V and Queen Mary, and the Royal Arms.

The seventh window illustrates the parable of the Good Samaritan (Luke 10:33), flanked by the MBE and BEM, Civil and Military, all ribbons bearing the emblem for gallantry in use from 1957 to 1974. These four gallantry decorations replaced the original proposal for the coats of arms of India, Pakistan, Sri Lanka and Ghana.

The eighth window illustrates three acts of mercy (Matthew 25:35) *I was hungry and you gave me food; I was thirsty and you gave me drink; I was a stranger and you welcomed me*. Here again can be seen the emblems and insignia of the Lay Officials of the Order: the book of the Registrar, the crossed quill pens of the Secretary, the purple rod of the Gentleman Usher, and the crown and rod of the King of Arms. The act of mercy towards thirst depicts water being poured into a basin. The original design showed a man up-ending a bottle to his lips, and brought forth the comment that he looked like a 'hardened toper'.[16] Brian Thomas duly redesigned the window to its present appearance. 'I so much hope that . . . the committee will feel that this latter imbibition is more decorous'.[17]

The ninth and last window illustrates the other three acts of mercy from Matthew 25:36: *I was naked and you clothed me, I was sick and you visited me, I was in prison and you came to me*. In the four corners of this window can be seen the badges of the four clerical Officials of the Order: the Prelate and the Prelate Emeritus (both incorrectly surmounted by a mitre), and the Dean and the Sub-Dean.

With the low roof, and the small amount of space, the hanging of large numbers of banners was never seriously considered. The committee decided in July 1959   *The banners* that only six royal banners should be hung – those of the Sovereign, the Grand Master, and four others. The possibilities were Queen Elizabeth The Queen Mother, the Duke of Windsor, the Duke of Gloucester, the Duke of Kent, the Princess Royal (Princess Mary, Countess of Harewood), the Duchess of Gloucester, the Duchess of Kent and Princess Alice, Countess of Athlone. As the Order was the first to admit women, it was not inappropriate that the chosen four should be Queen Elizabeth, the Princess Royal, the Duchess of Gloucester and the Duchess of Kent. To save unnecessary expenditure, the banners were painted (at a cost of £71) rather than embroidered (at a cost of £171).

The banners; were duly affixed in 1960, and there they remained until 1987. By that date, the Princess Royal (in 1965) and Princess Marina, Duchess of Kent (in 1968) had both long been dead, yet their banners were still in position. The options were either to remove the banners of deceased knights and dames, or to keep them in position to retain the symmetry and original appearance of the chapel. Some thought that the chapel would look less well with four rather than six banners; others thought it best to follow the precedent of the other Orders, especially the Order of the Garter at St George's Chapel, Windsor Castle, and to take down the banners of deceased knights and dames. The latter view prevailed, and the banners of the Princess Royal and Princess Marina were taken down in March 1988 and returned to their respective families.

The banners hanging in the chapel at the time of writing are, on the north side, those of the Duke of Edinburgh and Princess Alice, Duchess of Gloucester, and on the south side those of the Queen and Queen Elizabeth The Queen Mother.

The services   With work on the chapel largely complete by the early months of 1960, the first service of the Order was scheduled for Friday 20 May at 11.30 am. An accurate calculation of the size of the membership of the Order has never been possible, but in 1960 it was estimated at 85,000. Although conceivably just within the realms of administrative practicability, it would have been a costly and lengthy task to send out personal invitations to the last recorded address of every member of the Order. It might have produced so massive a list of acceptances as to provoke a ballot for places, the seating capacity of the cathedral being only about 3,000. For the same reason it was not even proposed to invite the 20,000 members who had subscribed to the chapel fund. Arrangements were made with Buckingham Palace accredited press agencies for notices to appear in a number of national and provincial newspapers some fourteen weeks before the date of the service, inviting applications for tickets. The procedure proved successful, with about 2,600 members applying to attend the service. The Order was represented by 60 Knights and Dames Grand Cross; 110 Knights and Dames Commanders; 520 Commanders; 850 Officers; 1,120 Members; and 220 holders of the British Empire Medal. The service was attended by the Queen and the Duke of Edinburgh, and by the Duchess of Gloucester and the Duchess of Kent. The Lesson, read by the Grand Master, was taken from Christ's Sermon on the Mount, reminding his hearers that they were the salt of the earth and the light of the world. The text of the service was drafted by the Sub-Dean and approved by the Prelate.

In order to maximise use of all available seating in the cathedral, the crypt itself is also used at Order services and seats about 400 people. At the 1960 service, the Sovereign, the Grand Master and the Officials, together with the twelve junior

Knights and Dames Grand Cross, formed a procession and went down to the crypt, during the singing of a hymn, for the dedication of the chapel. The procession then reformed and returned to the main body of the cathedral during the singing of another hymn. This format has been followed at every subsequent service. In 1963, the new cope, stole and altar plate were dedicated; in 1967, the windows of the chapel were dedicated; and in 1971, the new registry of the chapel was dedicated. Since that date, the chapel service has consisted only of the Lord's Prayer, and prayers for the living and departed members of the Order.

The Officials had envisaged that a service might be held every two years, and proposed 19 or 26 May 1962 as the date of the next service. Because of the absence of the Grand Master at the Commonwealth Study Conference in Canada, and the difficulty in finding an alternative date, the service was deferred until 30 October 1963. The service was as great a success as the first service, attracting 2,242 members of the Order. The current practice is for the Grand Master to be present at each service, and for the Sovereign to be present at alternate services, but their attendance will depend on their many commitments.

The Officials of the Order recommended, in the following year, that the best frequency would be every three years, and the next service was planned for May 1966. Difficulties again in finding a convenient date meant that the projected date was postponed to 28 October 1966. An observation that 1967 was the fiftieth anniversary of the foundation of the Order brought a further postponement until 24 May 1967. If a service was held in October 1966, it could hardly be followed by one held in May 1967, and Commonwealth Day in the 50th anniversary year was clearly the more significant. The service was attended by the Queen and the Grand Master, and also by the Duchess of Gloucester, Princess Marina Duchess of Kent, and Princess Alice Countess of Athlone.

On this occasion, the innovation of closed circuit television was introduced to enable the 400 or so members of the Order seated in the crypt to witness that part of the service taking place in the cathedral above. The experiment was not repeated at the 1971 service, and led to 'considerable adverse comment particularly by those situated in the Crypt Chapel'. The next service was at first scheduled for 1975, but as it would have clashed with the 250th anniversary service of the Order of the Bath, the date was brought forward to 1974, and closed circuit television was again used for the benefit of those in the crypt. In 1973 the Order paid for the re-seating of the cathedral with 2,500 new chairs at a cost of £37,000, and the chairs were used by the Order for the first time at the 1974 service.

After further services on a three-year basis, in 1977 and 1980, the present four-year pattern was adopted from 1984. Members of the Order were allowed to bring guests to the services from 1960–77, but in the latter year, the service was over-subscribed, 2,811 tickets being issued, and 60 guest names had to be cut from the list by means of a ballot. The 1980 service was limited to members of the Order, but even then a ballot had to be held and 920 applicants had to be turned down. The 1984 service was also over-subscribed by 400, but most of these were subsequently allocated returned tickets. In 1988, 662 applicants were balloted out, but 400 of these were subsequently accommodated by returned tickets. In 1992, all those members who applied, and did not withdraw, some 2,700, were accommodated.

The services of the Order are usually held in May for the historic reason that *The date of services* 24 May was celebrated as Empire Day. Commemoration of the day grew out of the Empire Day Movement at the end of the 19th century which proposed to celebrate the Empire on the 24 May, Queen Victoria's birthday. Empire Day was officially recognised in 1916 and commemorated as such until 1958 when its name was changed to Commonwealth Day. In 1966 Commonwealth Day was moved to the Queen's Official Birthday in June. From 1977 the day has been kept on the second Monday in March. The Statutes of the Order, however, continue to state: 'the Twenty-fourth day of May shall henceforth be taken and deemed to be the anniversary of the institution of this Order' despite the absence of any connection between this day and the creation of the Order in 1917.

Refurbishment of
the chapel

In 1990, Dean Eric Evans drew attention to the fact that the Chapel was in need of refurbishment. Lord Mottistone's work was now thirty years old, and time had taken its inevitable toll. The cost of total refurbishment of the chapel was estimated as being £1 million, and, since such a sum was beyond the in-hand finances of the Order, an appeal became necessary. Sir Robin Gillett, GBE, Gentleman Usher of the Purple Rod, was appointed Chairman of the Appeal Committee, the other members being Admiral Sir Anthony Morton, GBE, Dean Eric Evans, General Sir Anthony Farrar-Hockley, GBE, Sir Alexander Graham, GBE, Air Chief Marshal Sir Patrick Hine, GBE, Dame Simone Prendergast, DBE, and Leopold de Rothschild, CBE. On 13 May 1992 'The Most Excellent Order of the British Empire 75th Anniversary Appeal Fund' was launched. The brochure appealed for £750,000 and outlined the work to be done.

The organ is in poor condition and so badly sited that it has not proved possible to maintain the necessary stable conditions of temperature and humidity. The acoustic projection has been far from ideal, making both the acquisition of a new organ and its relocation matters of primary importance.

Liturgical changes in the past thirty years had rendered the chapel furnishings obsolete in the eyes of some, and in particular there was a perceived need for an altar that could be used for westward facing celebrations of the Eucharist. The chairs in the chapel had reached the end of their useful life; frequent repairs were necessary, and the cost of maintaining their leather covers was proving expensive. The lighting and wiring in the chapel was showing signs of age, and renewal would allow the installation of a more appropriate and imaginative system to enhance the overall appearance of the chapel. Greater numbers of visitors to the cathedral were now visiting the crypt, and the level of noise was such that when the chapel was in use for services, the crypt had to be closed. The volume of noise was expected to be even greater with the proposed transfer of the cathedral shop to the crypt, and the appeal would cover the cost of the provision of a screen of fumed oak to separate the chapel from the rest of the crypt. It was also proposed to replace the present vinyl floor tiling with a more suitable material.

Some 30,000 appeal letters were sent out to members of the Order in 1992, and by June 1995, £450,000 had been raised. The story of the appeal is still incomplete, but two substantial pieces of work have been undertaken. The decayed chairs were replaced, and a new screen of fumed oak and glass was erected, separating St Faith's Chapel from the rest of the crypt. The screen was in place by the end of October 1993 and incorporates representations of the insignia of the Order, carved by the cathedral craftsmen. Further plans include a presentation book in a display cabinet listing the names of all those who have contributed to the appeal.

FIFTEEN

Postscript

IN THE SERVICE OF THE NATION

And the culminating pleasure that we treasure beyond measure
Is the gratifying feeling that our duty has been done!
Sir William Gilbert, *The Gondoliers*, 1889

In relating the history of the Order of the British Empire, the text of this book has concentrated on institutional developments: the structure of the Order; the design of the robes and insignia; and the establishment of a chapel. Fascinating though their stories have been, it could be argued that more space might have been devoted to the stories of the tens of thousands of people who have been appointed to the Order since 1917. Structural changes are interesting but marginal, whereas the lives of men and women are the essence of the history of the Order: its reputation is no more than the lives of those who have accepted it, and its history is the record of their service to the nation. The point is well made. In one sense, the Order is the sum total of the people whose good deeds and well-performed duties have been so recognised and honoured. The reverse is also true; by their willingness to accept the Order, they have themselves conferred honour upon it and thereby raised its reputation. The flood of refusals in the early years has dwindled to a trickle, and the Order is now held in an esteem higher than at any other point in its history.

There is no satisfactory way, within the confines of a single volume, of doing justice to the lives of all those appointed to all grades of the Order since its inception in 1917. A list of names and dates alone would fill several books; but it would still convey nothing of the, often lifelong, service and achievement that culminated in those appointments. To have added brief biographies, even supposing they could have been found, would have been a colossal undertaking, and extended the project by many years. Attempting the task in 1921, *Burke's Handbook to the Order of the British Empire* became a 700-page book intended to produce brief biographies of the 25,000 appointments to the Order in the first four years of its existence; but even with such exhaustiveness, it proved impossible to trace a good number of the recipients, and many are listed without any biographical detail. Given the fact that many tens of thousands of people have been appointed since 1921, it would have been impractical to attempt something similar.

The alternative is to be selective and to say a little about some recipients whose achievements have established them in the public eye, but here there comes the temptation to focus attention on the names of the famous, and this gives no credit to the lifetimes of service performed by the many unremembered names; and fame, if public opinion is used as a measuring rod, can be notoriously transient. Many of those who were famous in their day, and recognised for their achievements, have long been forgotten. A great number of names, of national and lasting fame, have been added to the roll of the Order of the British Empire down the years; but a far greater number achieved fame only within their own profession, their own locality, or their own family, and somehow it seemed wrong to dwell upon the eminent achievements of the former at the expense of the equally eminent, though geographically restricted, achievements of the latter.

In trying to assess the breadth and depth of the membership of the Order and the recipients of its medal, the selection of a few famous names, and it would have to be only a few, would be a slight and inadequate testimony to the service of the total company. It is far better to look at the representative categories of service for which the Order has been used to accord recognition. The spirit of adventure, by explorers, mountaineers and aviators; courage, bravery and gallantry, by civilians and by the armed forces in war and peace, at home and abroad; the creative arts, by writers, dramatists, actors, composers, musicians, artists, sculptors and architects; education and learning, by teachers and academics; science, discovery and technology, by chemists, biologists, physicists, mathematicians, astronomers and inventors; those who work for the good of the community, by the doctors, nurses, policemen, firemen and local government officers; administration, by civil servants and the law; those whose work has contributed to the wealth of the nation, such as agriculturalists and farmers, and those employed in the world of commerce, industry and exports; the prowess of men and women in the world of sport; and those who give service in the voluntary organisations, such as the Women's Royal Voluntary Service, St John Ambulance, the British Red Cross Society, and the Scout and Guide movements; those who foster friendship with foreign and Commonwealth nations

Outstanding achievement in all these fields is recognised by membership of the Order of the British Empire, and no other United Kingdom honour is used to confer recognition on such a wide variety of professions, or lay claim to the titles of 'national' and 'nation-wide'.

If the system has any flaw, it lies in an area which is endemic to human nature. Those individuals whose service has indeed been unquestionable may feel disappointed that their names have not been included in an Honours List. For the one person who is honoured, there are many others who have also performed a lifetime of impeccable service but who have received no national honour. Many of their friends may sincerely believe that such people deserve to be honoured, and are puzzled when an honour fails to be forthcoming. The plain truth of the matter is that an honour, whether Order or Medal, of whatever level, is intended to recognise, not the diligence with which a duty is performed (that is required of everyone), but a level of service that is above and beyond the call of duty, in fact *exceptional* service. The statutory limits placed on the size of membership of, or annual quota of admissions to, the Order of the British Empire, are not pointless restrictions, but one way of ensuring that only *exceptional* service is recognised.

This postscript began with a quotation from Sir William Gilbert's satire *The Gondoliers*. At the beginning of Act 2, Giuseppe and Marco have been elevated from plying their trade as humble Venetian gondolieri to being enthroned as acting joint kings of Barataria. Overcome by the deference accorded to them by their subjects and courtiers, they resolved to make themselves useful by dedicating their days to the service of others, and at the end of each day they would retire to rest 'with the gratifying feeling that our duty has been done'.

When an individual is appointed to the Order, it can cause feelings of disappointment on the part of those not so recognised, especially if there is a sincere belief that their service was of a comparable standard to those being honoured. There should be no reason for the distribution of the Order of the British Empire to cause feelings of discontent. The process of selecting names is designed to ensure recognition of outstanding achievement or exceptional service, but the resulting award of an honour to one individual does not dismiss or downgrade the service of another, and there is neither need nor reason for it to cause disappointment. The gratifying feeling of duty well done, can be as much a culminating pleasure to a lifetime of service, as the receiving of an honour.

Those who are admitted to the ranks of the Order are receiving the recognition of a grateful nation. The almost innumerable host of the company of the Order of the British Empire, both living and departed, constitutes an impressive array of dedication, and brings forth thanksgiving for the fact that there were such people, and the prayer that there will be many more in the years ahead.

God save our gracious Sovereign,
God defend our Grand Master;
God bless the whole company
of the Most Excellent Order
of the British Empire.

(The Vivat of the Order)

APPENDIX I

The Grand Masters and the Officials of the Order

I THE GRAND MASTERS

His Royal Highness The Prince of Wales   1917–1936
   Born: 23 June 1894
   Appointed: 4 June 1917
   Died: 28 May 1972

Her Majesty Queen Mary   1936–1953
   Born: 26 May 1867
   Appointed: 27 March 1936
   Died: 24 March 1953

His Royal Highness The Prince Philip, Duke of Edinburgh   1953–
   Born: 10 June 1921
   Appointed: 22 May 1953

II THE PRELATES

The office has been held by successive Bishops of London since 1918, but it is not held ex officio.

The Right Reverend and Right Honourable Arthur Foley Winnington-Ingram   1918–1939
   Born: 26 January 1858
   Appointed: 12 April 1918
   Died: 26 May 1946

The Right Reverend and Right Honourable Geoffrey Francis Fisher   1939–1945
(*Archbishop of Canterbury 1945–1961*)
   Born: 5 May 1887
   Appointed: 10 November 1939
   Died: 15 September 1972

The Right Reverend and Right Honourable John William Charles Wand   1945–1956
(*Canon Residentiary of St Paul's Cathedral 1956–1969*)
   Born: 25 January 1885
   Appointed: 20 December 1945
   Died: 16 August 1977

The Right Reverend and Right Honourable Henry Colville Montgomery Campbell   1956–1961
   Born: 11 October 1887
   Appointed: 1 January 1956
   Died: 26 December 1970

The Right Reverend and Right Honourable Robert Wright Stopford   1961–1973
(*Vicar General of the Episcopal Church in Jerusalem and the Middle East 1974–1975;*
Bishop of Bermuda 1976)
   Born: 20 February 1901
   Appointed: 10 October 1961
   Died: 13 August 1976

The Right Reverend and Right Honourable Gerald Alexander Ellison   1973–1981
   Born: 19 August 1910
   Appointed: 26 October 1973
   Died: 18 October 1992

The Right Reverend and Right Honourable Graham Douglas Leonard   1981–1991
   Born: 8 May 1921
   Appointed: 4 August 1981

The Right Reverend and Right Honourable David Michael Hope   1991–1995
(*Archbishop of York 1995–*)
　Born: 14 April 1940
　Appointed: 20 August 1991

The Right Reverend and Right Honourable Richard John Carew Chartres   1995–
　Born: 11 July 1947
　Appointed: 29 November 1995

III THE KINGS OF ARMS

General the Right Honourable Sir Arthur Paget   1918–1928
　Born: 1 March 1851
　Appointed: 12 April 1918
　Died: 9 December 1928

Admiral Sir Herbert Leopold Heath   1929–1947
　Born: 27 December 1861
　Appointed: 28 June 1929
　Died: 22 October 1954

Queen Mary informally approved the choice of Air Marshal Sir Bertine Sutton to succeed Sir Herbert Heath in 1947, but Sir Bertine, who was also under consideration for another post, died suddenly before any announcement was made.

Air Marshal Sir Charles Roderick Carr   1947–1968
　Born: 31 August 1891
　Appointed: 14 February 1947
　Died: 15 December 1971

Lieutenant General Sir George Charles Gordon Lennox   1968–1983
　Born: 29 May 1908
　Appointed: 5 January 1968
　Died: 11 May 1988

Admiral Sir Anthony Storrs Morton   1983–
　Born: 6 November 1923
　Appointed: 21 June 1983

IV THE REGISTRARS

The Secretary of the Central Chancery of the Orders of Knighthood ex officio.

Brigadier General Sir Douglas Frederick Rawdon Dawson   1918–1921
　Born: 25 April 1854
　Appointed: 12 April 1918
　Died: 20 January 1933

Colonel the Honourable Sir George Arthur Charles Crichton   1921–1936
　Born: 6 September 1874
　Died: 5 March 1952

Major Sir Harry Hudson Fraser Stockley   1936–1946
　Born: 30 October 1878
　Died: 30 July 1951

Brigadier Sir Ivan De la Bere   1946–1960
　Born: 25 April 1893
　Died: 27 December 1970

Major General Sir Cyril Harry Colquhoun   1960–1968
　Born: 16 August 1903

Major General Sir Peter Bernard Gillett   1968–1979
  Born: 8 December 1913
  Died: 4 July 1989

Major General Sir Desmond Hind Garrett Rice   1980–1989
  Born: 1 December 1924

Lieutenant Colonel Walter Hugh Malcolm Ross   1989–1991
  Born: 27 October 1943

Lieutenant Colonel Anthony Charles McClure Mather   1991–
  Born: 21 April 1942

V THE SECRETARIES

This office was held by the Permanent Under Secretary of State in the Home Office 1918–1922, and has been held ex officio by the Head of the Home Civil Service since 1922.

Geoffrey Granville Whiskard (*Acting Secretary*)   1917–1918
  Born: 19 August 1886
  Died: 19 May 1957

Sir Charles Edward Troup   1918–1922
  Born: 27 March 1857
  Appointed: 12 April 1918
  Died: 8 July 1941

Sir Norman Fenwick Warren Fisher   1922–1939
  Born: 22 September 1879
  Died: 25 September 1948

Sir Horace John Wilson   1939–1942
  Born: 23 August 1882
  Died: 19 May 1972

The Right Honourable Sir Richard Valentine Nind Hopkins   1942–1945
  Born: 13 February 1880
  Died: 30 March 1955

The Right Honourable Sir Edward Ettingdean Bridges (Lord Bridges)   1945–1956
  Born: 4 August 1892
  Died: 27 August 1969

The Right Honourable Sir Norman Craven Brook (Lord Normanbrook)   1956–1962
  Born: 29 April 1902
  Died: 15 June 1967

Sir Laurence Norman Helsby (Lord Helsby)   1963–1968
  Born: 27 April 1908
  Died: 5 December 1978

The Right Honourable Sir William Armstrong (Lord Armstrong of Sanderstead) 1968–1974
  Born: 3 March 1915
  Died: 12 July 1980

Sir Douglas Albert Vivian Allen (Lord Croham)   1974–1977
  Born: 15 December 1917

Sir Ian Powell Bancroft (Lord Bancroft)   1978–1981
  Born: 23 December 1922

Sir Robert Temple Armstrong (Lord Armstrong of Ilminster)   1981–1987
  Born: 30 March 1927

Sir Frederick Edward Robin Butler   1988–
  Born: 3 January 1938

VI THE DEANS

The Dean of St Paul's Cathedral ex officio.

The Very Reverend Walter Robert Matthews   1957–1967
   Born: 22 September 1881
   Appointed: 13 June 1957
   Died: 5 December 1973

The Very Reverend Martin Gloster Sullivan   1967–1977
   Born: 30 March 1910
   Died: 5 September 1980

The Very Reverend Alan Brunskill Webster   1978–1987
   Born: 1 July 1918

The Very Reverend Thomas Eric Evans   1988–
   Born: 1 February 1928

VII THE GENTLEMEN USHERS OF THE PURPLE ROD

Sir Frederic George Kenyon   1918–1952
   Born: 15 January 1863
   Appointed: 12 April 1918
   Died: 23 August 1952

Sir Ernest Arthur Gowers   1952–1960
   Born: 2 June 1880
   Appointed: 30 September 1952
   Died: 16 April 1966

Sir Malcolm Trustram Eve (Lord Silsoe)   1960–1969
   Born: 8 April 1894
   Appointed: 2 December 1960
   Died: 3 December 1976

Sir Robert Ian Bellinger   1969–1985
   Born: 10 March 1910
   Appointed: 8 April 1969

Sir Robin Danvers Penrose Gillett   1985–
   Born: 9 November 1925
   Appointed: 10 March 1985

PRELATE EMERITUS

The Right Reverend John William Charles Wand   1956–1977
(Bishop of London 1945–1956 and Canon Residentiary of St Paul's Cathedal 1956–1969)
   Born: 25 January 1885
   Died: 16 August 1977

SUB-DEANS

The Venerable Oswin Harvard Gibbs-Smith   1957–1961
*(Archdeacon of London and Canon Residentiary of St Paul's Cathedral 1948–1961
and Dean of Winchester 1961–1969)*
   Born: 15 November 1901
   Died: 26 September 1969

The Reverend Canon Archibald Frederic Hood   1961–1971
(Canon Residentiary of St Paul's Cathedral 1961–1969)
   Born: 12 December 1895
   Died: 26 January 1975

The Venerable George Henry Cassidy   1996–
(Archdeacon of London and Canon Residentiary of St Paul's Cathedral 1987–)
   Born: 17 October 1942

APPENDIX 2

The Knights and Dames Grand Cross of the Order

The following list of the Knights and Dames Grand Cross of the Order of the British Empire is complete to 31 December 1995.

1 KNIGHTS GRAND CROSS

The prefix of a naval, military or air force rank normally indicates that the Knight Grand Cross has been appointed to the military division of the Order. In certain instances, those with service ranks have been appointed to the civil division. These have been noted by the word *Civil* appearing before the date of appointment.

H.R.H. the Duke of Windsor *(1894–1972)*	4 June 1917
H.R.H. the Duke of Connaught *(1850–1942)*	4 June 1917
The Lord Cunliffe *(1855–1919)*	4 June 1917
The Viscount Gladstone *(1854–1930)*	4 June 1917
The Lord Emmott *(1858–1926)*	4 June 1917
The Lord Moulton *(1844–1921)*	4 June 1917
The Lord Sydenham of Combe *(1848–1933)*	4 June 1917
The Lord Strathclyde *(1853–1928)*	4 June 1917
The Honourable Sir Arthur Stanley *(1869–1947)*	4 June 1917
Sir Eric Campbell Geddes *(1875–1937)*	4 June 1917
Sir Alexander McDowell *(1855–1918)*	4 June 1917
Sir Arthur Pearson *(1866–1921)*	4 June 1917
The Viscount Sankey *(1866–1948)*	4 June 1917
The Lord Blanesburgh *(1861–1946)*	4 June 1917
The Viscount Chelmsford *(1868–1933)*	4 December 1917
The Marquess of Willingdon *(1866–1941)*	4 December 1917
H.E.H. the Nizam of Hyderabad *(1886–1967)*	4 December 1917
H.H. the Maharajah of Mysore *(1884–1940)*	4 December 1917
H.H. the Maharajah of Gwalior *(1876–1925)*	4 December 1917
Sir Thomas Dunlop *(1855–1938)*	1 January 1918
Sir William Henry Ellis *(1860–1945)*	1 January 1918
Sir Richard Charles Garton *(1857–1934)*	1 January 1918
Sir David Harrel *(1841–1939)*	1 January 1918
Sir Robert Arundell Hudson *(1864–1927)*	1 January 1918
The Viscount Lee of Fareham *(1868–1947)*	1 January 1918
The Lord Plender *(1861–1946)*	1 January 1918
General Sir Francis Reginald Wingate *(1861–1953)*	1 January 1918
H.H. the Maharajah of Jammu and Kashmir *(1850–1925)*	1 January 1918
H.H. the Maharajah of Jaipur *(1861–1922)*	1 January 1918
H.H. the Maharao of Kotah *(1873–1941)*	1 January 1918
Lieutenant Colonel H.H. the Maharajah of Patiala *(1891–1938)*	1 January 1918
The Earl of Liverpool *(1870–1941)*	3 June 1918
Sir Arthur David Brooks *(1864–1930)*	3 June 1918
Sir William Edward Garstin *(1849–1925)*	3 June 1918
Sir Charles Blair Gordon *(1869–1937)*	3 June 1918
The Earl of Plymouth *(1857–1923)*	3 June 1918
The Very Reverend Thomas Banks Strong *(1861–1944)*	3 June 1918
Lieutenant General Sir Herbert Scott Gould Miles *(1850–1926)*	3 June 1918
The Reverend Sir John Pentland Mahaffy *(1839–1919)*	21 June 1918
Sir Henry Crichton Sclater *(1855–1923)*	1 January 1919
Colonel Sir Edward Willis Duncan Ward *(1853–1928)*	*(Civil)* 8 January 1919

The Lord Raglan (*1857–1921*)   8 January 1919
Sir Walter Durnford (*1847–1926*)   8 January 1919
Sir Charles Edward Ellis (*1852–1937*)   8 January 1919
The Earl Peel (*1867–1937*)   8 January 1919
Lieutenant Colonel H.H. the Maharajah of Navanagar (*1872–1933*)   3 June 1919
Major General Sir Frederick Hugh Sykes (*1877–1954*)   26 August 1919
Sir Alexander Baird (*1849–1920*)   1 January 1920
The Viscount Chilston (*1851–1926*)   1 January 1920
Brigadier General Sir Alexander Gibb (*1872–1958*)   (*Civil*) 1 January 1920
Colonel Sir James Gildea (*1838–1920*)   (*Civil*) 1 January 1920
Sir Charles Harris (*1864–1943*)   1 January 1920
Sir Nathaniel Joseph Highmore (*1844–1924*)   1 January 1920
The Viscount Horne (*1871–1940*)   1 January 1920
The Lord Kindersley (*1871–1954*)   1 January 1920
Sir Harry Livesey (*1860–1932*)   1 January 1920
The Earl of Meath (*1841–1929*)   1 January 1920
Sir Thomas Munro (*1866–1923*)   1 January 1920
Sir John Denison-Pender (*1855–1929*)   1 January 1920
Sir Edward Aurelian Ridsdale (*1864–1923*)   1 January 1920
Sir Arthur Everett Shipley (*1861–1927*)   1 January 1920
Sir Henry Babington Smith (*1863–1923*)   1 January 1920
Sir Percy Elly Bates (*1879–1946*)   5 June 1920
Sir John Lorne MacLeod (*1873–1946*)   5 June 1920
Lieutenant Colonel Sir Thomas Bilbe Robinson (*1853–1939*)   (*Civil*) 5 June 1920
The Viscount Samuel (*1870–1963*)   11 June 1920
Sir Edward Owen Cox (*1866–1932*)   15 October 1920
Lieutenant General Sir Richard Cyril Byrne Haking (*1862–1945*)   1 January 1921
Major General H.H. the Maharajah of Bikaner (*1880–1943*)   1 January 1921
Major General the Earl of Scarborough (*1857–1945*)   12 February 1921
The Lord Rockley (*1865–1941*)   2 January 1922
Sir Charles Scott Sherrington (*1857–1952*)   2 January 1922
Sir Laming Worthington-Evans (*1868–1931*)   3 June 1922
Sir John Herbert Lewis (*1858–1933*)   19 October 1922
Sir Philip Albert Gustave David Sassoon (*1888–1939*)   19 October 1922
The Viscount St Davids (*1860–1938*)   19 October 1922
Admiral Sir Reginald Godfrey Otway Tupper (*1859–1945*)   28 December 1922
Lieutenant General Sir Charles Harington (*1872–1940*)   28 December 1922
Sir John Malcolm Fraser (*1878–1949*)   30 December 1922
Sir Harry Harling Lamb (*1857–1948*)   2 June 1923
Major General Sir Lee Oliver Fitzmaurice Stack (*1868–1924*)   (*Civil*) 2 June 1923
Sir William Guy Granet (*1867–1943*)   2 June 1923
Sir Francis Drummond Percy Chaplin (*1866–1933*)   2 June 1923
Admiral Sir Alexander Ludovic Duff (*1862–1933*)   3 June 1924
Sir Robert Donald (*1861–1933*)   3 June 1924
Sir Howard George Frank (*1871–1932*)   3 June 1924
Sir Mansfeldt de Cardonnel Findlay (*1861–1932*)   3 June 1924
Field Marshal the Viscount Plumer (*1857–1932*)   (*Civil*) 3 June 1924
Major General the Lord Cheylesmore (*1848–1925*)   (*Civil*) 3 June 1925
Sir Frederic George Kenyon (*1863–1952*)   3 June 1925
Sir John Cleverton Snell (*1869–1938*)   3 June 1925
Sir Hugh Clifford (*1866–1941*)   3 June 1925
Lieutenant General Sir George Mark Watson Macdonogh (*1865–1942*)   17 July 1925
Lieutenant General Sir Travers Edwards Clarke (*1871–1962*)   (*Civil*) 19 January 1926
Admiral Sir Frederic Edward Errington Brock (*1854–1929*)   5 June 1926
The Lord Islington (*1866–1936*)   5 June 1926
Sir William Warrender Mackenzie (*1860–1930*)   5 June 1926
The Lord Queenborough (*1861–1949*)   5 June 1926
Lieutenant Colonel the Viscount Templewood (*1880–1959*)   (*Civil*) 3 June 1927
Sir Henry Frank Heath (*1863–1946*)   3 June 1927
Sir Henry Strakosch (*1871–1943*)   3 June 1927

Sir Otto Ernst Niemeyer (*1883–1971*)	3 June 1927
Sir Richard Threlfall (*1861–1932*)	3 June 1927
The Lord Kennet (*1879–1960*)	3 June 1927
General the Earl of Cavan (*1865–1946*)	(*Civil*) 27 June 1927
The Lord Ebbisham (*1868–1943*)	27 September 1927
H.H. the Maharajah of Kapurthala (*1872–1949*)	29 November 1927
General Sir James Frederick Noel Birch (*1865–1939*)	9 December 1927
Sir John Dewrance (*1858–1937*)	4 June 1928
Brigadier General Sir Henry Percy Maybury (*1864–1943*)	4 June 1928
Sir William Grenfell Max-Muller (*1867–1945*)	4 June 1928
The Lord Phillimore (*1845–1929*)	7 August 1928
Brigadier General Sir William Thomas Horwood (*1868–1943*)	(*Civil*) 2 November 1928
Sir Arthur Henry Crosfield (*1865–1938*)	1 March 1929
Sir William McLintock (*1873–1947*)	1 March 1929
Sir William Symington McCormick (*1859–1930*)	1 March 1929
Sir Henry Robert Conway Dobbs (*1871–1934*)	1 March 1929
Air Vice-Marshal Sir Philip Woolcott Game (*1876–1961*)	1 March 1929
Sir Arthur McDougall Duckham (*1879–1932*)	3 June 1929
The Lord Maenan (*1854–1951*)	3 June 1929
Sir Beilby Francis Alston (*1863–1929*)	3 June 1929
The Viscount Monsell (*1881–1969*)	28 June 1929
Sir Harold Bowden (*1880–1960*)	28 June 1929
The Earl of Swinton (*1884–1972*)	28 June 1929
Admiral Sir Edward Eden Bradford (*1858–1935*)	1 January 1930
Sir Robert Gibson (*1864–1934*)	3 June 1932
Admiral Sir William Archibald Howard Kelly (*1873–1952*)	1 January 1934
Sir Alan Garrett Anderson (*1877–1952*)	4 June 1934
Nawab Malik Sir Umar Hayat Khan (*1874–1944*)	4 June 1934
The Lord Reith (*1889–1971*)	4 June 1934
General Sir Felix Fordati Ready (*1872–1940*)	3 June 1935
Sir George Newman (*1870–1948*)	3 June 1935
Sir Ibrahim Rahimtoola (*1862–1942*)	3 June 1935
Sir Stephen Henry Molyneux Killick (*1861–1938*)	27 September 1935
Sir Sidney Barton (*1874–1946*)	1 January 1936
Admiral Sir Frederic Charles Dreyer (*1878–1956*)	11 May 1937
General Sir Archibald Rice Cameron (*1870–1944*)	11 May 1937
H.H. the Nawab of Jaora (*1883–1947*)	11 May 1937
Sir Ernest John Strohmenger (*1873–1967*)	11 May 1937
Sir Andrew Rae Duncan (*1884–1952*)	1 January 1938
Sir Frank Edward Smith (*1879–1970*)	2 January 1939
Lieutenant Colonel Sir George Stewart Symes (*1882–1962*)	(*Civil*) 2 January 1939
H.H. the Maharajah of Morvi (*1876–1857*)	8 June 1939
The Viscount Hyndley (*1883–1963*)	8 June 1939
Engineer Vice Admiral Sir Harold Arthur Brown (*1878–1968*)	8 June 1939
Sir Thomas Robert Gardiner (*1883–1964*)	1 January 1941
Sir William Arthur Robinson (*1874–1950*)	1 January 1941
Colonel Sir Reginald Hugh Dorman-Smith (*1899–1977*)	(*Civil*) 12 February 1941
Field Marshal the Lord Wilson of Libya (*1881–1964*)	4 March 1941
The Viscount Nuffield (*1877–1963*)	12 June 1941
The Lord Rushcliffe (*1872–1949*)	12 June 1941
Air Chief Marshal Sir Frederick William Bowhill (*1880–1960*)	1 July 1941
H.H. the Maharajah of Patiala (*1913–1974*)	1 January 1942
Sir Henry Shanks Keith (*1852–1944*)	1 January 1942
The Lord Riverdale (*1873–1957*)	11 June 1942
Admiral Sir Charles James Colebrooke Little (*1882–1973*)	11 June 1942
General Sir William Platt (*1885–1975*)	1 January 1943
Air Chief Marshal Sir Edgar Rainey Ludlow-Hewitt (*1886–1973*)	1 January 1943
Colonel Sir William Charles Wright (*1876–1950*)	(*Civil*) 1 January 1943
Sir Henry Hallett Dale (*1875–1968*)	1 January 1943
H.H. The Prince of Berar (*1907–1970*)	1 January 1943

General Sir Thomas Albert Blamey (*1884–1951*)   28 May 1943
The Lord Salter (*1881–1975*)   1 January 1944
Admiral Sir Percy Lockhart Harman Noble (*1880–1955*)   1 January 1944
Sir George Allan Powell (*1878–1948*)   1 January 1944
Sir Cowasjee Jehangir (*1879–1962*)   1 January 1944
H.H. the Maharajah of Rajpipla (*1890–1951*)   1 January 1945
The Viscount Finlay (*1875–1945*)   1 January 1945
Air Chief Marshal Sir Christopher Lloyd Courtney (*1890–1976*)   1 January 1945
Sir James Lithgow (*1883–1952*)   1 January 1945
H.H. the Maharao of Kutch (*1885–1948*)   14 June 1945
Sir Ernest Arthur Gowers (*1880–1966*)   14 June 1945
H.H. the Maharajah of Tripura (*1908–1947*)   1 January 1946
Major General Sir John Kennedy (*1878–1948*)   (*Civil*) 1 January 1946
Admiral of the Fleet Sir James Fownes Somerville (*1882–1949*)   1 January 1946
Admiral Sir Charles Edward Kennedy-Purvis (*1884–1946*)   1 January 1946
Sir Edward Victor Appleton (*1892–1965*)   1 January 1946
Sir Thomas Dalmahoy Barlow (*1883–1964*)   1 January 1946
Sir Henry Leon French (*1883–1966*)   1 January 1946
Sir Maurice Gerald Holmes (*1885–1964*)   1 January 1946
Sir Harold Gibson Howitt (*1886–1969*)   1 January 1946
Sir Francis Vernon Thomson (*1881–1953*)   1 January 1946
Admiral Sir Arthur John Power (*1889–1960*)   1 January 1946
Lieutenant General Sir Alexander Hood (*1888–1980*)   1 January 1946
Lieutenant General Sir Wilfred Gordon Lindsell (*1884–1973*)   1 January 1946
Field Marshal the Viscount Slim (*1891–1970*)   1 January 1946
Air Marshal Sir Douglas Claude Strathern Evill (*1892–1971*)   1 January 1946
The Lord Iliffe (*1877–1960*)   13 June 1946
The Lord Alness (*1868–1955*)   13 June 1946
Sir Thomas Williams Phillips (*1883–1966*)   13 June 1946
Sir William Henry Peat (*1878–1959*)   13 June 1946
Major General Sir Hubert Jervoise Huddleston (*1880–1950*)   (*Civil*) 13 June 1946
Vice Admiral Sir Henry Bernard Hughes Rawlings (*1889–1962*)   13 June 1946
Nawab Sir Muhammad Ahmad Sa'id Khan of Chhatari (*1888–1982*)   13 June 1946
Major General Sir Hubert Elvin Rance (*1898–1974*)   13 August 1946
Sir William Crawford Currie (*1884–1961*)   1 January 1947
Sir George Bailey Sansom (*1883–1963*)   1 January 1947
Sir Ellice Victor Sassoon (*1881–1961*)   1 January 1947
Admiral Sir Geoffrey Layton (*1884–1964*)   1 January 1947
Sir Frederick Joseph West (*1872–1959*)   1 January 1947
Lieutenant Colonel Sir John Robert Chancellor (*1870–1952*)   (*Civil*) 12 June 1947
The Viscount Radcliffe (*1899–1977*)   14 August 1947
Sir Edward Mellanby (*1884–1955*)   1 January 1948
Air Chief Marshal Sir Alfred Guy Roland Garrod (*1891–1963*)   1 January 1948
General Sir Alexander Frank Philip Christison (*1893–1993*)   1 January 1948
Sir Eubule John Waddington (*1890–1957*)   10 June 1948
Sir Reginald Wildig Allen Leeper (*1888–1968*)   10 June 1948
Sir William Wilson Jameson (*1885–1962*)   1 January 1949
Sir Walter Hamilton Moberly (*1881–1974*)   9 June 1949
Sir Robert George Howe (*1893–1981*)   9 June 1949
General The Lord Robertson of Oakridge (*1896–1974*)   9 June 1949
Admiral Sir Robert Lindsay Burnett (*1887–1959*)   2 January 1950
The Earl of Ilchester (*1874–1959*)   2 January 1950
The Lord Silsoe (*1894–1976*)   2 January 1950
Sir Donald St Clair Gainer (*1891–1966*)   2 January 1950
Sir Kenneth Dugald Stewart (*1882–1972*)   8 June 1950
Air Chief Marshal the Honourable Sir Ralph Alexander Cochrane (*1895–1977*)   8 June 1950
The Lord Porter (*1877–1956*)   1 January 1951
Admiral Sir Eric James Patrick Brind (*1892–1963*)   1 January 1951
The Earl of Crawford and Balcarres (*1900–1975*)   7 June 1951
General Sir Neil Methuen Ritchie (*1897–1983*)   7 June 1951

Air Chief Marshal Sir Leslie Norman Hollinghurst (*1895–1971*)	1 January 1952
Sir William Henry Bradshaw Mack (*1894–1974*)	5 June 1952
Lieutenant Colonel The Lord Brabazon of Tara (*1884–1964*)	(*Civil*) 1 January 1953
Admiral Sir Cecil Halliday Jepson Harcourt (*1892–1959*)	1 January 1953
The Earl of Limerick (*1888–1967*)	1 January 1953
Sir Alvary Douglas Frederick Gascoigne (*1893–1970*)	1 January 1953
Sir Charles Campbell Woolley (*1893–1981*)	1 January 1953
H.R.H. the Duke of Edinburgh (*1921–*)	25 March 1953
Sir Alexander Knox Helm (*1893–1964*)	1 June 1953
Sir Hilary Rudolph Robert Blood (*1893–1967*)	1 June 1953
Admiral the Honourable Sir Guy Herbrand Edward Russell (*1898–1977*)	1 June 1953
General Sir Frank Ernest Wallace Simpson (*1899–1986*)	1 June 1953
Air Chief Marshal Sir Hugh Pughe Lloyd (*1895–1981*)	1 June 1953
The Lord Llewellin (*1893–1957*)	1 August 1953
Sir Gilbert McCall Rennie (*1895–1981*)	1 January 1954
Air Chief Marshal Sir John Wakeling Baker (*1897–1978*)	1 January 1954
The Lord Aberdare (*1885–1957*)	10 June 1954
Air Chief Marshal Sir John Whitworth Jones (*1896–1981*)	10 June 1954
Sir Noel Vansittart Bowater (*1892–1984*)	9 November 1954
The Viscount Esher (*1881–1963*)	1 January 1955
Sir John Monro Troutbeck (*1894–1971*)	1 January 1955
Admiral Sir Geoffrey Nigel Oliver (*1898–1980*)	1 January 1955
The Lord Rootes (*1894–1964*)	9 June 1955
The Earl de la Warr (*1900–1976*)	2 January 1956
Sir John Morison (*1893–1958*)	2 January 1956
Sir Christopher Frederick Ashton Warner (*1895–1957*)	2 January 1956
General Sir Miles Christopher Dempsey (*1896–1969*)	2 January 1956
The Lord Erskine of Rerrick (*1893–1980*)	31 May 1956
General Sir John Francis Martin Whiteley (*1896–1970*)	31 May 1956
Sir Archibald Finlayson Forbes (*1903–1989*)	1 January 1957
Sir Geoffrey Harrington Thompson (*1898–1967*)	1 January 1957
Admiral Sir Charles Thomas Mark Pizey (*1899–1993*)	1 January 1957
Air Chief Marshal Sir Francis Joseph Fogarty (*1899–1973*)	1 January 1957
Sir Francis Edward Evans (*1897–1983*)	13 June 1957
General Sir Nevil Charles Dowell Brownjohn (*1897–1973*)	13 June 1957
General Sir Charles Frederic Keightley (*1901–1974*)	13 June 1957
The Earl of Dalhousie (*1914–*)	23 July 1957
The Lord Hailes (*1901–1974*)	25 September 1957
Sir Harold Edgar Yarrow (*1884–1962*)	1 January 1958
Air Chief Marshal Sir James Donald Innes Hardman (*1899–1982*)	1 January 1958
The Lord Citrine (*1887–1983*)	12 June 1958
Sir Denis Henry Truscott (*1908–*)	8 November 1958
The Viscount Kemsley (*1883–1968*)	1 January 1959
Sir John Balfour (*1894–1983*)	1 January 1959
Admiral Sir Frederick Robertson Parham (*1901–1991*)	1 January 1959
Sir William Palmer (*1883–1964*)	13 June 1959
Air Chief Marshal Sir Claude Bernard Raymond Pelly (*1902–1972*)	13 June 1959
Admiral Sir Gerald Vaughan Gladstone (*1901–1978*)	1 January 1960
Lieutenant General Sir Edward Ian Claud Jacob (*1899–1993*)	1 January 1960
Sir William Ivo Mallet (*1900–1988*)	1 January 1960
General Sir Cecil Stanway Sugden (*1903–1963*)	11 June 1960
The Lord Cottesloe (*1900–1994*)	11 June 1960
Air Chief Marshal the Earl of Bandon (*1904–1979*)	31 December 1960
Sir Ellis Hunter (*1892–1961*)	31 December 1960
Sir William Henry Tucker Luce (*1907–1977*)	31 December 1960
Sir Reginald James Bowker (*1901–1983*)	10 June 1961
Sir Hector James Wright Hetherington (*1888–1965*)	1 January 1962
Sir Kenneth William Blackburne (*1907–1980*)	1 January 1962
Admiral Sir Wilfrid John Wentworth Woods (*1906–1975*)	1 January 1963
Air Chief Marshal Sir Walter Merton (*1905–1986*)	1 January 1963

Sir Colville Montgomery Deverell (*1907–1995*)	1 January 1963
General Sir Harold English Pyman (*1908–1971*)	8 June 1963
The Earl of Selkirk (*1906–1995*)	17 December 1963
General Sir Roderick William McLeod (*1905–1986*)	1 January 1964
Sir Arthur Frederic Brownlow Fforde (*1900–1985*)	13 June 1964
Sir Clement James Harman (*1894–1975*)	13 June 1964
Admiral Sir Royston Hollis Wright (*1908–1977*)	13 June 1964
Sir George Peter Labouchere (*1905–*)	13 June 1964
Air Chief Marshal Sir Walter Graemes Cheshire (*1907–1978*)	1 January 1965
Lieutenant Colonel Sir Alexander Robert Gisborne Gordon (*1882–1967*)	(*Civil*) 1 January 1965
Sir James Miller (*1905–1977*)	12 June 1965
Lieutenant General Sir William Pasfield Oliver (*1901–1981*)	(*Civil*) 12 June 1965
General Sir Robert Napier Herbert Campbell Bray (*1903–1983*)	1 January 1966
Sir Hugh Southern Stephenson (*1906–1972*)	1 January 1966
Air Chief Marshal Sir Alfred Earle (*1907–1990*)	1 January 1966
Admiral Sir John Graham Hamilton (*1910–1994*)	11 June 1966
Sir Jonathan Lionel Percy Denny (*1897–1985*)	11 November 1966
The Lord O'Brien of Lothbury (*1908–1995*)	1 January 1967
Sir Robert Ian Bellinger (*1910–*)	10 June 1967
General Sir John D'Arcy Anderson (*1908–1988*)	10 June 1967
The Duke of Norfolk (*1908–1975*)	1 January 1968
Sir Gilbert Samuel Inglefield (*1909–1991*)	8 June 1968
Admiral Sir Nigel Stuart Henderson (*1909–1993*)	8 June 1968
Lieutenant General Sir Charles Henry Gairdner (*1898–1983*)	1 January 1969
General Sir Kenneth Thomas Darling (*1909–*)	1 January 1969
Air Chief Marshal Sir David John Pryer Lee (*1912–*)	1 January 1969
Sir Louis Halle Gluckstein (*1897–1979*)	14 June 1969
Sir Arthur Frank Kirby (*1899–1983*)	14 June 1969
Sir Arnold Charles Trinder (*1906–1989*)	14 June 1969
The Lord Thompson of Fleet (*1894–1976*)	1 January 1970
Sir Ian Frank Bowater (*1904–1982*)	13 June 1970
The Lord Benson (*1909–1995*)	1 January 1971
Lieutenant General Sir Ian Henry Freeland (*1912–1979*)	12 June 1971
Sir Peter Malden Studd (*1916–*)	12 June 1971
Sir Henry Frank Harding Jones (*1906–1987*)	1 January 1972
Sir Hamilton Edward de Coucey Howard (*1915–*)	3 June 1972
The Lord Martonmere (*1907–1989*)	1 January 1973
The Lord Cole (*1906–1979*)	2 June 1973
The Lord Mais (*1911–1993*)	2 June 1973
The Lord Shawcross (*1902–*)	1 January 1974
Sir Hugh Walter Kingwell Wontner (*1908–1992*)	15 June 1974
Sir John Ross Marshall (*1912–1988*)	4 October 1974
Sir Henry Murray Fox (*1912–*)	16 October 1974
The Lord Rothschild (*1910–1990*)	1 January 1975
Admiral Sir Derek Leslie Empson (*1918–*)	14 June 1975
General Sir William Godfrey Fothergill Jackson (*1917–*)	14 June 1975
Air Chief Marshal Sir Denis Graham Smallwood (*1918–*)	14 June 1975
Sir Lindsay Roberts Ring (*1914–*)	15 October 1975
Sir Ronald George Leach (*1907–*)	1 January 1976
General Sir Richard Erskine Ward (*1917–1989*)	1 January 1976
The Lord MacLehose of Beoch (*1917–*)	13 June 1976
Sir Robin Danvers Penrose Gillett (*1925–*)	12 October 1976
Sir Robert Mark (*1917–*)	31 December 1976
Admiral Sir Peter White (*1919–*)	31 December 1976
Air Commodore The Honourable Sir Peter Beckford Rutgers Vanneck (*1922–*)	
	(*Civil*) 18 October 1977
The Honourable Sir Ronald Keith Davison (*1920–*)	11 February 1978
Air Chief Marshal Sir Peter de Lacey Le Cheminant (*1920–*)	3 June 1978
Sir Kenneth Russell Cork (*1913–1991*)	11 October 1978
The Honourable Sir Yuet-Keung Kan (*1913–*)	16 June 1979

Sir Peter Drury Haggerston Gadsden (*1929–*)	17 October 1979
The Earl St Aldwyn (*1912–1992*)	31 December 1979
General Sir William Gerald Hugh Beach (*1923–*)	31 December 1979
Colonel Sir Ronald Lawrence Gardner-Thorpe (*1917–1991*)	(*Civil*) 14 October 1980
Air Chief Marshal Sir Robert William George Freer (*1923–*)	13 June 1981
Sir Christopher Leaver (*1937–*)	21 October 1981
Sir Francis Aimé Vallat (*1912–*)	31 December 1981
Admiral Sir Anthony Storrs Morton (*1923–*)	31 December 1981
General Sir Anthony Farrar-Hockley (*1924–*)	31 December 1981
Sir Anthony Stuart Jolliffe (*1938–*)	6 October 1982
Admiral of the Fleet The Lord Fieldhouse (*1928–1992*)	11 October 1982
Admiral Sir William Thomas Pillar (*1924–*)	11 June 1983
Air Chief Marshal Sir John Gingell (*1925–*)	31 December 1983
Sir Alan Towers Traill (*1935–*)	9 October 1984
General Sir Frank Edward Kitson (*1926–*)	31 December 1984
Sir William Allan Davis (*1921–*)	7 October 1985
Sir David Kenneth Rowe-Ham (*1935–*)	7 October 1986
Sir Kenneth Leslie Newman (*1926–*)	13 June 1987
The Lord Plowden (*1907–*)	31 June 1987
Sir Greville Douglas Spratt (*1927–*)	7 October 1987
Sir Joshua Abraham Hassan (*1915–*)	31 December 1987
Sir Kenneth Ernest Berrill (*1920–*)	11 June 1988
Sir Christopher Collett (*1931–*)	6 October 1988
Sir Sze-yuen Chung (*1917–*)	31 December 1988
Air Chief Marshal Sir David Harcourt-Smith (*1931–*)	31 December 1988
Sir Johann Thomas Eichelbaum (*1931–*)	6 February 1989
Admiral Sir John Forster Woodward (*1932–*)	17 June 1989
Sir Hugh Charles Philip Bidwell (*1934–*)	10 October 1989
Sir Tasker Watkins (*1918–*)	30 December 1989
Field Marshal Sir Richard Frederick Vincent (*1931–*)	30 December 1989
Sir Alexander Michael Graham (*1938–*)	9 October 1990
Admiral Sir John Jeremy Black (*1932–*)	15 June 1991
Air Chief Marshal Sir Patrick Bardon Hine (*1932–*)	29 June 1991
Sir Brian Garton Jenkins (*1935–*)	8 October 1991
Air Chief Marshal Sir Anthony Gerald Skingsley (*1933–*)	31 December 1991
Sir Francis McWilliams (*1926–*)	5 October 1992
Admiral Sir Kenneth John Eaton (*1934–*)	31 December 1993

II DAMES GRAND CROSS

With the exceptions of Dame Emma Maud McCarthy, Dame Ethel Hope Becher and Dame Sidney Jane Browne, all Dames Grand Cross have been appointed to the Civil Division of the Order.

H.M. Queen Mary (*1867–1953*)	4 June 1917
Dame Louise Margaret Leila Wemyss (Lady) Paget (*1881–1958*)	4 June 1917
The Honourable Dame Annie Allen (Lady) Lawley (*1863–1944*)	4 June 1917
Dame Flora Ann (Lady) Reid (*1867–1950*)	4 June 1917
Dame Katherine Furse (*1875–1952*)	4 June 1917
Frances Charlotte, Viscountess Chelmsford (*1869–1957*)	4 December 1917
Margaret, Baroness Ampthill (*1874–1957*)	1 January 1918
H.M. Queen Alexandra (*1881–1925*)	1 January 1918
Dame Edith Isobel Benyon (*1857–1919*)	1 January 1918
Dame Aimée Evelyn Dawson (*1864–1946*)	1 January 1918
Violet Hermione, Duchess of Montrose (*1854–1940*)	1 January 1918
Dame Mary Elizabeth (Lady) Hudson (formerly Viscountess Northcliffe) (*1868–1963*)	
	1 January 1918
H.H. the Begum of Bhopal (*1858–1930*)	1 January 1918

Annette Louise, Countess of Liverpool (*1875–1948*)	1 January 1918
Dame Emma Maud McCarthy (*1858–1949*)	(*Military*) 3 June 1918
Helen Hermione, Viscountess Novar (*1865–1941*)	3 June 1918
H.R.H. Princess Christian (*1846–1923*)	3 June 1918
H.R.H. Princess Louise, Duchess of Argyll (*1848–1939*)	3 June 1918
H.H. Princess Helena Victoria (*1870–1948*)	3 June 1918
Dame Ethel Hope Becher (*1867–1948*)	(*Military*) 3 June 1918
Mary Ethel, Viscountess Harcourt (*1873–1961*)	3 June 1918
Dame Agnes Weston (*1840–1918*)	3 June 1918
Charlotte Josephine, Marchioness of Winchester (*1851 or 1852–1924*)	3 June 1918
Dame Sidney Jane Browne (*1850–1941*)	(*Military*) 1 January 1919
H.R.H. Princess Beatrice (*1857–1944*)	8 January 1919
H.H. Princess Marie Louise (*1872–1956*)	8 January 1919
Adeline Marie, Duchess of Bedford (*1852–1920*)	8 January 1919
Mildred, Countess of Buxton (*1866–1955*)	8 January 1919
Dame Sarah Ann Swift (*1854–1937*)	8 January 1919
Beatrix Frances Beauclerk, Lady Osborne (*1877–1953*)	8 January 1919
Mabell Frances Elizabeth, Countess of Airlie (*1866–1956*)	1 January 1920
Maud Evelyn, Marchioness of Lansdowne (*1851–1932*)	1 January 1920
Alice Edith, Countess of Reading (*1866–1930*)	1 January 1920
Dame Annie Elizabeth de Sausmarez (*1896–1947*)	1 January 1920
Dame Margaret Lloyd George (*1864–1941*)	16 August 1920
Grace Elvina, Marchioness Curzon of Kedleston (*1877–1958*)	2 January 1922
Dame Mary Ethel Hughes (*1874–1958*)	2 January 1922
Marie Adelaide, Marchioness of Willingdon (*1875–1960*)	3 June 1924
Dame Ellen Alice Carew (Ellen Terry) (*1848–1928*)	1 January 1925
Dame Millicent Garrett Fawcett (*1847–1929*)	1 January 1925
Dame Ivy Muriel Chamberlain (*1878–1941*)	1 December 1925
Rachel Cecily, Baroness Forster (*1868–1962*)	1 January 1926
Dame Christina Allen Massey (*1882–1932*)	5 June 1926
H.R.H. The Princess Royal (*1897–1965*)	3 June 1927
Dame Nellie Melba (*1861–1931*)	3 June 1927
H.M. Queen Elizabeth the Queen Mother (*1900–*)	27 June 1927
Dame Edith Sophy Lyttleton (*1864 or 1865–1948*)	1 March 1929
Dame Helen Charlotte Isabella Gwynne-Vaughan (*1879–1967*)	3 June 1929
Ishbel Maria, Marchioness of Aberdeen and Temair (*1857–1939*)	1 January 1931
Annie, Viscountess Cowdray (*1860–1932*)	1 January 1932
Olave, Baroness Baden-Powell (*1889–1977*)	3 June 1932
H.R.H. Princess Alice, Duchess of Gloucester (*1901–*)	11 May 1937
H.R.H. Princess Marina, Duchess of Kent (*1906–1968*)	11 May 1937
H.R.H. Princess Alice, Countess of Athlone (*1883–1981*)	11 May 1937
Dame Enid Muriel Lyons (*1897–1981*)	11 May 1937
Lucy, Countess Baldwin of Bewdley (*1869–1945*)	28 May 1937
Irene Frances Adza, Marchioness of Carisbrooke (*1890–1956*)	9 June 1938
Stella, Marchioness of Reading (Baroness Swanborough) (*1894–1971*)	8 June 1944
Clementine, Baroness Spencer-Churchill (*1885–1977*)	13 June 1946
Dame Isobel (Lady) Cripps (*1891–1979*)	13 June 1946
Edwina, Countess Mountbatten of Burma (*1901–1960*)	14 August 1947
Dame Beryl Oliver (*1882–1972*)	1 January 1948
Gertrude Mary, Baroness Denman (*1884–1954*)	1 January 1951
Barbara, Baroness Freyberg (*1887–1973*)	1 January 1953
Margaret Diana, Countess Alexander of Tunis (*1905–1977*)	1 January 1954
Dame Pattie Maie Menzies (*1899–1995*)	1 January 1954
Angela Olivia, Countess of Limerick (*1897–1981*)	10 June 1954
The Baroness Horsbrugh (*1889–1969*)	18 October 1954
Dame Dehra Kerr Parker (*1888–1963*)	13 June 1957
The Baroness Sharp (*1903–1985*)	10 June 1961
Lady Dorothy Evelyn Macmillan (*1900–1966*)	10 February 1964
Dame Dorothy Mary Donaldson (*1921–*)	17 October 1983

III HONORARY KNIGHTS AND DAMES GRAND CROSS

Afghanistan

H.M. Queen Shah Khanum	13 March 1928

Argentina

Don Marcelo Torcuato de Alvear	20 September 1922
Don Angel Gallardo	19 February 1926
Admiral Don Manuel Domecq García	19 February 1926
General Agustín Justo	19 February 1926
Don Manuel Augusto Montes de Oca	19 February 1926
Don José Evaristo de Uriburu	24 March 1931
Don Guillermo Eduardo	7 February 1933
Don Manuel Esteban Malbrán	7 February 1933
Don Julio Argentino Roca	7 February 1933
Arturo Frondizi	22 March 1962

Austria

Josef Krainer	5 May 1969
Johann Lechner	5 May 1969
Alfred Maleta	5 May 1969
Bruno Marek	5 May 1969
Eduard Wallnöfer	5 May 1969
Hermann Withalm	5 May 1969

Bahrain

Sayed Mahmood Ahmed al Alawi	10 April 1984
Tariq Abdulrahman Almoayed	10 April 1984
Shaikh Mohamed al Khalifa	10 April 1984
Yousuf Ahmed al Shirawi	10 April 1984

Belgium

Jules Renkin	27 February 1918
Adolphe Eugène Henri Jean Max	20 January 1921
Camille Huysmans	24 June 1927
Philippe van Isacker	29 June 1935
Baron Emile Ernest de Cartier de Marchienne	16 November 1937
Pierre Ryckmans	8 June 1942
Achille van Acker	9 May 1966
Camille Gutt	9 May 1966
Paul Struye	9 May 1966

Bolivia

General Don Carlos Blanco	19 February 1931

Brazil

A. da Fontoura Xavier	4 June 1919
Raul Régis de Oliveira	5 July 1930
Getulio Vargas	8 March 1931
João Neves da Fontoura	14 January 1947
Juscelino Kubitschek	11 January 1956
João Belchior Marques Goulart	15 March 1962
Gilberto de Mello Freyre	3 February 1971
Celso da Rocha Miranda	3 February 1971
Ramiro Elysio Saraiva Guerreiro	4 May 1976

Brunei

Pehun Dato Haji Abdul Aziz	3 November 1992

Chile

Don Agustín Edwards	19 February 1926
Don Jorge Matte	19 February 1926
Don Carlos Ibáñez del Campo	22 February 1931
Jorge Alessandri Rodriguez	2 March 1962
Salvador Allende Gossens	11 November 1968
Osvaldo Illanes Benitez	11 November 1968
Hector Valenzuela Valderrana	11 November 1968
Tulio Marambio Marchant	11 November 1968

Cuba

Major General Mario García-Menocal	3 November 1921

Czechoslovakia

Edvard Beneš	22 October 1923

Denmark

Hans Niels Andersen	14 January 1919
Vice Admiral Anton Ferdinand Mazanti	11 February 1921
Lieutenant General Ellis Wolff	11 February 1921
Fin Lund	23 November 1939
Ole Bjørn Kraft	8 May 1951
Nils Thomas Svenningsen	21 February 1957
Anders Ejnar Andersen	16 May 1979
Jørgen Elkjaer-Larsen	16 May 1979

Egypt

Amin Pasha Osman	19 November 1937

Ethiopia

Ras Kassa Hailou	30 October 1930
H.I.H. Crown Prince Merd Azmerd Azmatch Asfa Wossen Haile Selassie	14 January 1932

Finland

Field Marshal Carl Gustav Emil, Baron Mannerheim	12 April 1938
Ralf Johan Gustaf Törngren	8 May 1961
Teuro Ensio Aura	24 May 1976
Veikko Kullervo Helle	24 May 1976
Martti Juhani Miettunen	24 May 1976

France

Sir Basil Zaharoff	14 March 1918
Albert Claveille	8 June 1918
Louis Loucheur	8 June 1918
Georges Pallain	8 June 1918
H.I.M. Empress Eugénie	24 February 1919
Victor Boret	1 May 1919
Paul Bignon	18 June 1919
Baron Edouard Alphonse James Rothschild	9 August 1919
Stéphane Dervillé	9 August 1919
William Martin	10 November 1919
Fernand Gérôme Urbain Raux	15 November 1920
Fernand David	25 February 1926
André Victor Laurent-Eynac	10 October 1930
Alexis Saint-Léger	19 July 1938
Général Alphonse Joseph Georges	9 December 1939
Marquis Louis de Vogüé	6 August 1937
Général Joseph Vuillemin	1 June 1940
Jean Monnet	29 August 1946

France (*continued*)

Général d'Armée Paul Henri Romuald Ely	8 April 1957
Louis Joxe	8 April 1957
Général d'Armée Henri Zeller	8 April 1957
Charles Corbin	14 December 1966
René Pleven	15 May 1972
Général d'Armée Aérienne François Louis Maurin	15 May 1972
Michel Debré	15 May 1972
Wilfrid-Siegfried Baumgartner	7 October 1976
Robert Badinter	23 October 1984
Jacques Chirac	9 June 1992
Jacques Michel Pierre Delmas	9 June 1992
Roland Louis Lern Dumas	9 June 1992

Germany

Felix von Eckardt	20 October 1958
Albert Hilger van Scherpenberg	20 October 1958
Kai-Uwe von Hassel	18 May 1965
Hermann Höcherl	18 May 1965
Ludger Wilhelm Franz Josef Westrick	18 May 1965
Klaus Bölling	22 May 1978
Peter Hermes	22 May 1978
Manfred Schüler	22 May 1978
Günther Wilhelm van Well	22 May 1978
Hans-Jürgen Wischnewski	22 May 1978
Hans-Dietrich Genscher	1 July 1986
Frau Ursula Albring	19 October 1992
Friedrich Bohl	19 October 1992
Pieter Kastrup	19 October 1992
Hans Werner Lautenschlager	19 October 1992
Helmut Schäfer	19 October 1992

Greece

Count Alexandre Mercati	26 November 1934
Field Marshal Alexander Papagos	15 March 1941
Lieutenant General Constantine Dovas	9 July 1963
Paul Leloudas	9 July 1963

Iceland

Guðmundur Benediktsson	25 June 1990

Iran

Lieutenant General Ahmad Vossough	2 March 1961
Manoutchehr Eghbal	21 March 1972

Iraq

H.R.H. Zeid ibn Hussein	19 May 1920
H.H. Saiyid Abdul Rahman Effendi Al Gailani, Naquib of Baghdad	1 August 1921
H.R.H. Feisal, Emir of the Hejaz and Nejd	14 May 1932

Italy

Don Prospero Colonna, Prince of Sonnino	23 September 1918
Raffaele Salvatore de Cornè	3 March 1919
H.R.H. The Duchess of Aosta	20 August 1919
Marquis Camillo Eugenio Garroni	23 August 1921
Prince Ludovico Spada Veralli Potenziani	11 June 1928
Antonio Chiaramante Bordonaro	20 March 1930
Balbino Giuliano	20 March 1930
Giuseppe, Conte di Misurata Volpi	11 November 1939

Italy (continued)

Adolfo Alessandrini	13 May 1958
Cristoforo Fracassi di Torre Rossano	13 May 1958
Giuseppe Cappi	29 April 1961
Giovanni Leone	29 April 1961
Cesare Merzagora	29 April 1961
Attilio Piccioni	29 April 1961
Signora Leonilde Iotti	14 October 1980
Amadei Leonetto	14 October 1980
Lelio Giuseppe Ernesto Lagorio	14 October 1980
Virginio Rognoni	14 October 1980
Arnaldo Squillante	14 October 1980

Japan

Viscount Shimpei Goto	24 June 1918
H.H. Prince Iyesato Tokugawa	24 June 1918
Count Sutemi Chinda	9 May 1921
Admiral Sojiro Tochinai	12 April 1922
Lieutenant General Hanzo Yamanashi	12 April 1922
H.H. Prince Ri Gin	30 September 1927
H.I.H. Princess Chichibu	23 July 1962
H.I.H. Prince Hitachi	7 May 1975
Ichitaro Ide	7 May 1975
Kenzo Kono	7 May 1975
Shigesaburo Maeo	7 May 1975
Tomokazu Murukami	7 May 1975
Mitsunori Ueki	7 May 1975

Jordan

H.H. Sherif Emir Abdulla ibn Hussein	11 March 1920
Field Marshal Habis Al Majali	19 July 1966
Sharif Abdulhamid Sharaf	19 July 1966
Hatem Zubi	19 July 1966
Leila A. Sharaf	26 March 1984
Suleiman Attallah Arar	26 March 1984
Taher N. Masri	26 March 1984
H.H. Lieutenant General Zeid Shakar	26 March 1984

Liberia

Stephen Allen Tolbert	10 July 1962
Ahamadu Zwannah	10 July 1962

Libya

H.M. King Mohammad Idris el Mahdi el Senussi	30 April 1954

Luxembourg

Joseph Bech	1 December 1958
Bernard Berg	8 November 1976
René van den Bulcke	8 November 1976
Emile Henri Kriepe	8 November 1976
Marcel Mart	8 November 1976
Joseph Wohlfart	8 November 1976

Malaysia

H.H. the Sultan of Johore	3 June 1935

Mexico

Adolfo López Mateos	21 October 1964
Alfonso Guzmán Neyra	3 April 1973
Almirante Luis M. Bravo Carrera	24 February 1975

Mexico (continued)

Euquerio Guerrero López	24 February 1975
Carlos Sansores Pérez	24 February 1975
José López-Portillo	24 February 1975
José Campillo Sainz	24 February 1975
Enrique Olivares Santana	3 April 1975
Héctor Hernández	11 June 1985
Jesús Silva-Herzog	11 June 1985
Antonio Riva Palacio	11 June 1985

Monaco

H.S.H. Prince Louis II	16 June 1947

Montenegro

Eugene Popovitch	16 April 1918

Morocco

Dey Ould Sidi Baba	27 October 1980
General Ahmed Dlimi	27 October 1980
Ahmed Osman	27 October 1980
Moulay Ahmed Alaoui	14 February 1987

Nepal

General Baber Shumsher Jang Bahadur Rana	19 December 1919
General Padma Shumsher Jang Bahadur Rana	8 March 1920
General Padma Bahadur Shumsher Jang Bahadur Rana	30 May 1934
Lieutenant General Mohum Shumsher Bahadur Rana	1 July 1937
Field Marshal Kaiser Shumsher Jang Bahadur Rana	29 April 1937
General Shanker Shumsher Jang Bahadur Rana	16 November 1949
H.R.H. Prince Himalaya Bir Bikram Shah Deva	8 May 1956
Narapratap Thapa	17 October 1960
Jagdish Shumsher Jung Bahadur Rana	18 November 1980
Lokendra Bahadur Chand	17 February 1986
Ranadir Subba	17 February 1986

Netherlands

Jonkheer Dirk Jan de Geer	11 June 1929
Jonkheer Alidius Warmoldus Lambertus Tjarda van Starkenborgh Stachouwer	
	3 February 1942
H.R.H. Prince Bernhard	10 January 1946
Dirk Uipko Stikker	21 November 1950
Pieter Sjoerds Gerbrandy	12 March 1958
Jozef Maria Laurens Theo Cals	25 March 1958
Ivo Samkalden	25 March 1958
Cornelis Staf	25 March 1958
Antonius Arnold Marie Struycken	25 March 1958
Vice Admiral Eric Roest	16 November 1982

Nigeria

H.H. The Sultan of Sokoto	1 June 1953

Norway

Admiral Karl Friedrich Griffin Dawes	22 June 1920
Andreas Tostrup Urbye	22 November 1929
Rasmus Ingvald Berentson	24 June 1955

Oman

H.H. Sayyid Fad bin Mahmoud al Said	16 March 1982
H.H. Sayyid Faisal bin Ali al Said	16 March 1982
Qais Abdul Munim Al Zawawi	16 March 1982

Panama

Colonel José Antonio Remón Cantera   29 November 1953

Peru

Don Augusto Leguía   12 November 1921
Don Luis M. Sánchez Cerro   11 February 1931
Manuel Prado   3 April 1957
Don Ricardo Rivera Schreiber   21 March 1962

Poland

Ignacy Paderewski   3 June 1925
General Wladyslaw Sikorski   15 March 1940
Count Edward Racyzinski   16 December 1991

Portugal

Affonso Costa   18 October 1917
Manuel Teixeira-Gomes   18 October 1917
Augusto Soares   18 October 1917
Alfredo Augusto Freire de Andrade   9 March 1920
José Bernadino Gonsalves Teixeira   9 March 1920
António Maria da Silva   5 October 1923
Don José Bacelar Bebiano   6 June 1929
António Oscar de Fragoso Carmona   25 April 1931
Francisco José Vieira Machado   1 June 1940
Luis Teixiera de Sampaio   1 June 1940
Eduardo Manuel Machado Bastos   25 March 1958
Rui Manuel de Medeiros D'Espiney Patricío   5 June 1973
Fernando Monteiro do Amaral   25 March 1985
Eduardo Ambar   25 March 1985
João de sá Coutinho   25 March 1985
Rui Manuel Parente Chancerelle de Machete   25 March 1985
Maria Manuela Aguiar Dias Moreira   25 March 1985
General Carlos Manuel Leme   27 April 1993
António Maria Pereira   27 April 1993

Qatar

Hassan Kamel   12 November 1985
Shaikh Ahmad bin Saif Al Thani   12 November 1985

Russia

Marshal Alexander Mikhailovich Vassilevsky   19 January 1944

Saudi Arabia

H.R.H. Emir Ali of the Hedjaz   11 March 1920
H.R.H. the Emir of the Hejaz and Nejd (later H.M. King Abdul Aziz)   14 May 1932
H.R.H. Prince Saud ibn Abdul Aziz (later H.M. King Saud)   20 June 1935
Shaikh Faisal Alhegelan   24 March 1987
Hisham M. Nazer   24 March 1987
Abdulaziz Al Zamil   24 March 1987

Spain

Don Juan Antonio Barranco Gallardo   17 October 1988
Don José Rodríguez de la Borbolla Camoyan   17 October 1988
Don José Federico de Carvajal y Pérez   17 October 1988
Don Felix Pons Irazasabal   17 October 1988
Don Felipe González Márquez   17 October 1988
Don Jordi Pujol   17 October 1988

Sudan

Bimbashi Mohammed Effendi Mustafa Abdulla   5 December 1931

Sweden

Leif Axel Lorentz Belfrage   8 June 1956

Thailand

H.R.H. Prince Devawongse Varophrakar   3 October 1918
H.H. Prince Fraidos Prabandh   5 January 1926
H.H. Prince Devawongse Varodaya   5 January 1926
Captain Luang Duamrong Navasvasti   27 December 1940
Air Chief Marshal Dawee Chullasapya   10 February 1972
Police General Prasert Rujirawongse   10 February 1972

Tonga

H.M. Queen Salote Tupou III   12 October 1945

Turkey

Feridun Cemal Erkin   1 November 1967
Talat Halman   18 October 1971
Ferit Melen   18 October 1971
Hamdi Omeroğlu   18 October 1971

United Arab Emirates

H.H. Shaikh Mohammed bin Rashid al Maktoum   18 July 1989
Ahmed Khalifa al Sowaidi   18 July 1989

United States of America

Abram Isaac Elkus   17 June 1920
Henry Morgenthau   17 June 1920
Frederick Courtland Penfield   17 June 1920
Admiral Harold R. Stark   20 January 1945
Lieutenant General Carl Spaatz   6 June 1945
Lieutenant General Walter Bedell Smith   11 June 1946
Clark Haynes Minor   10 July 1946
Winthrop Williams Aldrich   18 April 1947
John William Davies   30 March 1953
Lewis Williams Douglas   19 October 1957
Hugh Bullock   8 June 1976
Caspar Willard Weinberger   13 January 1988

Uruguay

Don Juan Carlos Blanco   19 February 1926
Don Luis Alberto de Herrera   11 February 1928
Gabriel Terra   21 March 1931

Yugoslavia

Jakor Blazević   17 October 1972
Rato Dugonjić   17 October 1972
Dragoslav Marković   17 October 1972
Mijalko Todorović   17 October 1972
Vidoje Zarković   17 October 1972

Zanzibar

H.H. Sultan Khalifa ibn Harub   3 June 1935

Specimen of Warrant of Appointment

Elizabeth R

Elizabeth the Second, by the Grace of God of the United Kingdom of Great Britain and Northern Ireland and of Her other Realms and Territories Queen, Head of the Commonwealth, Defender of the Faith and Sovereign of the Most Excellent Order of the British Empire

Greeting

Whereas We have thought fit to nominate and appoint you to be a   of the   Division of Our said Most Excellent Order of the British Empire

We do by these presents grant unto you the Dignity of a   of Our said Order and hereby authorise you to have hold and enjoy the said Dignity and Rank of a   of Our aforesaid Order together with all and singular the privileges thereunto belonging or appertaining.

Given at Our Court at Saint James's under Our Sign Manual and the Seal of Our said Order this   day of   19   in the   year of Our Reign.

By the Sovereign's Command.

Grand Master.

Grant of the Dignity of a
of the   Division of the Order of the British Empire
to

SOURCE REFERENCES

The text of this book is based mostly on the files of the Central Chancery of the Orders of Knighthood and the Ceremonial Branch of the Cabinet Office. These files are not open to public access at the time of writing. The detailed source references are given partly to enable historians, who may wish to, to quote from this book and to cite the location of the document, and partly to guide the next historian of the Order of the British Empire towards documents that the author's predecessor found significant.

> CCOK   Central Chancery of the Orders of Knighthood
> COCB   Cabinet Office, Ceremonial Branch
> PRO   Public Record Office
> RA   Royal Archives

Acknowledgements

1. CCOK, OBE Institution Letters Box, Sir Frederick Ponsonby to Sir Douglas Dawson, 1 September 1917.

Chapter 1. Conflict and Reward

1. CCOK, OBE Institution Letters Box, Sir Frederick Ponsonby to Sir Douglas Dawson, 6 December 1915.
2. CCOK, OBE Institution Letters Box, Memorandum by Sir Frederick Ponsonby, November 1915.
3. ibid.
4. ibid.
5. ibid.
6. ibid.
7. ibid.
8. CCOK, OBE Institution Letters Box, An undated and incomplete letter by Sir Douglas Dawson, probably to Sir Frederick Ponsonby, November or December 1915.
9. CCOK, OBE Letters, Box 1, Sir Frederick Ponsonby to M. Bonham Carter, 12 May 1916.
10. ibid.
11. CCOK, OBE Letters, Box 3, Sir Frederick Ponsonby to Sir Edward Troup, 23 November 1917.
12. CCOK, OBE Letters, Box 1, Sir Frederick Ponsonby to Sir Edward Troup, 12 May 1916.
13. CCOK, OBE Letters, Box 1, Memorandum on the proposed new Order from Sir Edward Troup to Sir Frederick Ponsonby, 16 May 1916.
14. CCOK, OBE Letters, Box 1, Sir Frederick Ponsonby to Sir Edward Troup, 20 May 1916.
15. ibid.
16. CCOK, OBE Letters, Box 1, Sir Frederick Ponsonby to Sir Edward Troup, 30 May 1916.
17. CCOK, OBE Letters, Box 1, Sir Edward Troup to Sir Frederick Ponsonby, 9 June 1916.
18. CCOK, OBE Letters, Box 1, Sir Frederick Ponsonby to M. Bonham Carter, 10 June 1916.
19. CCOK, OBE Letters, Box 1, Sir Frederick Ponsonby to M. Bonham Carter, 21 June 1916.
20. CCOK, OBE Letters, Box Misc., Report of the Committee appointed to enquire into the advisability of instituting a new decoration for services in connection with the war. Printed for the use of the Cabinet, 8 July 1916, p. 2.
21. CCOK, OBE Letters, Box 1, Sir Frederick Ponsonby to Sir Edward Troup, 3 July 1916.
22. CCOK, OBE Letters, Box Misc., Report of the Committee appointed to enquire into the advisability of instituting a new decoration for services in connection with the war. Printed for the use of the Cabinet, 8 July 1916, p. 2.
23. CCOK, OBE Institution Letters Box, Sir Frederick Ponsonby to the Comptroller, the Lord Chamberlain's Office, 23 June 1916.
24. CCOK, OBE Institution Letters Box, an unsigned and undated memorandum headed 'New Order. Note on Committee's Report'.

25. CCOK, OBE Institution Letters Box, Sir Frederick Ponsonby to Sir Douglas Dawson, 15 August 1916.
26. CCOK, OBE Letters, Box 1, Sir Frederick Ponsonby to Sir Edward Troup, 13 October 1916.
27. CCOK, OBE Letters, Box 1, Memorandum by Sir Douglas Dawson, 12 October 1916.
28. CCOK, OBE Letters, Box 1, Sir Edward Troup to Sir Frederick Ponsonby, 29 October 1916.
29. CCOK, OBE Letters, Box 1, Report of a discussion on questions relating to the institution of the Order of the British Empire, 6 December 1916.
30. ibid.
31. ibid.
32. CCOK, OBE Letters, Box 1, Memorandum from Sir Frederick Ponsonby to the Comptroller, the Lord Chamberlain's Office, 28 November 1916.
33. CCOK, OBE Letters, Box 1, Memorandum from Sir Frederick Ponsonby to the Comptroller, the Lord Chamberlain's Office, 29 December 1916.
34. CCOK, OBE Letters, Box 1, Sir Frederick Ponsonby to Sir Charles Matthews, 22 December 1916.
35. CCOK, OBE Letters, Box 1, Memorandum from Sir Frederick Ponsonby to the Comptroller, the Lord Chamberlain's Office, 28 November 1916.
36. CCOK, OBE Letters, Box 1, Memorandum from Sir Douglas Dawson, 11 December 1916.
37. CCOK, OBE Letters, Box 1, H. J. Bruce to Sir Frederick Ponsonby, 10 January 1917.
38. CCOK, OBE Letters, Box 1, Memorandum from Sir Frederick Ponsonby to the Comptroller, the Lord Chamberlain's Office, 29 December 1916.
39. CCOK, OBE Institution Letters Box, Memorandum by F. S. Osgood, 12 January 1917.
40. CCOK, OBE Letters, Box 1, Sir Frederick Ponsonby to Prince Louis of Battenberg, 10 February 1917.
41. CCOK, OBE Letters, Box 1, Sir Frederick Ponsonby to C. A. Harris, 16 February 1917.
42. CCOK, OBE Institution Letters Box, Sir Frederick Ponsonby to Sir Douglas Dawson, 17 February 1917.
43. CCOK, OBE Letters, Box 1, Sir Frederick Ponsonby to Prince Louis of Battenberg, 26 February 1917.
44. ibid.
45. CCOK, OBE Letters, Box 1, Sir Frederick Ponsonby to Prince Louis of Battenberg, 5 March 1917.
46. ibid.
47. CCOK, OBE Letters, Box 2, Sir Frederick Ponsonby to the Earl Curzon of Kedleston, 21 March 1917.
48. COCB, BE 1A, War Cabinet 122, Appendix 3, 1 April 1917.
49. ibid.
50. CCOK, OBE Letters, Box 2, Sir Frederick Ponsonby to Sir Douglas Dawson, 5 April 1917.
51. CCOK, OBE Letters, Box 2, Memorandum from Sir Frederick Ponsonby to Lieutenant Colonel Clive Wigram, 27 April 1917.
52. CCOK, OBE Letters, Box Miscellaneous, (J. R. Oswald Smith?) to Sir Frederick Ponsonby, 17 May 1917.
53. CCOK, OBE Letters, Box 3, Sir Arthur Pearson to Sir Frederick Ponsonby, 1 May 1918.
54. CCOK, OBE Institution Letters Box, Sir Thomas Heath to M. Bonham Carter, 1 November 1916.
55. CCOK, OBE Institution Letters Box, Sir Frederick Ponsonby to M. Bonham Carter, 2 November 1916.
56. CCOK, OBE Institution Letters Box, Sir Thomas Heath to Sir Frederick Ponsonby, 4 November 1916.
57. CCOK, OBE Institution Letters Box, Memorandum by Prince Louis of Battenberg, 6 December 1916.
58. CCOK, OBE Institution Letters Box, Memorandum from Sir George Fiddes to Sir Frederick Ponsonby, 13 December 1916.
59. CCOK, OBE Letters, Box 1, Sir Edward Troup to Sir Frederick Ponsonby, 15 December 1916.
60. CCOK, OBE Letters, Box Misc., G.140, Order of the British Empire. Memorandum by the Earl Curzon of Kedleston. Printed for the use of the Cabinet, 1 April 1917.
61. CCOK, OBE Letters, Box 2, Sir Douglas Dawson to Sir Frederick Ponsonby, 2 May 1917.
62. CCOK, OBE Letters, Box 2, Sir Frederick Ponsonby to H. H. Asquith, 22 May 1917.

63. CCOK, OBE Letters, Box 2, Memorandum, 15 May 1917.
64. CCOK, OBE Letters, Box 2, Sir Frederick Ponsonby to H. H. Asquith, 22 May 1917.
65. CCOK, OBE Letters, Box 2, Sir Frederick Ponsonby to the Earl Curzon of Kedleston, 24 May 1917.
66. CCOK, OBE Institution Letters Box, Sir Frederick Ponsonby to Sir Douglas Dawson, 11 September 1917.

Chapter 2. Allocation and Management

1. CCOK, OBE Letters, Box Misc., Memorandum by Sir Frederick Ponsonby, 27 October 1916, re-issued 26 January 1917.
2. CCOK, OBE Letters, Box Misc., Sir Frederick Ponsonby to the Earl Curzon of Kedleston, 30 March 1917.
3. ibid.
4. CCOK, OBE Letters, Box Misc., Memorandum by Sir Frederick Ponsonby, 26 April 1917.
5. CCOK, OBE Letters, Box Misc., Memorandum, 27 April 1917.
6. CCOK, OBE Letters, Box Misc., Sir Frederick Ponsonby to Sir Derek Keppel, 26 April 1917.
7. CCOK, OBE Letters, Box Misc., Sir Derek Keppel to Sir Frederick Ponsonby, 27 April 1917.
8. COCB, BE 1A, Minutes of committee meeting, 1 May 1917, p. 5.
9. *Burke's Handbook to the Order of the British Empire*, (London, 1921), p. 9.
10. COCB, BE 1A, Minutes of committee meeting, 1 May 1917, p. 6.
11. Sir Frederick Ponsonby, *Recollections of Three Reigns*, (London, 1935), p. 56.
12. COCB, BE 1A, Minutes of committee meeting, 1 May 1917, p. 11.
13. ibid., p. 15.
14. ibid.
15. CCOK, OBE Letters, Box 1, Sir Frederick Ponsonby to the Marquess of Lincolnshire, 5 February 1917.
16. COCB, BE 1A, Minutes of committee meeting, 1 May 1917, p. 13.
17. CCOK, OBE Letters, Box 2, Prince Louis of Battenberg to Sir Frederick Ponsonby, 8 May 1917.
18. CCOK, OBE Letters, Box 2, Sir Frederick Ponsonby to Sir Douglas Dawson, 31 May 1917.
19. CCOK, OBE Letters, Box 2, Sir Frederick Ponsonby to the Prime Minister, 30 May 1917.
20. CCOK, OBE Letters, Box 2, Memorandum from Sir Frederick Ponsonby to the Prime Minister, 30 May 1917.
21. CCOK, OBE Letters, Box 2, Sir Frederick Ponsonby to C. A. Harris, 25 June 1917.
22. CCOK, OBE Letters, Box 2, Memorandum from Lord Stamfordham to Sir Frederick Ponsonby, 20 August 1917.
23. CCOK, OBE Letters, Box 2, Sir Frederick Ponsonby to the Earl of Derby, 17 September 1917.
24. CCOK, OBE Letters, Box 3, Memorandum from Sir Frederick Ponsonby to the Earl of Derby, 25 September 1917.
25. CCOK, OBE Institution Letters Box, Sir Douglas Dawson to Prince Louis of Battenberg, 14 December 1916.
26. CCOK, OBE Institution Letters Box, Prince Louis of Battenberg to Sir Douglas Dawson, 15 December 1916.
27. CCOK, OBE Institution Letters Box, Sir Frederick Ponsonby to Sir Douglas Dawson, 4 September 1917.
28. CCOK, OBE Letters, Box 2, Sir Frederick Ponsonby to the Earl of Derby, 17 September 1917.
29. CCOK, OBE Letters, Box 2, Memorandum from Sir Frederick Ponsonby to Lieutenant Colonel Clive Wigram, 20 September 1917.
30. CCOK, OBE Letters, Box 3, Memorandum by Walter H. Long, 26 September 1917.
31. CCOK, OBE Letters, Box 1, Report on the meeting of the departmental committee appointed to enquire into certain questions relating to the Order of the British Empire, 28 September 1917.
32. ibid.
33. ibid.
34. ibid.
35. CCOK, OBE Letters, Box 2, Memorandum from Sir Frederick Ponsonby to Willliam Sutherland, 28 September 1917.
36. CCOK, 45/23. Colonel Clive Wigram to Colonel the Honourable George Crichton, 27 February 1923.

Chapter 3. Anxiety and Concern

 1. CCOK, OBE Letters, Box 3, Sir Douglas Dawson to Sir Frederick Ponsonby, 10 October 1917.
 2. CCOK, OBE Letters, Box 3, Sir Frederick Ponsonby to Sir Douglas Dawson, 10 October 1917.
 3. RA, GV, 1102/9, Lord Stamfordham to A. J. Balfour, 6 April 1917.
 4. CCOK, OBE Letters, Box 3, Sir Frederick Ponsonby to the Earl of Crawford and Balcarres, 6 November 1917.
 5. CCOK, OBE Letters, Box 3, Sir Frederick Ponsonby to William Sutherland, 29 September 1917.
 6. COCB, BE 1B, *Hansard*, House of Commons, 3 July 1918.
 7. CCOK, OBE Letters, Extract from War Cabinet Meeting, 17 October 1917.
 8. CCOK, OBE Letters, Box 3, Cabinet Minute, 28 September 1917.
 9. CCOK, OBE Letters, Box 3, The Earl of Crawford and Balcarres to Sir Frederick Ponsonby, 23 October 1917.
10. CCOK, OBE Letters, Box 3, G.T. 2392, Report by the Earl of Crawford and Balcarres, 25 October 1917.
11. CCOK, OBE Letters, Box 3, The Earl of Crawford and Balcarres to Sir Frederick Ponsonby, 28 October 1917.
12. CCOK, OBE Letters, Box 3, The Earl of Crawford and Balcarres to Sir Frederick Ponsonby, 7 November 1917.
13. CCOK, OBE Letters, Box 3, G.T. 2577, Memorandum by the Earl of Crawford and Balcarres, 11 November 1917.
14. CCOK, OBE Letters, Box 3, Extract from the Minutes of a meeting of the War Cabinet, 14 November 1917.
15. CCOK, OBE Letters, Box 3, The Earl of Crawford and Balcarres to Sir Frederick Ponsonby, 14 November 1917.
16. CCOK, OBE Letters, Box 3, Sir Frederick Ponsonby to Sir Edward Troup, 7 January 1918.
17. CCOK, OBE Letters, Box 3, Sir Frederick Ponsonby to J. T. Davies, 5 January 1918.
18. CCOK, OBE Letters, Box 3, Sir Edward Troup to Sir Frederick Ponsonby, 9 January 1918.
19. CCOK, OBE Letters, Box 3, Draft minutes of a meeting of the Advisory Committee, 30 January 1918.
20. CCOK, OBE Letters, Box 3, Sir Frederick Ponsonby to Lieutenant General Sir Francis Davies, 26 April 1918.
21. CCOK, OBE Letters, Box 3, Sir Frederick Ponsonby to Lord Knutsford, 26 June 1918.
22. CCOK, OBE Letters, Box 3, Lord Southborough to Thomas Jones, 1 July 1919.
23. ibid.
24. ibid.
25. CCOK, OBE Letters, Box 3, Lord Southborough to Sir Frederick Ponsonby, 8 July 1919.
26. CCOK, OBE Letters, Box 3, Sir Frederick Ponsonby to Lord Southborough, 9 July 1919.
27. CCOK, OBE Letters, Box 3, Sir Frederick Ponsonby to The Honourable Theophilus Russell, 29 December 1917.
28. CCOK, OBE Letters, Box 3, The Honourable Theophilus Russell to Sir Frederick Ponsonby, 29 December 1917.
29. CCOK, OBE Letters, Box 3, Berkeley Levett to Sir Frederick Ponsonby, 17 May 1918.
30. CCOK, OBE Letters, Box 3, Sir Frederick Ponsonby to G. G. Whiskard, 17 May 1918.
31. CCOK, OBE Letters, Box 3, Sir Frederick Ponsonby to Sir Edward Troup, 4 December 1917.

Chapter 4. Annoyance and Discontent

 1. Ivan De la Bere, *The Queen's Orders of Chivalry*, (London, 1964), pp 156-7.
 2. CCOK, OBE Letters, Box 3, The Earl of Durham to Lord Stamfordham, 4 February 1918.
 3. CCOK, OBE Letters, Box 3, Sir Frederick Ponsonby to G. G. Whiskard, 22 February 1918.
 4. CCOK, OBE Letters, Box 3, Sir Douglas Dawson to Sir Frederick Ponsonby, 9 July 1918.
 5. CCOK, OBE Letters, Sir Frederick Ponsonby to Sir Douglas Dawson, 10 July 1918.
 6. COCB, H 25, Sir Douglas Dawson to Sir Edward Troup, 11 July 1918.
 7. CCOK, OBE Letters, Box 4, Transcript of a letter from Henry G. R. Aldridge to G. G. Whiskard, 27 June 1918.
 8. CCOK, OBE Letters, Box 4, G. G. Whiskard to Lord Stamfordham, 26 June 1918.
 9. Kenneth Macfarlane Walker, *I talk of dreams. An experiment in autobiography*, (London, 1946), pp 205-7.

10. COCB, BE 1A, Lord Stamfordham to Sir Edward Troup, 29 July 1918.
11. CCOK, OBE Letters, Box 3, Sir Frederick Ponsonby to Lord Stamfordham, 1 August 1918.
12. ibid.
13. ibid.
14. ibid.
15. Ivan De la Bere, *The Queen's Orders of Chivalry*, (London, 1964), pp 156-7.
16. CCOK, OBE Letters, Box 3, The Earl of Crawford and Balcarres to Sir Frederick Ponsonby, 9 November 1917.
17. *The Times*, 31 August 1918, p. 9.
18. *The Times*, 14 November 1918, p 10.
19. CCOK, OBE Letters, Box 4, *Truth*, 21 August 1918, p. 235.
20. ibid.
21. PRO, HO 45/18984/352070/39, M. D. Graham to Sir Douglas Dawson, 26 July 1920.
22. CCOK, OBE Letters, Box 4, Sir Frederick Ponsonby to Lieutenant General Sir Francis Davies, 12 November 1918.

Chapter 5. Retrenchment and Consolidation

1. CCOK, OBE Letters, Box 3, Sir Frederick Ponsonby to Sir Edward Troup, 23 November 1917.
2. CCOK, 45/22, J. T. Davies to Sir Douglas Dawson, 10 January 1919.
3. CCOK, 45/22, Sir Douglas Dawson to J. T. Davies, 14 January 1919.
4. CCOK, OBE Letters, Box 3, Sir Douglas Dawson to Sir Frederick Ponsonby, 21 July 1919.
5. CCOK, OBE Letters, Box 5, Memorandum from Sir Frederick Ponsonby to the Comptroller, the Lord Chamberlain's Office, 24 November 1919.
6. ibid.
7. CCOK, OBE Letters, Box 5, Sir Douglas Dawson to Sir Frederick Ponsonby, 16 December 1919.
8. CCOK, OBE Letters, Box 5, Memorandum from Sir Frederick Ponsonby to the Comptroller, the Lord Chamberlain's Department, 20 December 1919.
9. CCOK, OBE Letters, Box 5, Lord Stamfordham to Sir Frederick Ponsonby, 25 January 1920.
10. CCOK, OBE Letters, Box 5, Sir Frederick Ponsonby to Lord Stamfordham, 27 January 1920.
11. COCB, BE 1, Minute by E. C. E. Leadbitter to Sir Warren Fisher, 10 June 1922.
12. CCOK, 45/22, Note of a meeting, 15 January 1920.
13. COCB, BE 1, Lord Stamfordham to Sir Warren Fisher, 1 December 1920.
14. COCB, BE 1, J. T. Davies to Sir Warren Fisher, 3 December 1920.
15. COCB, BE 1, M. D. Graham to Sir Douglas Dawson, 27 August 1920.
16. COCB, BE 1, Sir Douglas Dawson to R. E. Harwood, 8 March 1921.
17. COCB, BE 1, Memorandum from Sir Warren Fisher to the Prime Minister, 11 November 1921.
18. ibid.
19. COCB, H 24, Minute from Sir Robert Knox to D. B. Pitblado, 4 November 1952.
20. COCB, BE 1, Sir Warren Fisher to Lord Stamfordham, 15 June 1922.
21. ibid.
22. COCB, BE 1, Memorandum from Sir Warren Fisher to the Prime Minister, 9 October 1922.
23. ibid.
24. ibid.
25. COCB, BE 1, Sir Warren Fisher to Sir Herbert Creedy, 6 November 1922.

Chapter 6. Stability and Popularity

1. COCB, H 13, Robert Knox to Harry Stockley, 26 March 1931.
2. COCB, H 13, Harry Stockley to Robert Knox, 1 April 1931.
3. COCB, H 13, Robert Knox to Harry Stockley, 10 April 1931.
4. COCB, H 13, Sir Herbert Samuel to Ramsay Macdonald, 26 January 1932.
5. COCB, H 13, Memorandum from Sir Warren Fisher to the Prime Minister, 21 March 1933.
6. COCB, H 13, Note on the title 'Dame' by Sir Christopher Bullock, Permanent Secretary, Air Ministry, 18 July 1933.
7. ibid.
8. COCB, H 13A, Sir George Coldstream to Derek Mitchell, 15 September 1965.
9. COCB, H 13A, Derek Mitchell to Sir Michael Adeane, 22 September 1965.

10. COCB, H 13A, Sir Laurence Helsby to the Prime Minister, 1 October 1965.

11. COCB, H 13, Sir Laurence Helsby to the Prime Minister, 10 November 1965.

12. COCB, H 13, Derek Mitchell to Alan Wyatt, 22 November 1965.

13. COCB, H 13, Kenneth Stowe to Norman Warner, 24 June 1975.

14. COCB, H 13, P. S. Milner-Barry to Kenneth Stowe, 10 July 1975.

15. ibid.

16. COCB, H 24, Minute from Sir Robert Knox to D. B. Pitblado, 4 November 1952.

17. COCB, H 25/3, Part 2, Sir Warren Fisher to Sir Herbert Creedy, 21 April 1936.

18. CCOK, 45/31, P.Y. 66/31, J. P. Gibson to the Registrar, Central Chancery of the Orders of Knighthood, 30 January 1931.

19. CCOK, 45/36, P. Mason to the Secretary, Military Department, India Office, 14 May 1936.

20. CCOK, 45/47/65, This letter is dated 15 April 1965, but presumably it was written on, and meant to be dated, 15 June 1965.

21. COCB, H 11A, E. J. Emery to Sir Charles Dixon, 26 July 1965.

Chapter 7. Foreign and Commonwealth

1. CCOK, OBE Letters, Box 3, The Honourable Theophilus Russell to Sir Frederick Ponsonby, 21 May 1917.

2. CCOK, OBE Letters, Box 3, Sir Frederick Ponsonby to The Honourable Theophilus Russell, 25 May 1917.

3. ibid.

4. ibid.

5. ibid.

6. CCOK, OBE Letters, Box 3, Sir Frederick Ponsonby to Sir Edmund Wyldbore-Smith, 3 December 1917.

7. CCOK, OBE Letters, Box 3, O137/4/76, Procedure with regard to the Award of the Order of the British Empire to Foreigners, 20 July 1918.

8. COCB, BE 13, Sir Frederick Ponsonby to Sir Warren Fisher, 14 October 1921.

9. COCB, BE 13, A. Akers Douglas to Sir Frederick Ponsonby, 21 October 1921.

10. ibid.

11. COCB, BE 13, Sir Warren Fisher to Sir Frederick Ponsonby, 26 October 1921.

12. RA, GeoV AA 43/291, Empress Eugénie to King George V, 6 March 1919.

13. CCOK, OBE Letters, Box 3, The Honourable Sir Arthur Stanley to Sir Frederick Ponsonby, 12 April 1918.

14. COCB, BE 2/6, Part 1, H. J. Neethling to Commonwealth Relations Office, 29 August 1952.

15. COCB, BE 53, Annexe to a letter from David Mandie, President of the Victorian Association of the Order of the British Empire, to the author, 31 March 1995.

16. COCB, BE 23, HD 6411, Committee on the Grant of Honours, Decorations and Medals. Order of the British Empire. Description, 8 January 1963, pp 1-2.

17. ibid., p. 4.

18. ibid., p. 4.

19. ibid., p. 5.

20. COCB, BE 23, Christopher Eastwood to Sir Neil Pritchard, 6 December 1963.

21. COCB, BE 23, Annexe to a letter from Sir Charles Dixon to Sir Robert Knox, 12 February 1964.

22. ibid.

23. COCB, BE 23, Sir Robert Black to Sir Hilton Poynton, 27 December 1964.

24. CCOK, OBE Letters, Box 2, W. Graham Greene to Sir Frederick Ponsonby, 21 May 1917.

25. COCB, BE 23, HD 6927, Committee on the Grant of Honours, Decorations and Medals. One thousand and third report. Order of the British Empire, 7 October 1966, p. 3.

26. COCB, BE 23, Draft note for Sir Laurence Helsby to send to Michael Halls, 25 July 1966.

Chapter 8. The Robes and Insignia of the Order: 1 The Old Pattern

1. CCOK, OBE Letters, Box 1, Sir Frederick Ponsonby to Prince Louis of Battenberg, 12 July 1916.

2. ibid.

3. CCOK, OBE Letters, Box 1, Sir Frederick Ponsonby to Sir Douglas Dawson, 15 August 1916.

4. CCOK, OBE Letters, Box 1, Sir Frederick Ponsonby to M. Bonham Carter, 12 July 1916.

5. CCOK, OBE Letters, Box 1, Sir Frederick Ponsonby to Prince Louis of Battenberg, 12 July 1916.

6. ibid.

7. CCOK, OBE Letters, Box 1, Prince Louis of Battenberg to Sir Frederick Ponsonby, 13 July 1916.

8. ibid.

9. CCOK, OBE Letters, Box 1, Sir Frederick Ponsonby to Prince Louis of Battenberg, 25 July 1916.

10. CCOK, OBE Letters, Box 1, Prince Louis of Battenberg to Sir Frederick Ponsonby, 26 July 1916.

11. CCOK, OBE Letters, Box 1, Sir Frederick Ponsonby to Prince Louis of Battenberg, 28 July 1916.

12. ibid.

13. CCOK, OBE Letters, Box 1, Sir Frederick Ponsonby to Prince Louis of Battenberg, 12 July 1916.

14. ibid.

15. CCOK, OBE Letters, Box 1, Prince Louis of Battenberg to Sir Frederick Ponsonby, 13 July 1916.

16. ibid.

17. ibid.

18. ibid.

19. CCOK, OBE Letters, Box 1, Sir Frederick Ponsonby to Prince Louis of Battenberg, 28 July 1916.

20. CCOK, OBE Institution Letters Box, H. Farnham Burke to Sir Douglas Dawson, 22 September 1916.

21. ibid.

22. CCOK, Institution Letters Box, Sir Douglas Dawson to The Honourable Sir Derek Keppel, 21 September 1916.

23. CCOK, OBE Letters, Box 1, Miss Elinor Hallé to Sir Frederick Ponsonby, 7 July, 1916.

24. CCOK, OBE Institution Letters Box, Miss Elinor Hallé to Sir Douglas Dawson, 25 September 1916.

25. CCOK, OBE Letters, Box 1, Memorandum from Sir Frederick Ponsonby to the Comptroller, Lord Chamberlain's Office, 2 October 1916.

26. CCOK, OBE Letters, Box 1, Prince Louis of Battenberg to Sir Frederick Ponsonby, 26 July 1916.

27. CCOK, OBE Letters, Box 1, Sir Frederick Ponsonby to Prince Louis of Battenberg, 25 July 1916.

28. CCOK, OBE Letters, Box 1, Prince Louis of Battenberg to Sir Frederick Ponsonby, 13 July 1916.

29. CCOK, OBE Letters, Box 1, H.M. Queen Mary to Sir Frederick Ponsonby, no date.

30. CCOK, OBE Letters, Box 1, Sir Douglas Dawson to Prince Louis of Battenberg, 29 September 1916.

31. CCOK, OBE Letters, Box 1, Prince Louis of Battenberg to Sir Douglas Dawson, 30 September 1916.

32. CCOK, OBE Letters, Box 1, Memorandum, Sir Frederick Ponsonby to the Comptroller, Lord Chamberlain's Office, 2 October 1916.

33. CCOK, OBE Institution Letters Box, Sir Frederick Ponsonby to Sir Douglas Dawson, 7 September 1916.

34. CCOK, OBE Institution Letters Box, Miss Elinor Hallé to Sir Douglas Dawson, 25 September 1916.

35. CCOK, OBE Letters, Box 1, Prince Louis of Battenberg to Sir Douglas Dawson, 30 September 1916.

36. CCOK, OBE Institution Letters Box, Sir Douglas Dawson to Sir Frederick Ponsonby, 4 October 1916.

37. CCOK, OBE Institution Letters Box, Sir Frederick Ponsonby to Sir Douglas Dawson, 11 October 1916.

38. CCOK, OBE Letters, Box 1, Sir Frederick Ponsonby to Sir Douglas Dawson, 9 March 1917.

39. ibid.

40. ibid.

41. CCOK, OBE Letters, Box 1, Memorandum from Sir Frederick Ponsonby to Sir Douglas Dawson, 10 March 1917.
42. CCOK, OBE Institution Letters Box, Garrard to Sir Douglas Dawson, 13 March 1917.
43. CCOK, OBE Letters, Box 3, Sir Frederick Ponsonby to Sir Edward Wallington, 7 March 1918.
44. CCOK, 45/24, The Honourable Sir Derek Keppel to Colonel the Honourable Sir George Crichton, 15 July 1924.
45. CCOK, 45/24, Colonel the Honourable Sir George Crichton to Sir Warren Fisher, 4 September 1924.
46. CCOK, 45/24, Lord Stamfordham to Sir George Crichton, 26 August 1924.
47. CCOK, OBE Letters, Box 1, Prince Louis of Battenberg to Sir Frederick Ponsonby, 13 July 1916.
48. CCOK, OBE Letters, Box 1, Sir Frederick Ponsonby to Prince Louis of Battenberg, 18 July 1916.
49. COCB, BE 10, Ralph Harwood to Sir Warren Fisher, 13 February 1923.
50. COCB, BE 10, Sir Warren Fisher, to the Earl of Cromer, 27 November 1924.
51. ibid.
52. COCB, BE 10, Sir Warren Fisher to the Earl of Cromer, 11 December 1923.
53. CCOK, 45/26, Order of the British Empire Collars Correspondence 1923-6, draft letter from Sir Douglas Dawson to Sir Warren Fisher, no date, probably November or December 1923.
54. COCB, BE 10, The Earl of Cromer to Sir Warren Fisher, 28 November 1924.
55. CCOK, 45/26, Order of the British Empire Collars Correspondence 1923-6, The Keeper of the Privy Purse to the Lord Chamberlain, 12 December 1924.
56. COCB, BE 10, The Earl of Cromer to Sir Warren Fisher, 13 December 1924.
57. COCB, BE 10, Memorandum by Sir Warren Fisher, 18 December 1924.
58. CCOK, 45/26, Order of the British Empire Collars Correspondence 1923-6, draft letter from Sir Douglas Dawson to Sir Warren Fisher, no date, probably November or December 1923.
59. COCB, BE 10, Memorandum by Sir Warren Fisher, 18 December 1924.
60. CCOK, 45/26, Order of the British Empire Collars Correspondence 1923-6, Colonel Robert A. Johnson to the Earl of Cromer, 7 May 1925.
61. COCB, BE 10, Sir Warren Fisher to Colonel Robert A. Johnson, 10 June 1925.
62. COCB, BE 10, 1264/25, Colonel Robert A. Johnson to Sir Warren Fisher, 12 June 1925.
63. COCB, BE 10, Colonel the Honourable Sir George Crichton to Sir Warren Fisher, 26 February 1927.
64. COCB, BE 10, Colonel the Honourable Sir George Crichton to Sir Warren Fisher, 3 July 1928.
65. COCB, BE 10, Note by E. C. E. Leadbitter, 13 February 1925.
66. CCOK, 45/26, Order of the British Empire Collars Correspondence 1923-6, Brief by E. C. E. Leadbitter to Sir Warren Fisher, 9 February 1925.
67. COCB, BE 10, Major Harry Stockley to E. B. Athawes, 25 July 1929.

Chapter 9. The Robes and Insignia of the Order: 2 The New Pattern

1. COCB, H 28, Part 2, ODM 18, Committee on the alteration of the insignia of Orders and the alteration of decorations and medals, with the change of reign, 12 May 1936, p. 7.
2. ibid., p. 8.
3. COCB, BE 27, Robert Knox to Gerald Chichester, 21 March 1936.
4. ibid.
5. ibid.
6. ibid.
7. COCB, BE 27, Gerald Chichester to Robert Knox, 23 March 1936.
8. COCB, BE 27, Sir Warren Fisher to Gerald Chichester, 23 March 1936.
9. COCB, BE 27, Gerald Chichester to Robert Knox, 23 March 1936.
10. COCB, BE 27, Robert Knox to Gerald Chichester, 18 April 1936.
11. ibid.
12. COCB, BE 27, Sir Robert Johnson to Robert Knox, 8 June 1936.
13. COCB, BE 27, Robert Knox to Lord Wigram, 22 December 1936.
14. CCOK, 45A/1936-7, 10 May 1937.
15. CCOK, 45A/1936-7, 13 June 1937.
16. Ivan De la Bere, *The Queen's Orders of Chivalry*, (London, 1964), p. 162.
17. CCOK, 45/23/66, Letter dated 24 March 1966.

Chapter 10. The Robes and Insignia of the Order: 3 The Officials

1. COCB, H 9, Colonel Sir Clive Wigram to Sir John Maffey, 22 February 1934.
2. COCB, BE 10, Sir Warren Fisher to Colonel the Honourable Sir George Crichton, 18 May 1928.
3. COCB, BE 10, Major Harry Stockley to E. B. Athawes, 25 July 1929.
4. COCB, BE 27/1. L. Taylor to Sir Robert Knox, 7 April 1960.
5. COCB, BE 30, Part 1, Memorandum from Sir Robert Knox to Sir Warren Fisher, 27 February 1936.
6. COCB, BE 30, Part 1, Sir Warren Fisher to the Prime Minister, 17 March 1936.
7. COCB, BE 30, Part 1, Minute from Sir Robert Knox to Sir Edward Bridges, 14 April 1953.
8. COCB, BE 30, Part 3, Minute from Sir Robert Knox to Sir Norman Brook, 10 October 1961.

Chapter 11. The Robes and Insignia of the Order: 4 The Medal of the Order and the Emblem for Gallantry

1. COCB, BE 1A, Minutes of committee meeting, 1 May 1917, p. 26.
2. CCOK, OBE Letters, Box 4, Report of the Munitions Medals Committee, 17 January 1918.
3. CCOK, OBE Letters, Box 4, Sir Frederick Ponsonby to Sir Edward Troup, 13 June 1918.
4. CCOK, OBE Letters, Box 2, Sir Frederick Ponsonby to Edmund B. Phipps, 23 May 1917.
5. CCOK, OBE Institution Letters Box, F. S. Osgood to H. Farnham Burke, 3 May 1917.
6. *The Times*, 25 August 1917, p. 8.
7. PRO, HO 45/18984/352071/11. Report of medal sub-committee, 5 December 1917.
8. CCOK, OBE Letters, Box 4, Report of the British Empire Medal Sub-Committee on the basis to be adopted for the distribution of the Medal, 21 February 1918.
9. CCOK, OBE Letters, Box 4, Sir Frederick Ponsonby to Sir Edward Troup, 6 June 1918.
10. CCOK, OBE Letters, Box 4, Sir Frederick Ponsonby to Sir Edward Troup, 26 June 1918.
11. PRO, HO 45/18984/352070/39. M. D. Graham to Sir Douglas Dawson, 26 July 1920.
12. COCB, BEM 2A, Lord Stamfordham to J. T. Davies, 9 June 1921.
13. COCB, BE 2A, Statutes of the Order of the British Empire, 1922.
14. COCB, BE 1, Memorandum from Sir Warren Fisher to the Prime Minister, 9 October 1922.
15. COCB, BEM 2A, Colonel Robert A. Johnson to E. C. E. Leadbitter, 20 July 1922.
16. COCB, BE 1, Submission from Sir Warren Fisher to the Prime Minister, 9 October 1922.
17. COCB, BEM 2B, Lord Stamfordham to Sir Warren Fisher, 4 October 1922.
18. COCB, BEM 2B, Sir Warren Fisher to Colonel the Honourable George Crichton, 30 November 1922.
19. COCB, BEM 2A, Memorandum from the Keeper of the Privy Purse to Lord Stamfordham, 17 July 1922.
20. COCB, BEM 2B, Sir Frederick Ponsonby to Sir Warren Fisher, 22 November 1922.
21. COCB, BEM 2B, Colonel Robert A. Johnson to Sir Frederick Ponsonby, 1 February 1923.
22. COCB, BEM 2A, Sir Frederick Ponsonby to Sir Warren Fisher, 25 May 1925.
23. COCB, BEM 2B, Note circulated to Selection Committee for the Medal of the Order of the British Empire, 19 March 1931.
24. ibid.
25. COCB, BEM 2B, Memorandum by Sir John Anderson, 24 March 1931.
26. ibid.
27. COCB, BEM 2A, Sir Warren Fisher to Sir Frederick Ponsonby, 23 May 1925.
28. COCB, H 5, Part 3, *Hansard*, House of Commons, 4 March 1993.
29. COCB, BE 36, HW 549, 21 September 1942.
30. COCB, BE 36, HW 582, 12 November 1942.
31. COCB, BE 36, Sir Robert Knox to Sir Norman Brook, 21 November 1957.
32. COCB, BE 36, HD 7221, Draft of a proposed oral statement by the Prime Minister, and background note, 16 May 1974.

Chapter 12. The Quest for a Chapel: 1 St Margaret's Church, Westminster and others

1. COCB, BECh 1, Memorandum by Sir Lawrence Weaver, 1917.
2. COCB, BECh 5, Sir Charles Peake to the Earl of Halifax, 19 January 1950.
3. ibid.
4. COCB, BECh 1, Note by Sir Warren Fisher to the Committee of 1937 on the distribution of the permanent establishment, 14 July 1937.
5. CCOK, 45/24, Colonel the Honourable Sir George Crichton to Sir Edward Ward, 13 May 1924.

6. CCOK, 45/25, Colonel the Honourable Sir George Crichton to F. J. Warren, 12 June 1925.

7. COCB, BECh 1, Sir Frederic Kenyon to Sir Warren Fisher, 13 April 1933.

8. COCB, BECh 1, Lord Cromer to the Bishop of London, 28 June 1932.

9. COCB, BECh 1, Note by Sir Warren Fisher to the Committee of 1933 on the distribution of the permanent establishment, 8 July 1933.

10. COCB, BECh 1, Note by Sir Robert Knox to the Committee of 1937 on the distribution of the permanent establishment, 14 July 1937.

11. COCB, BECh 1, Sir Edward Barton to the Bishop of London, 30 March 1937.

12. COCB, BECh 1, Sir Alexander Hardinge to the Bishop of London, 5 April 1937.

13. COCB, BECh 1, Note by Sir Warren Fisher to the Committee of 1937 on the distribution of the permanent establishment, 14 July 1937.

14 ibid.

15. ibid.

16. ibid.

17. ibid.

18. ibid.

19. ibid.

20. COCB, BECh 1, Gerald Chichester to Sir Robert Knox, 23 July 1937.

21. COCB, BECh 1, The Bishop of London to Sir Warren Fisher, 25 October 1937.

22. COCB, BECh 1, Sir Warren Fisher to the Bishop of London, 11 November 1937.

23. COCB, BECh 1, Canon Vernon Storr to Sir Warren Fisher, 29 November 1937.

24. COCB, BECh 2, Sir Robert Knox to Canon Vernon Storr, 4 March 1938.

25. COCB, BECh 2, Canon Vernon Storr to Sir Robert Knox, 4 March 1938.

26. COCB, BECh 2, Sir Charles Peers to Sir Robert Knox, 5 March 1938.

27. COCB, BECh 2, Canon Vernon Storr to Sir Robert Knox, 13 April 1938.

28. ibid.

29. COCB, BECh 2, Sir Charles Nicholson to Sir Robert Knox, 5 May 1938.

30. COCB, BECh 2, Sir Charles Nicholson to Sir Robert Knox, 29 September 1938.

31. COCB, BECh 2, Part 1, Sir Charles Nicholson to Sir Robert Knox, 5 October 1938.

32. COCB, BECh 2, Part 1, Sir Charles Nicholson to Sir Robert Knox, 10 October 1938.

33. COCB, BECh 2, Part 1, Canon Vernon Storr to Sir Robert Knox, 3 November 1938.

34. ibid.

35. COCB, BECh 2, Part 1, Canon Vernon Storr to Sir Robert Knox, 21 November 1938.

36. COCB, BECh 2, Part 1, Canon Vernon Storr to Sir Robert Knox, 22 November 1938.

37. COCB, BECh 2, Part 1, Sir Charles Nicholson to Sir Robert Knox, 23 November 1938.

38. COCB, BECh 2, Part 1, Canon Vernon Storr to Sir Robert Knox, 27 November 1938.

39. COCB, BECh 2, Part 1, Sir Robert Knox to Archdeacon Vernon Storr, 1 December 1938.

40. COCB, BECh 2, Part 3, Dr F.C. Eeles to Archdeacon Vernon Storr, 3 July 1939.

41. COCB, BECh 2, Part 3, Hansard, House of Commons, 18 July 1939.

42. COCB, BECh 3, Sir Robert Knox to Sir Edward Bridges, 30 January 1947.

43. COCB, BECh 2, Part 3, Sir Robert Knox to Archdeacon Vernon Storr, 27 September 1939.

44. COCB, BECh 2, Part 2, The Bishop of London to Sir Robert Knox, 1 June 1939.

45. COCB, BECh 3, Minute from Sir Robert Knox to Sir Richard Hopkins, 19 July 1943.

Chapter 13. The Quest for a Chapel: 2 Southwark Cathedral and others

1. COCB, BECh 3, Sir Robert Knox to Sir Richard Hopkins 12 April 1944.

2. COCB, BECh 3, Sir Harry Stockley to Sir Robert Knox, 28 July 1945.

3. COCB, BECh 3, The Bishop of London to Sir Edward Bridges, 26 April 1947.

4. COCB, BECh 3, Draft report by Sir Robert Knox, 30 April 1947.

5. ibid.

6. ibid.

7. ibid.

8. COCB, BECh 3, Major J. L. Wickham to Sir Edward Bridges, 30 April 1947.

9. ibid.

10. COCB, BECh 3, Note for the record by Sir Edward Bridges, 2 May 1947.

11. COCB, BECh 3, Minute by Sir Robert Knox to Sir Edward Bridges, 8 May 1947.

12. COCB, BECh 3, Major J. L. Wickham to Sir Alan Lascelles, 14 October 1947.

13. COCB, BECh 3, Sir Alan Lascelles to Sir Edward Bridges, 6 December 1947.

14. COCB, BECh 3, Major J. L. Wickham to Sir Robert Knox, 7 July 1948.

15. COCB, BECh 3, Provost Edward Ashdown to Sir Robert Knox, 12 July 1948.

16. COCB, BECh 3, Conclusions of a meeting of Officials at Southwark Cathedral, 26 October 1948.
17. COCB, BECh 3, Major J. L. Wickham to Sir Edward Bridges, 26 October 1948.
18. COCB, BECh 3, Part 1, BEC ('49) 6, Proposed chapel and services. Conclusions of a meeting held at Southwark Cathedral, 3 February 1949.
19. COCB, BECh 3, Sir Edward Bridges to Sir Robert Knox, 25 January 1949.
20. COCB, BECh 3, Part 1, Note by Major J. L. Wickham, January 1949.
21. COCB, BECh 3, Part 1, Note for the record by Sir Robert Knox, 15 January 1949.
22. COCB, BECh 3, Part 1, Note for the record by Sir Robert Knox, 26 January 1949.
23. COCB, BECh 3, Sir Ivan De la Bere to Sir Edward Bridges, 29 January 1949.
24. COCB, BECh 3, Part 1, Air Marshal Sir Roderick Carr to Sir Edward Bridges, 1 February 1949.
25. COCB, BECh 3, Part 1, Sir Frederic Kenyon to Sir Edward Bridges, 12 February 1949.
26. COCB, BECh 3, Part 1, The Bishop of London to Sir Edward Bridges, 16 February 1949.
27. COCB, BECh 3, Part 1, BEC ('49) 6D, Proposed Chapel and Services. First Report, 22 February 1949.
28. COCB, BECh 3, Part 1, Sir Edward Bridges to Major J. L Wickham, 28 February 1949.
29. COCB, BECh 3, Part 1, Minute from Sir Robert Knox to Sir Edward Bridges, 1 April 1949.
30. COCB, BECh 3, Part 1, Sir Edward Bridges to Sir Alan Lascelles, 5 April 1949.
31. COCB, BECh 3, Part 1, Sir Alan Lascelles to Sir Edward Bridges, 19 April 1949.
32. ibid.
33. COCB, BECh 3, Part 1, Major J. L. Wickham to Sir Edward Bridges, 3 May 1949.
34. ibid.

Chapter 14. The Quest for a Chapel: 3 St Paul's Cathedral
1. COCB, BECh 3, Part 1, Dean W. R. Matthews to Sir Edward Bridges, 17 February 1953.
2. COCB, BECh 4, Dean W. R. Matthews to the Bishop of London, 29 March 1954.
3. COCB, BECh 4, Canon G. L. Prestige to the Bishop of London, 19 April 1954.
4. COCB, BECh 4, Note for the record by Sir Edward Bridges, 30 July 1954.
5. COCB, BECh 4, Part 1, Minute to Sir Robert Knox from Sir Edward Bridges, 3 February 1955.
6. COCB, BECh 4, Part 1, Note for the record by Sir Edward Bridges, 8 February 1955.
7. CCOK, Chapel of the Order, Box 1954-58, BEC 1-55, The Earl of Scarborough to Brigadier Norman Gwatkin, 24 August 1956.
8. COCB, BECh 4, Part 2, BEC 42, Note of a meeting, 28 September 1956.
9. COCB, BECh 9, Agreement as to Chapel of the Order, 20 March 1957.
10. COCB, BECh 4, Part 2, Minute from Sir Robert Knox to Sir Edward Bridges, 30 May 1956.
11. COCB, BECh 5, Part 1, Memorandum by Brigadier Ivan De la Bere, 19 May 1958.
12. CCOK, British Empire Chapel Fund, Furnishings 1957-63, Personal and confidential note for the information of Sir Norman Brook, from Brigadier Ivan De la Bere, 10 June 1958.
13. Frederic Hood, *The Chapel of the Most Excellent Order of the British Empire*, (Oxford, 1967), pp 21-2.
14. COCB, BECh 13A, Part 2, Sir Alexander Clutterbuck to Sir Norman Brook, 28 March 1961.
15. COCB, BECh 13A, Part 2, Brian Thomas to Sir Robert Knox, 1 January 1963.
16. COCB, BECh 13A, Part 2, James Orr to Sir Laurence Helsby, 11 January 1963.
17. COCB, BECh 13A, Part 2, Brian Thomas to Sir Robert Knox, 21 March 1963.

INDEX